WEST COUNTRY TREASURY

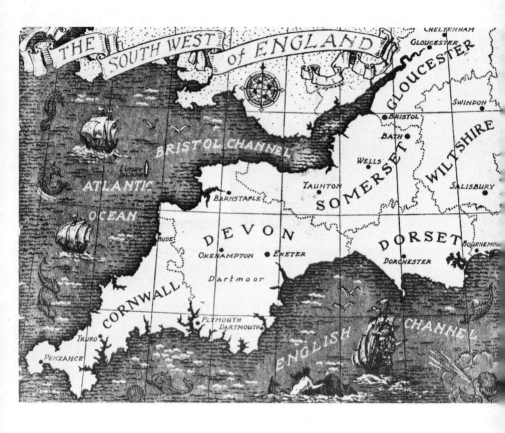

WEST COUNTRY TREASURY

*A Compendium of
Lore and Literature,
People and Places*

Alan Gibson
and
Anthony Gibson

EX LIBRIS PRESS

First published in 1989 by
Ex Libris Press
1 The Shambles
Bradford on Avon
Wiltshire

Cover by 46 Design, Bradford on Avon
Book originated by Ex Libris Press on
Apple Macintosh SE Computer
using Pagemaker Software
Typeset in Plantin by Manuscript, Trowbridge
Printed by BPCC Wheatons, Exeter

ISBN 0 948578 19 X

To Olwen, wife and mother

CONTENTS

INTRODUCTION

These essays are of varying length, and cover various subjects. They all, however, relate to some aspect of life in the West of England, where we both live and which we both love. They are not intended to be a comprehensive history of the West, but they are all subjects with which our lives have brought us, at some time or another, into contact. Alan Gibson spent much of his life working for the West of England Home Service of the B.B.C. Anthony, his son, was born in Devon, and is at present Secretary of the National Farmers' Union for the South-West Region. Although all the pieces have been re-written to a greater or less extent, most are based on broadcasts and articles of the past. It is therefore appropriate to pay acknowledgements to the B.B.C., *The Times, The Guardian, The Western Morning News, The Somerset County Gazette, The Journal of the Royal Agricultural Society, The Bristol Evening Post, The Listener, The Southampton Evening Echo, The Plymouth Evening Herald, The Spectator, Time and Tide,* with apologies to any we may have forgotten. The articles have been written over many years, and have been up-dated so far as we could. We have avoided subjects on which we have made longer broadcasting contributions, or written about in books. (This accounts, for instance, for a rather noticeable gap concerning the Armada).

The West Country, R.A.J.Walling suggests in his delightful book of that name, begins at Taunton. This is dutifully, indeed warmly accepted by all Devonians and Cornishmen, and those Somerset men born in Taunton or near it (not very many, since the county town is perilously near the Devon border). We have taken a broader view. Anthony, though he still lives in Devon (just over the border) is prepared to admit a total of six counties to his picture of the West Country, adding Dorset, Wiltshire and Gloucestershire. Alan is inclined to admit Hampshire and even parts of Sussex (though our publisher cannot stretch his West Country to include the latter), which came within the boundaries of the West of England Home Service. We have tried to avoid the use of the first person singular. Where the occasional "I" has slipped through, the context will, we hope, usually indicate which of us was concerned.

Alan Gibson and Anthony Gibson
Taunton, 1989

EARLY DAYS

*Arthur,
Avalon
and
Sedgemoor*

Arthur, Avalon, and Sedgemoor

No story of the west, or legend of the west, or romance of the west — whatever you decide to call it — is so persistent and so telling as that of Arthur.

In a book which we value greatly, *Avalon and Sedgemoor*, Desmond Hawkins has written of the "Somerset Plain", or, as some call it "The Somerset Levels": "The tract of land, much of it reclaimed distantly or recently from the sea, which stretches, roughly, from the Mendip shelf to the line Ilminster - Taunton - Bridgwater where the Blackdowns and Quantocks begin." He calls the part nearer to Bristol, the north-eastern part, "Avalon"; and the part further from Bristol, on the other side of the Poldens, "Sedgmoor". Not everyone would agree with this classification, but it is a handy one which we propose to follow.

"Sedgemoor": the last battle on English soil, is probably how we usually react to the word. There used long ago to be a cigarette card in a series called "English Battles" or something of the kind. The card had a picture of a vague kind of moor, with James II, the theoretical victor over the unhappy Duke of Monmouth, encapsulated in a corner. Monmouth's men, knowing the tricky swamps, might have won that battle but for a gunshot in the middle of the night, set off by ill-luck or an enemy agent. As it turned out, it hardly mattered, except to the unfortunate combatants. "Sedgemoor": leave aside memories of the battle, and it is a self-explanatory name. The *Shorter Oxford Dictionary* defines sedge as "any of various coarse, grassy, rush-like or flag-like plants growing in wet places", and some of Sedgemoor is still like that. Much more of it used to be, before the long and often frustrated efforts at reclamation. "Avalon": that has quite a different ring. The very name is like a bell. It tells of history and majesty, and we were disappointed when we looked it up and found that it means only a piece of low ground where the water is always coming in, as it used to do when Glastonbury was reduced, in winter, to a scattering of islands. But it is a name which has acquired its own dignity, because of its associations with King Arthur, and because so many English writers have taken Arthur, and therefore Avalon, as their theme:

I stand upon the lone, high hill
Ruling the Vale of Avalon,
  By Glastonbury in Avalon,
And in the heat-hazed distance still
  Comes Lancelot, this summer's eve,
With shield and breastplate, sword and greave,

10

EARLY DAYS

A-riding to his lady's bower,
To Glastonbury, Our Lady's Dower,
A-riding down by Camelot
To Glastonbury, in Avalon.

And from the hill so green and fair
That guards the Vale of Avalon,
  By Glastonbury, in Avalon,
I see the little village where
The best and holiest of our line
Did break the bread and sup the wine
And shed a wistful tear — they say —
That he must rise and haste away,
A-riding down to Calvary,
  From Glastonbury, in Avalon.

There is a great deal more of it, which gets no better, but those were the thoughts of a sentimental mid-twentieth-century young man upon a summer's day on Glastonbury Tor. The Vale of Avalon was, wasn't it? — where the boy Jesus came, with his uncle, Joseph of Arimathaea; and where Joseph came for retirement, perhaps bringing Mother Mary as well. And it was where, centuries later, Arthur defended Christian civilisation against the barbarian hordes.

There is no serious evidence for such things, but Avalon has dwelt so long amidst the legends, it does sometimes seem to communicate a sense of mystery and awe. Even the forlorn drop-outs, or hippies, or whatever you would call them, who gather round Glastonbury now — presumably even they are groping after some felt but incomprehensible beauty. You would not expect to find them, for instance, at Yeovil.

In his book, Desmond Hawkins discusses these legends in a calm and scholarly way. His poetic turn of mind might easily have lured him unduly on the subject of Arthur, but he recognises readily enough that Arthur may be a myth, and that if there ever was such a place as Camelot, many other places have as good a claim as South Cadbury, which is the fashionable favourite. He does, however, quote a note made as recently as 1890 by a rector of South Cadbury, who was in turn preserving an account by one of his parishioners:

Folks do say that on the night of the full moon, King Arthur and his men ride round the hill, and their horses are shod with silver, and a silver shoe has been found in the track where they do ride; and when they have ridden round the hill, they stop to water their horses at the Wishing Well.

11

But we are not now concerned with the historical and archaeological evidence about the Arthurian legend. All we are proposing to do is to say something about its influence on English literature, and to comment on one interesting comparison to which Desmond Hawkins draws attention.

Most of us make the acquaintance of Arthur and his knights in our childhood. We had a big book about them, suitable for ten years old or thereabouts: it had a bright blue and orange cover, with a shining silver Lancelot in the middle. It is those early images, the bold British King, surrounded by his galaxy of knights, the Round Table (as in Winchester Cathedral and elsewhere), the mighty wars they fought, the errands of chivalry, the damsels they rescued — it is these which stay with us all our lives. Our book was, as recollection goes, a much abbreviated and much edited version of *Le Morte D'Arthur*, by Sir Thomas Malory. Now *Le Morte D'Arthur* was completed, Malory tells us, in 1469, and was printed by Caxton, the first British printer, in 1485. It is the most famous version of the tales of Arthur, so much so that when we think of Arthur, we think of Malory; but of course it is not the only one, nor even the first. Malory tells us that he was working from earlier sources, mostly French, and most of his sources are known. In 1959 a symposium was published called *Arthurian Literature in the Middle Ages*, and Malory was allotted 12 pages out of a total of 563. That is how wide the field is.

The Arthurian legends first bloomed among the Celtic bards, especially in Wales. Arthur was thought of as a mighty Celtic king in an unspecified past age. The bards sang of a land of fantasy and enchantment: although Arthur was often not the central character in the tales, he was always there, omnipotent, in the background. The existence of these romances was known elsewhere in Britain, and in Europe, but they were largely ignored, even despised. William of Malmesbury, a sound historian, writing in the twelfth century, accepts the historical existence of Arthur, but he has no time for the Celtic legends. Indeed, he says:

This is that Arthur concerning whom the idle tales of the Britons rave wildly even today, a man truly worthy to be celebrated, not in the foolish dreams of deceitful fables, but the truthful history, since for a long time he sustained the declining fortunes of his country, and incited the unbroken spirit of the people to war.

So even in the twelfth century a distinction has grown up between the Arthur of history, and the Arthur of romance.

But only a few years after William of Malmesbury wrote, Geoffrey of Monmouth published his *History of the Kings of Britain*, a book which really set the whole Arthurian movement rolling. For Geoffrey treated much of the mythical material of the legends as historical fact, and ever since then the myth and the history have been inextricably mixed up. Geoffrey was a man of some note, a bishop; he wrote in Latin, and his work was read in that international language in all the libraries of Europe. He was not an historian. He was a propagandist. He rewrote history, from the fall of Troy to the death of the British king Cadwallader in 689, a period of 2,000 years, entirely in the interests of the British, that is to say Celtic race. Through all this time, we learn, the British had a series of successes which, such was their valour and nobility, ought to have enabled them to rule the world. They had inherited both the glories of Troy and the glories of Greece. Roman Britain only existed by courtesy of the Britons, with whom the Romans treated on equal terms, as fellow master-races. The alliance with Rome was sealed by the marriage of the daughter of the Emperor Claudius to the British king Arviragus.

Of course, as he drew nearer to his own age, Geoffrey of Monmouth was faced with the discrepancy that the British, despite always winning, had been nearly wiped out. This, he explained, was due to treachery, or bad luck, or bad refereeing by the superior powers.

Nevertheless, Geoffrey claimed to be a serious historian, and for a long time was taken as such, except by other historians. His influence was vast and continuing. He had told people what they wanted to hear: that Britain had a history no less illustrious than that of Greece or Rome. Let us take an example of his continuing influence. Brutus the Trojan, the destined founder of the British race, on his way over here to found us, won a battle against the Gauls with much glorious slaughter. However, he still found himself in some difficulties:

> Wherefore he chose rather to retire to his ships while the greater part of his army was still whole and the glory of the victory still fresh, and to set sail in quest of the island which the divine monition had prophesied should be his own. And after loading his ships with all the treasures and luxuries he had acquired, he re-embarked, and with a prosperous wind sought out the promised island, where he landed at last in safety at Totnes.

This is said to be Totnes, in Devon (or possibly Totton, near Southampton) and at Totnes there is still a stone, halfway up the main street, on which Brutus landed to found the British race. Quite a recent issue of the Totnes guide tells us:

> Upon this stone has been observed 'time out of mind' the proclamation of a new sovereign by the mayor, uniting the House of Windsor with the House of Troy.

13

Geoffrey of Monmouth had brought Arthur, so to speak, within the pale of European civilisation: it was French writers who took up the cycle, and so it came about that when Sir Thomas Malory decided to write what he called "the whole book" of King Arthur, it was upon French sources that he depended (he spent some time in France as a prisoner-of-war). The stories had travelled from Celtic Britain to France, and when Malory brought them home again, the Celtic nature of the story had been largely lost. That historical Arthur whom William of Malmesbury had been so anxious to distinguish from the Welsh barbarian legend, had merged with it. Arthur was now king of all England, and a hero of all England, a name to make every Saxon breast swell with pride. Whether there had been an historical Arthur or not — for ourselves we are doubtful, rather more doubtful than Desmond Hawkins — he was now submerged in the legend: but if this has blurred our history, it has certainly enriched our literature.

A gentle knight was pricking on the plain,
Y-clad in mighty arms and silver shield,
Wherein old dints of deep wounds did remain,
The cruel marks of many a bloody field;
Yet arms till that time did he never wield:
His angry steed did chide his foaming bit,
As much disdaining to the curb to yield:
Full jolly knight he seem'd, and fair did sit,
As one for knightly jousts and fierce encounters fit.

Thus Spenser in *The Faerie Queene*, writing about a hundred years after Malory. He set out to write a poem about Queen Elizabeth, but only published six volumes of his intended twelve, and so the Queen, who was planned to appear in the last book, only looks in peripherally. The poem is really about Arthur and his knights: Prince Arthur, Spenser calls him, and his knights, in their endeavours to serve the Faerie Queene, have many Arthurian adventures, full of jousts and damsels:

A lovely Lady rode him fair beside,
Upon a lowly Ass more white than snow,
Yet she much whiter, but the same did hide
Under a veil, that wimpled was full low,
And over all a black stole she did throw,
As one that only mourn'd; so was she sad,
And heavy sat upon her palfrey slow:
Seemed in heart some hidden care she had,
And by her in a line a milk-white lamb she lead.

Spenser's treatment of the Arthurian theme takes colour from its own age, and so have most: it is in this sense that Arthur, if not exactly immortal, is long-lasting. There are passages in Malory when he was clearly thinking of Henry V. Tennyson sang the praises of that modern and improbable Arthur, the Prince Consort, thus providing us with some of his funniest lines. Fortunately Tennyson had become interested in Arthur for much better reasons, and because he was a great poet his Arthurian verses contain much great poetry.

> So all day long the noise of battle roll'd
> Among the mountains by the winter sea;
> Until Arthur's table, man by man,
> Had fallen in Lyonnesse about their Lord,
> King Arthur: then, because his wound was deep,
> The bold Sir Bedivere uplifted him,
> Sir Bedivere, the last of all his knights,
> And bore him to a chapel nigh the field,
> A broken chancel with a broken cross,
> That stood on a dark strait of barren land.
> On one side lay the Ocean, and on one
> Lay a great water, and the moon was full.

Tennyson was handicapped in dealing with Arthur by Victorian standards of propriety. The Arthurian knights were less chivalrous in bed than out of it. Swinburne, in his long poem, *Tristram of Lyonesse*, was bolder, but he was better at arranging patterns of words than patterns of thought. Matthew Arnold wrote movingly of the story of Tristram's death. It is the poets, of whom we have only mentioned some of the more famous, who have kept Arthur alive, and kept him changing, as all live things must change. Theirs has been, for the Arthurian legend, one of the classical functions of poetry, when:

> as imagination bodies forth
> The form of things unknown, the poet's pen
> Turns them to shapes, and gives to airy nothing
> A local habitation and a name.

Milton contemplated writing an Arthurian epic — how tantalizing it is not to know what he would have made of it! In *Paradise Regained* he speaks, disapprovingly, of

> Ladies of th' Hesperides, that seemed
> Fairer than feign'd of old, or fabled since

15

Of faery damsels met in forest wide
By knights of Logres, or of Lyonnesse,
Lancelot, or Pelleas, or Pellinore.

Logres and Lyonesse, Lancelot, Pelleas, Pellinore — such airy nothings, such habitations, such names.

Logres and Lyonesse are not the same place, though they have often been interwoven: Lyonesse is usually supposed to be the sunken land beyond Cornwall. On a summer evening, on Garrison Hill, on St Mary's in the Isles of Scilly, it is easy to convince oneself that one can hear, faintly, the dim tolling of the bells in the lost churches, fathoms deep between Scilly and Land's End.

Low in the waves she lies,
Sea-sepulchred, and monodied by winds,
That ever sigh o'er Lyonnesse the fair.

Lyonnesse is a real but lost land, in the story. Logres is a magic land. It might be a fair comparison to say that Lyonnesse is Sedgemoor — before they drained it, and who knows but that the seas will come again? And Logres is Avalon, the Avalon of the poets.

Malory uses the word "Logres" to describe one of Arthur's kingdoms, and it has a routine enough derivation, from Locrine, one of the sons of Brutus the Trojan. But it has long had a deeper mystical sense. This is how it is put by a character in a novel by C.S.Lewis:

Something we may call Britain is always haunted by something we may call Logres. Haven't you noticed that we are two countries? After every Arthur, a Mordred: behind every Milton, a Cromwell; a nation of poets, a nation of shopkeepers: the home of Sidney — and of Cecil Rhodes. Is it any wonder that they call us hypocrites? But what they mistake for hypocrisy is really the struggle between Logres and Britain.

The leader of Logres is the Pendragon, the successor of Uther and Arthur and Cassibelaun.

Some of the Pendragons are well known to history, though not under that name. Others you have never heard of. But in every age they and the little Logres which gathered about them have been the fingers which gave the tiny shove or the almost imperceptible pull, to prod England out of the drunken sleep or to draw her back from the final outrage into which Britain tempted her.

EARLY DAYS

C.S.Lewis was only writing what he called "a fairy-tale for grown-ups" (*That Hideous Strength*) and does not suggest we are to take his notions too seriously. But that is the kind of way in which many people have thought, and do think, of the Arthurian legend. It is the classical British myth.

Yet it is, on the face of it, odd that the myth of Britain should have centred on Arthur, to the exclusion of a genuine hero-saint who lived about three hundred years after Arthur is supposed to have done, and who has been seriously described as "the only perfect man of action recorded in history." Desmond Hawkins brings out the contrast clearly, in his chapters on "Arthur and Avalon" and "Alfred and Athelney". Alfred of Wessex, Alfred the Great, made his headquarters at Athelney, in Sedgemoor, at the crisis of his battles against the Vikings.

The Vikings, mostly Danish, in their long ships with the stripe sails and dragon prows, were the dreaded invaders from the north. They had swept through the East and the Midlands, until they beset the last of the Saxon kingdoms, the quiet peasant country of Wessex. Ethelred, the king, was defeated and killed in battle, and so the men of the Witan, the council of Essex, chose his brother for king. This was Alfred.

How much do you know about Alfred? You will have heard the story of how he burnt the cakes. When University College, Oxford, in 1880, purported to celebrate its thousandth anniversary, the Regius Professor of History sent along a burnt cake as his contribution to the festivities. But whatever the dubiety of the cakes story (it is supposed to have happened at Altheney), there is no doubt that he beat back the Northmen. The first year of his reign was always known as the year of the nine battles. Every one was hardly fought, but at the end the kingdom of Wessex was safe. More than that, Alfred built a navy, and beat the Vikings at sea as well. And then, after several more years of fighting, with Alfred winning again and again, Guthrum, the king of the Danes, admitted defeat, and came to the village of Aller in Somerset, not to be executed, as you might have expected in those days, but to be baptised. The chronicler says that Alfred was so pleased about this that his face shone as though it were the face of an angel.

But Alfred was much more than a fighter. A Welsh monk, whose name was Asser, taught him to read and write, and he proved so apt a pupil that he began writing books of his own. He wanted the young men of Wessex to be wise as well as strong. He and his monks translated many of the great Roman writers into the Anglo-Saxon language. He used to say that he wanted to model himself on the Roman Emperor Titus, of whom it was said that "he was so anxious to serve his people that he counted the day lost on which he did no good." In those days, people lived by the sun, getting up when it rose and going to bed when it set. Alfred thought this a waste of time, and so he invented a

17

candle clock — six candles lasted just twenty-four hours. It sounds simple enough now, but it was quite a remarkable idea then. And he invented a horn case, so that his candles should be both light and time to him.

He rebuilt the city of London. When the Northmen attacked it, he beat them off. This time he beat them off for good, and his last years were years of peace. The chronicler wrote "Thanks be to God, the enemy host has not utterly broken down Angelkin." He was king of a country which was beginning to be England. His last work was to finish the translation of a work of the good Pope Gregory. And when he had finished it, he wrote at the end these words of his own, about the spring of knowledge which always above all he had sought:

> This is now the watering which the world's Creator
> For refreshment promised to us who till the field.
> Let us not spill the sparkling water
> Or of life's drink depart forlorn.

Well, that is a summary of what is known about Alfred, whereas nothing is really known about Arthur at all. Even Leslie Alcock, a scholarly Arthurian devotee, and author of *Arthur's Britain* (Penguin, 1973), concludes that Arthur, "apt symbol though he is for the period between the break with Rome in 407-10 and the emergence of the Heptarchy in the seventh century, in terms of *realpolitik* his achievement is negligible."

Yet the poets have largely neglected Alfred. There was the laureate Alfred Austin, who perhaps is better forgotten, and a poem by Chesterton, *The Ballad of the White Horse*, which contains some fine passages:

> I tell you naught for your comfort,
>   Yea, naught for your desire,
> Save that the sky grows darker yet
>   And the sea rises higher.

But Alfred has not generally proved to be the stuff of which poetry and romance are made. Too much is known about him. His achievements and character are too plainly recorded, to stir the instinct for the pursuit of the invisible which lies in Arthurian breasts. Arthur may have dwelt in Avalon, but Alfred dwelt in Sedgemoor.

At the heart of the Arthurian romances lies the Holy Graal. The Graal was the cup from which Jesus and his disciples drank at the last supper. Alternatively, it was the platter used at the last supper, and then used by Joseph of Arimathaea to receive the Saviour's blood at the cross. For our present purposes it does not matter which. Joseph of Arimathaea is supposed to have brought it to Glastonbury. It was doubtless a commonplace enough platter or cup, but it acquired mystical qualities, since it had contained the blood of God.

That is a rough summary of the story. In fact, it is a story which in one form or another is recognizable in many ancient cultures, a story which the Christian religion picked up as it went along. So in the Graal stories you have a primitive fairy-tale mixed up with a series of what claimed to be historical events, and it is this mixture which continues to make the Graal a force to be reckoned with, by historians, by writers, and — be sure — by psychiatrists.

There was a supposed Graal at Genoa, an emerald graal, and Napoleon pinched it and took it back to Paris, where it was found to be made of moulded glass. Herodotus, centuries before Christ, wrote of a bowl which dropped from heaven, and glowed with fire, and only a youngest son could extinguish the fire, after which he was made king. Confucians have an egg-shaped void at the centre of eternity, and something like a graal in the centre of the void. Orpheus knew the magic cup of Dionysus, and introduced many to the magic table where it could be drunk. There is a magic table, and at least the implication of a graal, in the Koran. For details of such events you may turn to *The Grail Legend*, by Emma Jung and Marie-Louise Von Franz.

In the Arthurian legend, it was the ambition of every good knight to find the Graal, which was to be found in the country of Logres. It was thought that its finding would bring miraculous benefits to the kingdom. But only a knight of exceptional purity and bravery could seize it. Lancelot was not good enough. It needed Galahad.

> I Galahad, saw the Graal,
> The Holy Graal, descend upon the shrine:
> I saw the fiery face as of a child
> That smote itself into the Bread, and went;
> And hither am I come; and never yet
> Hath what my sister taught me first to see,
> This Holy Thing, failed from my side, nor come
> Cover'd, but moving with me night and day,
> Fainter by day, but always in the night
> Blood-red, and sliding down the blacken'd marsh,
> Blood-red; and in the sleeping mere below,
> Blood-red.

(Tennyson once more). The Graal story has become central to the Arthurian myth: not itself invisible, or not always, but a representative in time of an invisible world.

Let us return to Sir Thomas Malory, whose work had so much to do with the subsequent outpourings of Arthurian writings in English literature. Malory is not anxious to stress the deeper religious significance of his stories. Compared with his sources, he plays down the magical and sacramental aspects. He is a story-teller, not a mystic, and though he writes beautiful prose, he is not a poet. But even Malory seems to feel a sense of awe when he comes close to the Graal. There is the time when Lancelot, though so noble and courageous a knight, learns that because of his past sins, the Graal can never be won by him.

> Then Sir Lancelot went to the cross and found his helm, his sword and his horse taken away. And then he called himself a very wretch, and most unhappy of all knights: and there he said:
>
> "My sin and my wickedness have brought me unto great dishonour. For when I sought wordly advantages in wordly desires, I ever achieved them and had the better in every place, and never was I discomfit in no quarrel, were it right or wrong. And now I take upon me the adventures of holy things, and now I see and understand that mine old sin hindreth me and shameth me, so that I had no power to stir nor speak when the holy blood appeared afore me."
>
> So thus he sorrowed till it was day, and heard the fowls sing: then somewhat he was comforted.

And this is how Malory describes the moment when Galahad does at last find his heart's desire:

> Now at the year's end, and the self day after Galahad had bourne the crown of gold, he arose up early and his fellows, and came to the palace, and saw before him the holy vessel, and a man kneeling on his knees in the likeness of his bishop, that had about him a great fellowship of angels as it had been Jesus Christ himself; and then he arose and began a mass of our Lady. And anon he called Galahad, and said to him,
>
> "Come forth the servant of Jesu Christ! and thou shalt see that thou hast much desired to see."
>
> And then Galahad began to tremble right hard when the deadly flesh began to behold the spiritual things.

It is the meeting, the mixture of the deadly flesh and the spiritual things that gives the Arthurian legend its permanence and its power. It has something to do with the relationship between Celt and Saxon; between Avalon and Sedgemoor; between Britain and Logres. But most of all it is a mingling of the human and the divine: nothing less, and nothing more, than the perpetual mystery of the incarnation; of God mixed up with man.

PEOPLE

Roger Bacon
Thomas Coryate
John Hicks
Hannah More
Joseph Cottle
John Skinner
Francis Kilvert
Charles Kingsley
George Muller
Arnold Thomas
Hugh Redwood

Roger Bacon

With all the excitement over the Shakespeare quatercentenary in 1964, it seemed unfortunate that so little was done to celebrate the anniversary of Bacon. We do not speak of Francis, the essayist, lawyer, and crooked financier, whose misfortune it has been to be chiefly remembered as the man who did not write somebody else's plays. The reference is to Roger Bacon, who was born in Ilchester, Somerset, three hundred and fifty years before Shakespeare. The year was 1214, though the month and the day are unknown.

Roger Bacon certainly had one of the most brilliant minds of the thirteenth century. He was a religious, of course, as all scholars and scientists then were, and this explains a certain dichotomy in his work which seems strange to modern eyes. For instance, his experimental research in optics was an enormous advance on anything that had gone before. But he also spent a great deal of time seeking the philosopher's stone, which was to transmute all metal into gold. He was chained to some extent by the credulities of his age. Even so, he fell into trouble with his superiors in the Franciscan order, and spent at least two long periods in confinement, denied the opportunity of carrying out research which it was felt might have heretical implications. Before, however, we condemn the church too readily, we must remember that at least it provided a channel whereby such men as Bacon could pursue a scholarly career. His family seems to have been good solid Somerset stock, but with no great wealth or noble connections to advance him.

Scholars then disdained specialisation. Knowledge of any kind was what Bacon sought. It was he who mastered the properties of the concave and convex lens. It was equally he who discovered gunpowder. Whether he also invented the telescope and burning-glasses has been argued, but without any doubt he played a key part in their development. He led a great advance in physics, and even in astronomy, though here again he was handicapped by the preconceptions of his time. He invented the magic lantern. It irritated him that it was this comparatively trivial achievement which brought him most fame in his own lifetime (the thirteenth century was preoccupied with toys as much as the twentieth).

The *Admirable Power of Art and Nature in the Production of the Philosopher's Stone* was a treatise which showed an astonishing depth and variety of learning. The title rather suggests he has found it; but in fact, though he describes several hot scents, he had not.

Thomas Coryate

In 1611 was published *Coryate's Crudities hastily gobbled up in five months travells in France, Savoy, Italy, Helvetia, alias Switzerland, some parts of High Germany and the Netherlands; newly digested in the hungry air of Odcombe, in ye county of Somerset, and now dispersed to the nourishment of the travelling members of this kingdome.* That is the full title.

Tom Coryate had been born in Odcombe, the son of the rector, probably in 1577. He went to the royal court, and became a fool or jester to Prince Henry, the eldest son of James I. Court fools were very rarely fools, as Shakespeare makes clear enough. But it could be a hazardous job, and Coryate decided to travel, a practice to which Englishmen, apart from their seamen, were not then much addicted. He travelled through France and Italy, getting a lift when he could on the outward trip, but walking back, a thousand miles or so, from Venice to Flushing. When he was safely home he hung up the shoes he had used in Odcombe church.

Coryate's Crudities is the account of his journey: a witty, rambling, lengthy book, though not particularly crude as the word is understood today. He set out again in 1612, this time for Greece, the Holy Land, Persia and India. He became familiar with oriental languages, an almost unknown branch of study, and when he was presented to the Great Mogul was able to make a speech in Persian. He declares he only spent three pounds all the way between Aleppo and Agra, and often lived "competently" — his own word — for a penny a day. He was still abroad when he died, at Surat in 1617. His last words were reputed to have been "Sack, sack, is there such a thing as sack? I pray you give me some sack." He never wrote an account of this second and greater journey, but we have knowledge of it from letters he sent home.

Tom Coryate is traditionally the man who introduced forks into England. This has been described as an exaggerated claim, if only because the Saxons had used forks for eating a thousand years earlier. But the habit had died out, and Coryate certainly helped to reintroduce it. "I observed", he says, "a custom in all these Italian cities and towns through which I passed that is not used in any other country that I saw in my travels; neither do I think any other nation in Christendom doth use it. The Italians do always at their meals use a little fork when they cut their meat. For while with their knife which they hold in one hand, they cut out the meat of the dish, they fasten their fork, which they hold in their other hand, upon the same dish, so that whatsoever he be that sitting in the company of any other at meat should inadvisedly touch the dish of meat with his fingers from which all the table do cut, he will give occasion of offence unto the company. The Italian cannot by any means endure to have his dish touched with fingers, seeing all men's fingers are not alike clean."

For this, his friend Lawrence Whitaker of Yeovil christened Coryate "Furcifer". And though it was another century before forks came into general use in England, there seems, on this evidence, no reason to deny Coryate his customary accolade. And after all, the fork is an exceptionally useful instrument.

John Hicks

"There is only one denomination that has never persecuted", declared John Clifford once to a Baptist Assembly, "and that is the Baptists!" Resounding applause. "And that", added Clifford as the cheers died away, "is because we have never had the chance."

In this account of John Hicks, an Independent — or Congregationalist, as we would latterly say — minister who was persecuted in the reign of Charles II, we are not seeking to draw any inference that Hicks was necessarily better than his persecutors. The ministers of the Church of England had suffered during the 1640s. The Nonconformist ministers suffered during the 1660s. Both sides were equally zealous in persecution and equally manful in suffering it. The only major exception we are prepared to make is that great and good man Oliver Cromwell, who was the first English ruler to accept the idea of religious liberty, even if in a limited sense, and whose supporters could never understand why he was so tender to prelacy and even papacy.

Oliver Cromwell died in 1658. Two chaotic years later, Charles II came to the throne. Charles was not by nature a persecuting type either — one doubts if he believed in any religion at all, accepting whatever suited him at the time — but he was scared of the puritans, who had chopped off his father's head and kept him many years in exile, and thus he assented readily enough to what was called the Clarendon Code, a series of Acts named after his chief minister, designed to prevent the Dissenters, or Nonconformists, from having any say in national affairs, and to prevent them from gathering to worship in public.

Devon at this time was a stronghold of Dissent. One hundred and twenty clergy were ejected from their livings upon the return of Charles, a higher number than in any other county. Among them were well-known contemporary figures such as John Flavell, of Dartmouth; Francis Whiddon, of Totnes; Allan Geare, of Fleming. These men, and many others, were more distinguished pastors, more distinguished theologians than John Hicks: but none of them had quite his richness of character, his determination to fight against all odds. Perhaps his Yorkshire birth and upbringing, and Irish education, had

24

something to do with it, although he was to spend the greater part of his life in the West Country.

He was born at Kirkby Moorhouse, Yorkshire, in 1633. He went to Trinity College, Dublin, where he became a Fellow. From 1657 to 1662 he held the living of Saltash, and then he was ejected under the Act of Uniformity. He stayed on at Saltash for some years, and in 1665 a government agent reported his as one of six ministers, "all", says the agent, "notoriously disaffected", living in the Saltash area. Later he moved to Kingsbridge, in the South Hams of Devon, and became the leading spirit among the Dissenters there.

He was not, of course, allowed to hold public services. But he got over that by preaching on the Saltstone Rock, in the Kingsbridge Estuary. It is not a very large island, nearly submerged at high tide, but its jurisdiction was disputed between neighbouring parishes, and since nobody would take the responsibility of keeping law and order there, Dissenting preachers could get away with it, without being arrested. Another place Hicks is known to have preached is Tacket Wood, and one rather dubious explanation of the name is that it is a corruption of "Ticket Wood", and that admission to Dissenting services there was by ticket only (presumably to keep out agents).

As there was no police force, the enforcement of the various Acts passed against Dissenters after 1660 depended on the Justices of the Peace. Where there were lenient J.P.s, there was a reasonable degree of toleration. Those J.P.s who were determined to carry out the law had to rely on the services of informers. One of these informers was murdered, and Hicks, with nine others, was charged with the crime at Exeter Assizes, but was acquitted. He published a pamphlet, the title of which was almost as long as the pamphlet itself, describing his vindication, and the "horrid perjuries" of witnesses for the prosecution. He was particularly severe on an informer called John Bear. This John Bear nevertheless became a justice, and he was known all over South Devon for his severity. He was "called by a nickname", Hicks said, "Cockey Bear".

This trial over, Hicks went back to his hazardous and irregular ministry. On one occasion, an apparitor — an agent of the bishop's court — called to see him with a citation to appear. The apparitor said that he came to enquire for one Mr. Hicks, gentleman. Hicks, who was a large man, and habitually carried a cudgel, came to the door and said: "I am John Hicks, Minister of the Gospel." There was a pause; and then the apparitor, possibly in response to a suggestive twitch of the cudgel, went on his way. But not all troubles were countered so easily. Sometimes Hicks had to go into hiding. The publication of his pamphlet infuriated the bishop's court, and this time two messengers were sent with a citation, apparently to maintain one another's courage. They fell in with a stranger on the Exeter road, lunched with him, and told him they were trying to arrest this desperate and malignant fellow Hicks. After lunch they repaired to the stables and the stranger, who had listened to all they had to say, suddenly set about them with his cane and "corrected them till they begged his pardon." For of course it was Hicks himself. This sounds a bit too good to be true, but there is sound authority for it, as there is for the next episode in this extraordinary man's life.

For Hicks decided to go to London to see the king, and actually managed to obtain an interview. Charles II, characteristically, was intrigued rather than angered by so unconventional a visitor. He nevertheless rebuked Hicks for his behaviour, at which the minister replied: "Oppression, may it please your majesty, makes a wise man mad. The justices, beyond all law, have very much wronged your majesty's loyal subjects, the nonconformists in the west." This was a statement of doubtful truth. However, this was the time when Charles, for reasons of his own, was meditating a Declaration of Indulgence, designed to extend some liberty to Protestant Dissenters provided that it could also be extended to Roman Catholics. Hicks received a royal pardon for his offences, and three months later he presented to the king a "Grateful Acknowledgment for Indulgence", signed by seventy-two West Country ministers. He helped to obtain from the king a restitution of a third part of the fines paid by the Dissenters under the Clarendon Code, and with some of the proceeds he built a new meeting-house for his congregation at Kingsbridge.

But most Dissenters thought that to obtain an Indulgence from the king was supping with the devil, and the spoon was not long enough. The king's ministers and parliament, unsympathetic to Protestant Dissenters and Catholic Dissenters alike, would have none of the Indulgence, and it was withdrawn.

Hicks cheerfully went on preaching, and was promptly fined £20. He earned a tribute at this time, from the Bishop of Exeter, who spoke of

> Mr. Hicks, famous or infamous rather in these parts and bold at court, who is come down and disturbs the quiet and peace, to the by my late Lord Chancellor for doing his duty [this is a reference to "Cockey" Bear]. I for the same reason got restored by my Lord Keeper.

Hicks was preaching once on Lincombe Hill, near Kingsbridge. His text — the kind of text one might expect in those circumstances — was, "The sufferings of this present time are not worthy to be compared with the glory which shall be revealed." The meeting was broken up by the justices and their men. Hicks hid in the outbuildings of a neighbouring farm; a pitchfork was thrust into the hay with which he had covered himself. But it narrowly missed, and he avoided capture.

Another time, along with James Burwood of Batson (an ancestor of Field-

Marshal *Sir* William Birdwood of Anzac) and another minister, Hicks took part in a joint service on the Saltstone. Hicks and Brand had walked out from Kingsbridge, and when they reached the rock found Burdwood already there, with the people singing "God is our refuge and our strength". All three ministers addressed the congregation in turn. Brand spoke on "A remnant according to the election of grace", Hicks on "The Rocks of Ages", Burdwood upon "Christ is All in All". After that, the brethren prayed until night and the tide drove them back to their homes. Even at low tide, the Saltstone is only about a hundred feet long and fifty broad. The spiritual endurance of the seventeenth century puritans is something to be marvelled at.

After some years, Hicks moved on from Kingsbridge to Portsmouth, and then to Keynsham. In 1685, Monmouth landed at Lyme and launched his madcap expedition for the English crown. Hicks was fifty-two, but along with thousands of others in the west, flocked to the motley ranks. The morning after the savage chaos of Sedgemoor, he and a lawyer called Nelthorpe were flying together for their lives.

After a day of desperation, they were granted a refuge in the home of Lady Alice Lisle, the widow of one of Cromwell's ministers of government, a lady who was widely loved in the locality and (according to Macaulay) had on previous occasions given shelter to royalist fugitives in distress. Next morning, the king's troops were around the house. Hicks hid in the malthouse, Nelthorpe in the chimney. But luck was no longer with them: they were discovered and arrested, and so was Lady Alice.

Lady Alice was the first victim of Judge Jeffreys upon his Bloody Assize. If she had indeed sheltered traitors, knowing them to be traitors, she was indeed guilty of a capital crime, since technically all Monmouth's forces were traitors. She declared that she had thought the fugitives to be persecuted ministers, with warrants out against them for field-preaching. Even if the court disbelieved this explanation, which they presumably might have done, it seemed inconceivable that in such circumstances the death penalty would be enforced. In any case Lady Alice was tried before Hicks and Nelthorpe had been tried, and consequently could not be legally found guilty (a point which was made in the reversal of her attainder some years later). It took all the bullying and cursing of which Jeffreys was capable to obtain a verdict of guilty from the jury. This was the occasion when he made his famous pronouncement:

> There is not one of those lying, snivelling, canting Presbyterians but, one way or another, had a hand in the rebellion. Presbyter has all manner of villainy in it. Nothing but Presbytery could have made Dunne [one of the witnesses] such a rogue. Show me a Presbyterian, and I'll show thee a lying knave.

Attempts have been made, at one time and another, to whitewash practically every bad character in history. With Jeffreys the whitewash has never clung, and those few sentences are sufficient reason to explain why. Apart from anything else, they show him to be an ignorant man. He used the word "Presbyterian" as an equivalent to Dissenter. The bulk of Monmouth's forces, including Hicks, were Independents, and would have rejected the description "Anglican" or "Royalist" or "Roman Catholic".

Jeffreys sentenced Lady Alice Lisle to death by burning the same afternoon. The combined remonstrances of the king's general, of the Earl of Clarendon, of the clergy of Winchester Cathedral, and scores of others, could do no more than persuade him to commute the sentence to beheading, and postpone it for five days.

So Lady Alice died; and Hicks died too, hanged at Taunton on 6 October 1685, another of Jeffreys' three hundred and twenty victims. He had had a stormy life and perhaps, in that age, it was not altogether an inappropriate end. Certainly he died for the things in which he believed, and he died sure in the promises. A picture of his arrest, painted by Ward, is in the Houses of Parliament. Otherwise he has no memorial. His body was one of those left to rot away in the market-places of western towns, a reminder from Jeffreys of the unwisdom of rebellion.

Three years later, no more, it appeared that the people had not learnt their lesson. William of Orange landed at Brixham, the West rose again, and the Stewarts were swept from the throne for good. One wishes Hicks could have survived to see it. At the same time, he cannot be said to have been the ideal seventeenth-century puritan: the gentle Flavell, on Hicks's ow doorstep at Dartmouth, the wise and majestic Milton, the sweet-tongued Andrew Marvell, showed the qualities which John Hicks lacked. The great tragedy of that age in England is that so many good men, for what seemed to them genuinely good reasons, were in violent opposition to each other. And though one admires John Hicks for his character and courage, the parson in South Devon who was really in tune with Christian belief was a long-forgotten Rector of Diptford called George Nosworthy, who must have known Hicks well. Nosworthy decided to stay with the established church: his kinsman, Francis Whiddon of Totnes, chose to take his place with the ejected. But at Whiddon's funeral, Nosworthy risked the displeasure of authority by preaching, and his words included these:

> Of late, one pulpit hath not held us; but I trust in due time, one heaven shall; where there is no discord in the saints' harmony; where Calvin and Luther are made friends.

They are words which ring across the centuries, both as a reproach and an inspiration.

Hannah More

It is hard to know where to begin, with Hannah More. She had several lives, and they overlapped from time to time. She is not much remembered now, though she had a great name in her days, which were long. She was born in 1745, the year of the last Jacobite rebellion, and she died in 1833, the year after the passing of the Reform Bill: from the last of the English civil wars, you might say, to the first act of modern politics. It is worth emphasizing the great changes that occurred during her life span, for she herself, who had been an eighteenth century belle, became a nineteenth century bluestocking.

She was the fourth daughter of Jacob More, a schoolmaster at Stapleton, Bristol. She began writing plays, suitable for young ladies to act, at the age of twelve. A broken engagement to a Mr. Turner left her heart-whole and financially assured, and in her twenties she went to London, where she stormed without difficulty the exclusive circle of Johnson, Reynolds and Garrick. She wrote a tragedy which was performed successfully at Covent Garden, Garrick himself writing the prologue and epilogue. She wrote a comedy, also fairly successful. Johnson, who was of course much older and liked the flattery of young and vivacious women, flattered her in turn, telling her (one cannot believe convincedly) how good her poems were. She wrote to one of her sisters in Bristol:

> I had the happiness to carry Johnson home from Hill Street, though Mrs. Montagu publicly declared she did not think it prudent to trust us together, with such a declared affection on both sides. She said she was afraid of a Scotch elopement!

And on another occasion,

> Keeping bad company leads to all other bad things. I have got the headache all day, by raking out so late with that young libertine Johnson!

Johnson once said,

> I dined yesterday at Mrs. Garrick's, with Mrs. Carter, Miss Hannah More and Miss Fanny Burney. Three such women are not to be found. I know not where I could find a fourth, except Mrs. Lennox, who is superior to them all.

At least the memory of Hannah More is recalled more readily than that of Mrs. Carter and Mrs. Lennox. Such dinners were meat and drink to Johnson in more than one sense. He did once say to Hannah,

> You should consider what your flattery is worth before you choke me with it.

But it was not a serious reproof, and when she told him how delighted she was with his praise of some piece of her work, he replied

> And so you may be, for I have given you the opinion of a man who does not rate his opinion in these things very low, I can tell you.

It was to her, however, that he made one of his best-known literary judgments. She had been expressing surprise that the poet who had written *Paradise Lost* should write such poor sonnets, which produced the answer:

> Milton, madam, was a genius that could cut a Colossus from a rock, but could not carve heads from cherry stones.

An odd judgment, that one, though a memorable phrase. But Johnson, as Robert Lynd has pointed out, does not appear at his best in his conversations with Hannah More. And Boswell did not like her, because she had once sharply rebuked him for being drunk.

Her period in the Johnson circle appears now to be little more than a prelude to her life. When she was 35 she published her *Sacred Dramas,* and thereafter her mind took an increasingly serious bent. Three years later she bought a house at Cowslip Green, near Wrington, and settled down to country life with one of her sisters. It was quite a change from living with the Garricks' in the Adelphi. But she kept up her literary acquaintances, and sometimes visited them. Horace Walpole was one: too flippant a man, it might be thought, even though he was now an old one, for Hannah. But he seems to have enjoyed her earnestness. She wrote:

> Except the delight he has in teazing me for what he calls over strictness, I never heard a sentence from him which savoured of infidelity. Neither age nor suffering can abate the entertaining powers of the pleasant Horace, which rather improve than decay; though he himself says he is only fit to be a milkwoman, as the *chalk-stones* at the fingers' ends qualify him for nothing but *scoring.*

The reference is to Walpole's gout — to "score", in this sense, was to make a notch on a stick, as a milkwoman did on her tally-stick. She dedicated her poem "Florio" to him, and received a suitably elegant reply:

> I don't believe that the deity who formerly practised both poetry and physic, when gods got their livelihood by more than one profession, ever gave a recipe in rhyme. I wish you may get a patent for life for exercising both faculties. Since I cannot wait on you to thank you, nor dare ask you "to call your doves yourself", and visit me in your Parnassian quality, I might send for you as my *physicianess.* Yet why should not I ask you to come and see me? You are not such a prude as to "blush to show compassion", though it should "not chance this year to be the fashion."

This was a delicate quotation from Hannah's poem. It was an effective plea, for she did go to see him, and

> Notwithstanding his sufferings, I never found him so pleasant, so witty, and so entertaining. He said a thousand diverting things about "Florio"; but accused me of having imposed on the world by a dedication full of falsehood, meaning the compliment to himself.

By this time, you will be beginning to realise that there is something of a mystery about Hannah More. She was growing older, probably had never been an outstanding beauty, and yet the great men of her age, if they do not exactly dance attendance upon her, still clearly like her to dance attendance upon them. It is not as if her poetry had any special merit. It has long lain unread, save by the curious. No doubt she had a lively style in her conversation, for she is repeatedly described as 'vivacious', but it is not reflected in her writing, nor even her letters, which though much praised and much published are mostly rather dull.

Well, her life has some way to go yet. At about this time occurred the episode of Ann Yearsley. Ann Yearsley was a milkwoman. Possibly Walpole had her in mind when he described himself to be "only fit to be a milkwoman." Indeed, Ann Yearsley delivered the milk to the home of Hannah's family in Bristol, and turned out to have poetic leanings, and Hannah, as we would say today, "discovered" her. She set to among her friends and raised a sum of money so that Ann could stop being a milkwoman and devote all her time to her muse. It was a successful appeal, and Hannah decided that the money should be put in trust. To this Ann Yearsley strongly objected. It was her money, and she wanted it. She called on Hannah and spoke her mind. Hannah was deeply pained at this ingratitude. Ann ultimately got her money, but at the cost of bitter feelings on both sides.

The Bristol bookseller Joseph Cottle was involved in, or at any rate informed about, this to-do; as he was in most Bristol affairs in those days. He is inclined to take Ann Yearsley's side, pointing out that she wanted the capital because she had two sons she wished to educate, and also because she planned to open, for her maintenance, a circulating library. Cottle says,

> Here was a strong-minded illiterate woman on one side, impressed with a conviction of the justice of her cause; and further stimulated by a deep consciousness of the importance of success to herself and family;

(He does not seem to think there is anything contradictory in being both illiterate and a poet)

> and, on the other side, a refined mind, delicately alive to the least approximation of indecorum, and, not unreasonably, requiring deference and conciliation. Could such incongruous materials coalesce? Ann Yearsley's name was branded with ingratitude. Gloom and perplexities in quick succession oppressed the Bristol milkwoman, and her fall became more rapid than her ascent. The eldest of her sons, whom she had apprenticed to a eminent engraver, with a premium of one hundred guineas, prematurely died; and his surviving brother soon followed him to the grave. Ann Yearsley, now a childless and desolate widow, retired, heart-broken from the world, on the produce of her library; and died many years after, in a state of almost total seclusion, at Melksham. She lies buried in Clifton churchyard.

So much for Ann Yearsley, who was probably an awkward customer with few gifts. But this does not leave us with an altogether comfortable feeling about Hannah's part. She complained a good deal of what had happened, and Horace Walpole wrote to her:

> You fancied that Mrs. Yearsley was a spurious issue of a Muse; and to be sure, with all their immortal virginity, the parish of Parnassus has been sadly charged with their bantlings! And as nobody knows the fathers, no wonder some of the misses have turned out woeful reprobates!

By the end of the century, at Cowslip Green and then at Barley Wood, not far away, Hannah More was well into her next life, which might be called that of a "religious writer", though the phrase conveys little about her work. She wrote a series of tracts, mostly for children, expressing the attitudes of the evangelical party in the Church of England. They were extraordinarily successful. Not only did they sell in large numbers, but the children who read them were those who raised the evangelical movement to such power and influence in the century about to begin.

She caught a tide, for there was a great increase in the number of people who could read, in her lifetime. All round England penny chapbooks were being hawked, most of them bawdy. Hannah More's tracts, published anonymously, were produced in the same style, even to the coloured covers, and often sold in the same way. They were stories from real life, or fiction — more and more of them fictional as time went on — pointing a moral. It was recorded that in the year 1795, in one period of six weeks, no less than 300,000 copies were sold of her first series of "Repository Tracts", as she called them.

The fictional ones were far the most popular (though she also had a gift for retelling Bible stories effectively). There is a touch of Dickens about a title as this:

BETTY BROWN: a St. Giles' Orange Girl, with some account of Mrs. Sponge, the Money-Lender.

This was a tale of virtue triumphing over adversity; sometimes, however, there is no happy ending, and vice brings its destined disaster. *The Cheapside Apprentice* ends suitably at Tyburn. In *The Good Mother's Legacy*, the daughter is betrayed by the butler, returns home with her bastard child, and both die in the snow on the way:

Betty Adams tried to speak, but in vain: a ghostly hue overspread her features, her limbs shivered, her jaws fell, and with a deep groan, she expired.

This is a favourite theme. It recurs in one of her tracts in verse, called *Robert and Richard, or the Ghost of Poor Molly*: the same trail of weakness leading to, wickedness, leading to retribution,

Till Molly and Molly's poor baby were found
One evening in Richard's own mill-pond, both drowned.

One of the remedies is a sterner attitude by parents. This Hannah feels, is especially needed in the poorer classes.

Poor parents must not fall into that sad mistake, that because their children are poor, and have little of this world's goods, the mothers must make it up to them in false indulgence. The children of the gentry are much more reproved and corrected for their faults, and bred up in far stricter discipline.

And there is a really rather horrible scene at the end of *The Execution of Wild Robert: a Warning to Parents*. At Robert's inevitable execution, his mother begs a last kiss, but he refuses, with the words

You gave me life, but with it gave
What made that life a curse;
My sins uncurbed, my mind untaught,
Soon grew from bad to worse.

From quotations such as these, Hannah More does sound a sour old termagant. What had happened to the girl who had laughed with Garrick and flirted with Johnson, and written for the London stage? Well, she had not altogether disappeared, and it is quite clear from those who knew her that she could never bring herself to be as stern as her writings. She wrote that "Young people are apt to imagine that the world is full of pleasure and enjoyment", and it was a weakness which, try as she might, she could not help herself from sharing. She was a teacher as well as a writer, and much loved by many of her pupils. Her friends sometimes thought her too indulgent. Although she declared she regretted having written secular plays, she continued to write sacred ones for children. At her school for young ladies in Bristol she taught French and Italian, and music and dancing, a very frivolous syllabus according to the thinking of many of the evangelicals, who were inclined to believe that education need not go much beyond the Bible. Indeed their argument for education, and Sunday Schools, was that without it children would not be able to read the Bible.

But there was a distinction between the education considered fitting for the poor and for the rich. It lingered long, and perhaps there are places where it lingers still. It was another gentle nineteenth-century lady, Mrs. Alexander, who no doubt had been brought up on Hannah More, who wrote the famous lines in "All things bright and beautiful",

The rich man in his castle,
The poor man at his gate,
God made them high and lowly,
And ordered their estate.

Yet Hannah More did care about the poor, and apart from her school for young ladies in Bristol, she founded schools, not only Sunday Schools but day schools, all over the Mendips, and superintended them herself. She could not bring herself to treat these children, the children of colliers mostly, with any less kindness than she treated her Bristol young ladies. Most of her accounts of her educational theories were written on the defence, because she was often attacked for troubling them with education at all, and she tries to explain that she was really not trying to do too *much* for them. Thus to the Bishop of Bath and Wells:

> When I settled in this country thirteen years ago, I found the poor in many villages sunk in a deplorable state of ignorance and vice. There were, I think, no Sunday Schools in the whole district, except one in my own parish which had been established by our respectable rector, and another in the adjoining parish of Churchill. This drew me to the more neglected villages. Not one school there did I ever attempt to establish without the hearty concurrence of the clergyman of the parish. My plan of instruction is extremely simple and limited. They learn on week days such coarse work as may fit them for servants. I allow of no writing for the poor. My object is not to make fanatics, but to train up the lower classes in habits of industry and piety. I know of no way of teaching morals but by teaching principles; or of inculcating Christian principles without imparting a good knowledge of Scripture.... To teach the poor to read without providing them with *safe* books, has always appeared to me an improper measure, and this consideration induced me to enter upon the laborious undertaking of the Cheap Repository Tracts.

This certainly sounds harsh and rather stupid, but there is a warmer note in the same letter — though she is still on the defensive, for she had been accused of rabble-rousing, a subject on which everyone was very sensitive, since it was only a few years after the French Revolution.

> In some parishes where the poor are numerous, such as Cheddar, and the distressed mining villages of Shipham and Rowberrow, I have instituted, with considerable expense to myself, friendly benefit societies for poor women, which have proved a great relief to the sick and lying-in, especially in the late seasons of scarcity. We have in one single parish an accumulation of between two and three hundred pounds — the others in proportion. This I have placed out in the funds. The late lady of the Manor of Cheddar, in addition to her kindness to my institutions during her life, left at her death a legacy to the club, and another for the school, as a testimony of her opinion of the utility of both. We have two little annual festivities for the children and poor women of these clubs, which are always attended by a large concourse of gentry and clergy.

The last phrase spoils it a bit, but that does shows us a better side of Hannah. She enjoyed herself at the little annual festivities and did her best to see that everyone else did.

She also retained her habit of being on familiar terms with the influential and important people. Wilberforce was her friend, and she supported the campaign against slavery. She had known Johnson, and she knew the man who was to be the nineteenth century's nearest equivalent to Johnson; for at the special request of his father, Mr. Zachary Macaulay, she became for a while the governess to his child, a child who was something of a prodigy, Thomas Babington Macaulay. This acquaintance began when she called one day at Zachary Macaulay's house:

> I was met by a pretty, slight child, with an abundance of light hair, about four years of age. He came to the front door to receive me, and told me that his parents were out, but that if I would be good enough to step into the sitting-room he would bring me a glass of old spirits.

Hannah More liked recounting this story, and accepted the invitation — not to the old spirits, but to the sitting-room. When he was questioned as to what he knew of old spirits, the child could only reply — but a perfectly accurate reply it was — that Robinson Crusoe often had some.

It was about this time that the same infant, out visiting, had some hot coffee spilt over him, much to the pain and the concern of his hostess. When he had been mopped up, the hostess asked him how he was feeling, and he replied — aged four or thereabouts — "Thank you, madam; the agony is abated." It has been said that the lady concerned was Hannah More herself, but Trevelyan, in the *Life and Letters of Lord Macaulay*, says it happened on a visit to Lady Waldegrave at Strawberry Hill, Walpole's old home; and as Trevelyan was Macaulay's nephew he must be supposed to be right. But no doubt Hannah knew the story and retold it.

Now mark a sequel. When Macaulay was at the height of his fame, and when Hannah was four years dead, the suggestion arose that he might review her collected works. Macaulay knew that there was not much in her output which he could conscientiously praise, and he was not a man to give praise falsely. He therefore wrote to the publisher who had made the request,

> She was exactly the very last person in the world about whom I should choose to write a critique. She was a very kind friend to me from childhood. Her notice first called out my literary tastes. Her presents laid the foundation of my library. She was to me what Ninon was to Voltaire — begging her pardon for comparing her to a bad woman, and yours for comparing myself to a great man. She really was a second mother to me. I have a real affection for her memory. I therefore could not possibly write about her unless I wrote in her praise; and all the praise which I could give to her writings, even after straining my conscience in her favour, would be far indeed from satisfying any of her admirers.

It is a good example of the way in which her friends loved her, even though they might not always agree with her.

She had put the child Macaulay in a novel. He and his sister are supposed to be the originals of the Stanley children in the book, *Coelebs in Search of a Wife*. This was the best known of her later works, and although it is only nominally a novel — much more a moral tract — it had a great success amongst the pious. Unfortunately the Stanley children were very much duller than the Macaulay children, and find few readers today. She had, herself, previously condemned novels as "the most pernicious source of moral corruption": another example of her inconsistency. She was in fact a good deal of a pragmatist. If she found something worked effectively, she did not concern herself whether it fitted her theories. Consider her teaching methods. She starts from a gloomy premise.

> If I were asked what quality is most important in an instruction of youth, I should not hesitate to reply, such a strong impression of the corruption of our nature, as should ensure a disposition to counteract it.

This is the evangelical doctrine of Total Depravity, which Toplady enshrined in "Rock of Ages", a hymn which is still earnestly sung by people who would not dream of taking its doctrine seriously. Nor did Hannah always act as if she believed such a doctrine. Cheerfulness would keep breaking in.

> My grand endeavour is to make everything as entertaining as I can, by familiar homely language, full of anecdotes of the people round about, as well as of the good people that lived in old times, and full of practical piety. A teacher should instruct, as Christ did, by interesting parables, should seize on surrounding objects and local circumstances; should call on all creation to her aid, and so make religion and her ways appear, what they really are, the ways of pleasantness. Learning by rote should be replaced by animated conversation and lively discussion.

Very few teachers held such views at that time, or for long afterwards. No wonder she was popular with her pupils, one of whom said of her, "Good woman as she was, she taught me to believe in Tom Thumb nearly as implicitly as in Joseph and his brethren."

There is a modern ring, too, about her assertion that women are superior to men, though the reason she gave was not a modern one. It was, she said, because women, since they had no opportunity of reading classical tongues, were not subject to pagan influence. There was a little of the tongue in the cheek when she said this. All the leading evangelicals, so often critical of her libertarianism, had by this standard to admit that they themselves had been subjected to corrupt influences, and were therefore in no position to criticise the education of others. Hannah More read the classical authors widely herself, as the young Macaulay testifies. But this apart, she did stand up for the rights and duties of women in society, as all her later life shows; and she was not to be put upon. When a row broke out at Blagdon between the stupid schoolmaster and the stupid clergyman — a row which had national echoes — she put them both in their place without difficulty.

There is also a touch of feminist pride in this recollection, written in her old age to a parent of one of her children.

> The young race, of course, have all forgotten me; but I have not forgotten the energy with which your eldest son, at seven years old, ran into the drawing room, and said to me, "After all, Ferdinand would never have sent Columbus to find out America if it had not been for Isabella: it was entirely *her* doing."

The seven-year-old was not Macaulay, but a member of the Pepys family, a descendant of Samuel himself, and later Lord Cottenham, twice Lord Chancellor of England.

Hannah More outlived her four sisters, who had gravitated towards her, and had in various degrees helped her with her work in the Mendips. At the age of 83, she decided to go into semi-retirement at Clifton, where she lived at 4, Windsor Terrace. From there she wrote to Wilberforce,

> I am diminishing my worldly cares. I have sold Barley Wood. I have exchanged what you called the eight "pampered minions" for four sober servants. As I have sold my carriage and horses, I want no coachman: as I have no garden, I want no gardener. I have greatly lessened my house expenses, which enables me to maintain my schools, and enlarge my charities.

She was visited by the assiduous Cottle, accompanied by the formidable Baptist minister from Broadmead, Robert Hall. Cottle has given us this glimpse of her:

> She brought us to the windows of her spacious drawing room, and there, in the expanse beneath, invited us to behold the new docks, and the merchants' numerous ships, while the hill of Dundry appeared, at a distance of four miles, far loftier than her own Mendip, and equally verdant. From the window of her back room also, directly under her eye, a far more exquisite prospect presented itself than any Barley Wood could boast; Leigh Woods, St. Vincent's Rocks, Clifton Down, and to crown the whole, the winding Avon, with the continually shifting commerce of Bristol; and we left her with the impression that the change in her abode was a great accession to her happiness.

Cottle does not mention her two cats. One was called "Passive Obedience" and the other "Non-Resistance": a little, just slightly irreverent, theological joke.

What do we make of her? There are few characters whom we have at all studied more baffling. Let us quote the judgment of Paul Sangster, on whose book, *Pity My Simplicity*, we have considerably drawn.

> Hannah More, the old Bishop in Petticoats, as William Cobbett so aptly called her, was a mass of contradictions. She never knew enough theology to be sure what Calvinism meant, yet she indulged in theological writings; she was methodistic, yet openly opposed the Methodists; she mixed with the great freely, and opposed nearly all their ways in her writings; and she attacked secular writings for children and devoted her life to producing them. In addition to all this, or in spite of it, she was a very clever woman, in some ways far ahead of her times.

A fair judgement, if an inconclusive one. Compare with the opinion of another judge: John Opie, who painted her in 1786. That was about the time she had put the world behind her. Her dress and mien are proper and puritanical. And yet — John Opie spotted it, and he was a Cornishman, and just the kind of man who would — there *is* a wink in the eye of that pretty face. It would have been fun to take her home in a cab, as Dr. Johnson did, provided one was rather younger than Dr. Johnson was then. What was wrong with poor forgotten Mr. Turner?

Joseph Cottle

In the year 1770, a Bristol poet died, and a Bristol poet was born. The poet who died was Chatterton, "the marvellous boy". Resisting, at least for now, the temptation to dwell on Chatterton, we will just allow ourselves to say that it was characteristically irritating of him to die at the age of 17, so that we can never discover whether he was a genius, or just a juvenile prodigy.

The poet who was born was Wordsworth. It is too partisan a claim to say that Wordsworth was a Bristol poet. He was born at Cockermouth, in Cumberland, and it was the Lake District, where he in due course returned, which became the traditional Wordsworth country. Yet it was in Bristol that the *Lyrical Ballads* were published, one of his greatest works, certainly the one which transformed English poetry. Indeed we are prepared to argue, and to the boredom of our friends often do, that no other event in the history of Bristol has been nearly so important, or so splendid, as the publication of *The*

Lyrical Ballads.

If you count Shakespeare apart, if only because he was a dramatist as much as a poet, you can make a case for saying that Wordsworth is the best of English poets. Perhaps Keats is better, perhaps Milton. Perhaps Joe Bumbleby Binks of Quaker's Yard Low Level is better, and perhaps the name of Bumbleby Binks will resound as that of Shakespeare has done throughout the empyrean. We are too close to modern poetry to make guesses (though perhaps Charles Causley will be found to be a major poet, as the centuries sort themselves out).

As to Wordsworth, here is just a little from the beginning of "Tintern Abbey", one of the most famous of *The Lyrical Ballads*. Wordsworth himself has told us how it was written:

> No poem of mine was composed under circumstances more pleasant to remember than this. I began it upon leaving Tintern, after crossing the Wye, and concluded it just as I was entering Bristol in the evening, after a ramble of four or five days with my sister. Not a line of it was altered, not any part of it written down till I reached Bristol.

So this is a Bristol poem if ever there was one. It is not an easy poem from which to pick a quotation. It is a unity. So perhaps it is just to catch the flavour from the opening lines, with Wordsworth describing the revisited scene:

> Five years have past; five summers, with the length
> Of five long winters! and again I hear
> These waters, rolling from their mountain-springs
> With a soft inland murmer. Once again
> Do I behold these steep and lofty cliffs,
> That on a wild secluded scene impress
> Thoughts of more deep seclusion; and connect
> The landscape with the quiet of the sky.
> The day is come when I again repose
> Here, under this dark sycamore, and view
> These plots of cottage-ground, these orchard-tufts,
> Which at this season, with their unripe fruits,
> Are clad in one green hue, and lose themselves
> 'Mid groves and copses. Once again I see
> These hedgerows, hardly hedgerows, little lines
> Of sportive wood run wild: these pastoral farms,
> Green to the very door: and wreaths of smoke,
> Sent up, in silence, from among the trees!
> With some uncertain notice, as might seem

Of vagrant dwellers in the houseless woods,
Or of some Hermit's cave, where by his fire
The Hermit sits alone.

Before we leave Wordsworth, we must add that apart from writing much magnificent poetry he also wrote some that was comically bad. Some of his worst lines have achieved almost as much fame as some of his best. Even the *Ballads* contained, beside "Tintern Abbey", these lines from "The Idiot Boy":

This piteous news it so much shocked her,
She quite forgot to send the Doctor.

And these, from "Peter Bell":

For me are homelier tasks prepared;
To the stone table in my garden
The Squire is come, and as I guess
His little ruddy daughter Bess
With Harry the Churchwarden.

It was this endearing way Wordsworth had, of hopping between the sublime and the ridiculous, that caused a friendly parodist to write:

Two voices are there: one is of the deep,
And one is of an old half-witted sheep,
And Wordsworth, both are thine.

But we must press on, for we have not yet reached our proper subject. When *The Lyrical Ballads* was first published, the name of Wordsworth did not appear on the title page. Nor did that of Coleridge, who had made some, for ever undefinable, contribution to them. The only name to appear was that of Joseph Cottle. He was a Bristol bookseller, and a publisher, in a small way, and they had sold him the book.

In 1797 Wordsworth and his sister Dorothy had moved, from Dorset, to Alfoxden, on the Bristol Channel. They moved in order to be nearer their friend Coleridge, who was then living at Nether Stowey. The Wordsworths stayed in Alfoxden only a year, but it was at the end of this year that *The Lyrical Ballads* were published. They had been Coleridge's idea, but it was, not surprisingly, Wordsworth who did nearly all the work. They hoped they could sell the poems for the cost of a walking holiday abroad. In this they were not quite successful. The holiday cost thirty-five pounds, and Cottle paid them thirty.

This Cottle was a poet himself. As it happened he too had been born in the bodeful year, so Bristol can boast another poet of that vintage even if the claim of Wordsworth is disallowed. Cottle was not, it must be said, much of a poet. Some of his lines bear a compelling resemblance to a bad bit of Wordsworth. On climbing in the Malvern hills:

> Still I toil,
> How long and steep and cheerless the ascent!
> It needs the evidence of close deduction
> To know that I shall ever reach the height!

But it is not fair to laugh at Cottle's bad lines. He had so few good ones to set against them, and bad poetry only becomes funny when it is written by good poets.

Cottle set up as a bookseller in Bristol when he was 21, by which time, he proudly tells us, he had read more than a thousand volumes of "the best English literature". He does not seem to have been a very successful book-seller. Even the whereabouts of his shop seems to be unknown. But he had some private means, and he was helpful from time to time to Wordsworth, and Coleridge, and Southey, all three of whom were in and around Bristol at that period. Indeed, though it has become customary to depict him as rather a mean man, it is arguable that he was generous to them, and certainly they all at that time counted him as a friend. He retired from selling and publishing books in 1799, after only eight years at it. This was the year after *The Lyrical Ballads*, though he did not realise there was any special significance in the book at the time. He then wrote his first epic poem, on the very proper subject of King Alfred, and pottered about in literary circles, cheerfully and fussily, maintaining a copious correspondence with the great, until his death at the age of 83.

When he was 67, he published a book of memoirs, called *Early Recollections*: chiefly relating to the late S.T.Coleridge, during his long residence in Bristol. Ten years later, he published his *Remiscences of Coleridge and Southey*. This second book contained most of the first, sometimes recast, and with additional material touching generally on the literary life of his period. It was these books which gave Cottle his fame, or, as some were quick to say, his infamy. D.B.Wyndham Lewis, writing in 1930, says "In these memoirs Mr. Cottle is perceived to be a forerunner of what is known in our times as the Cads' Concert." Even the *Dictionary of National Biography* ticks the man off for "vanity and self-righteousness". For Cottle had set down, in some detail, his financial services to the poets; had reminded the admirers of Southey and

Wordsworth, both of whom had become sternly conservative men with age, that they had been more than mildly radical in youth; and — this was the part that shocked — had revealed Coleridge's addiction to drugs. It cannot have been all that much of a revelation. According to his own account, Cottle must have been about the last of Coleridge's friends to realise what was going on. He wrote to Coleridge a letter telling him to stop it, and relations were later broken off. But a "Cads' Concert"? It does not strike a reader quite like that, at this time of day.

Cottle has one serious fault. He garbles some of the letters he prints. In many cases the originals have been found, and exist to confute him. This does of course cast a general doubt on his reliability on points of detail. But the garbling is a random affair, often no more than the casualness of a man with no proper academic training. If it has a purpose, it is usually to project a more favourable image of Cottle himself, rather than to denigrate Coleridge or any of the others.

As against this, it is a deeply interesting book, which carries you along despite its pomposities, about a deeply interesting period in the history of Bristol. Let us take an extract. This is part of an account by Cottle of an expedition to the Wye valley. He had invited Southey and Coleridge to be his guests, and also two young ladies, sisters; one of whom was to become, happily, Mrs. Southey, and the other, disastrously, Mrs. Coleridge. They have lunched well at the Beaufort Arms, Chepstow, and set off for Tintern — Cottle riding, because (be sure he explains) of an old ankle injury, the rest walking. They lost their way, were overtaken by storm, and then darkness.

> I dismounted, resolving to lead my steed who trembled as though conscious of the perilous expedition on which he had entered. Mr. Coleridge who had been more accustomed to rough riding than myself, upon understanding that I through cowardice had forsaken the saddle, without speaking a word put his foot in the stirrup and mounting, determined to brave at all hazards, the dangers of the campaign.

This is perhaps a little dig at Coleridge, who had at one time run away from Cambridge and joined the Dragons; in his brief enlistment it was said he spent most of his time falling off his horse:

> We had arrived at a spot, where there was just light enough to descry three roads, in this bosom of the wood, diverging off in different directions. We now shouted aloud, in the faint hope that some solitary woodman might hear, and come to our relief. All was silence! One in the company now remarked, "Of what service is it to boast a pioneer, if we do not avail ourselves of his service?" Mr. Coleridge received the hint, and set off up one of the lanes at his swiftest speed, namely, a cautious

creep. From his long absence, we almost feared whether hard necessity might not force us to go in search of our way-bewildered or quagmired companion.

To our great joy, we heard the horse's hoofs sliding over the loose stones. Mr. Coleridge approached and pensively said, that could not be the way, for it led to an old quarry which the quick sight of his steed discovered just in time to save both their necks. Mr. C was next ordered instantly to explore one of the other two ominous lanes; when like a well-disciplined orderly man, he set off gallantly on his new commission. After waiting a time, he leisurely returned, significantly saying that neither man nor beast could pass that way! rubbing his thorn-smitten cheek. Now came the use of the syllogism, in its simplest form. "If the right road by A, B, or C, and A and B were wrong, then C must be right." Under this conviction, we marched boldly on, without further solicitude or exploration, and at length joyfully reached — Tintern Abbey!

This kind of reminiscence gives us pleasing glimpses of the young lions at play, and at the end of the eighteenth century, Bristol was full of young lions of one kind and another. While Coleridge was experimenting with new metres for poetry, and with opium, Humphry Davy was experimenting with the medical properties of gases at the Pneumatic Institution in Hotwells. Among others who worked there were T.L.Beddoes and the editor of the Thesaurus, P.M.Roget. The place was buzzing with intellectual activity, and Cottle, the benevolent busybody, was at the heart of it all, and recording much of it. Coleridge called him "a well-meaning creature, but great fool" — but that was after Cottle had found out about the drugs. Although Wordsworth did not stay very long, Southey, growing priggish young, stayed longer and maintained contacts with Cottle throughout his life. There was Thelwall, the dangerous radical with the police on his tail. There are glimpses of Hazlitt, the genius of prose, a sad rather than sour man; of Charles Lamb, who was cross when Coleridge called him "gentle-hearted", but who was indeed gentle-hearted, in the best sense; a calm hollow amid the buffeting winds of his friends — Lamb, who travelled always with his beloved sister, and with a straight-jacket, lest she should be seized again with the madness which had caused her to kill her mother... it was all a startling mixture of the graceful and the grotesque, a society which can properly be called romantic in almost any of the innumerable meanings of that word. And it needed such unromantic chroniclers as Cottle.

Above anyone else, his scene is dominated by Coleridge. Coleridge was not the best of the romantic poets. He wrote comparatively little that has lasted. But he was much the most interesting person among them, and Cottle, though often irritated by him almost beyond endurance, was clearly captivated by him. Also, Coleridge spent longer in Bristol than the others; kept coming back to earn a few extra pounds by lecturing, and — in latter years — to keep away from his wife, tucked away in Lakeland with the Southeys. Cottle had published Coleridge's first book of poems, several years before *The Lyrical Ballads* appeared. The publication was not achieved without difficulty.

On my expressing to him a wish to begin the printing as early as he found it convenient, he sent me the following note.

My dear friend,

The printer may depend on copy on Monday morning, and if he can work a sheet a day, he shall have it.   S.T.C.

A day or two after, and before the receipt of the copy, I received from Mr. C the following cheerful note.

Dear Mr. Cottle,

By the thick smoke that precedes the volcanic eruptions of Etna, Vesuvius, and Hecla, I feel an impulse to fumigate, at 25 College Street, and if thou wilt send me by the bearer four pipes, I will write a panegyrical epic poem upon thee, with as many books as there are letters in thy name. Moreover, if thou wilt send me "the copy book", I hereby bind myself, by tomorrow morning, to write out enough copy for a sheet and a half. God bless you! S.T.C.

This promising commencement was soon interrupted by successive and long-continued delays. The permission I had given to anticipate payment was remembered and complied with, before the work went to the press. These delays I little heeded, but they were not quite so acceptable to the printer, who grievously complained that his types were locked up week after week, to his great detriment. I continued to see Mr. Coleridge every day, and occasionally said to him, smiling, "well how much copy?" "None, today" was the general reply, "but tomorrow you shall have some." Tomorrow produced, if any, perhaps a dozen lines; and, in a favourable state of mind, so much, it might be, as half a dozen pages.

It may amuse the reader to receive one or two more of Mr. C's little apologies.

My dear Friend,

The printer may depend on copy by tomorrow. S.T.C.

Dear Cottle,

A devil, a very devil, has got possession of my left temple, eye, cheek, jaw, throat and shoulder. I cannot see you this evening. I write in agony. Your affectionate Friend and Brother, S.T.C.

Sometimes his other engagements were of a pressing nature.

Dear Cottle,

Shall I trouble you (I being over the mouth and nose, in doing something of importance, at Lovell's) to send your servant into the market, and buy a pound of bacon, and two quarts of broad beans; and when he carries it down to College St. to desire the maid to dress it for dinner, and tell her I shall be home by three o'clock. Will you come and drink tea with me, and I will endeavour to get the etc. ready for you. Yours affectionately, S.T.C.

When ingenuity was fairly taxed with excuses, Mr. C would candidly admit, that he had very little "finger industry", but then, he said, his mind was always on "full stretch". The Herculean labour now appeared to be drawing to a close.

My dear, very dear Cottle,

I will be with you at half past six; if you will give me a dish of tea, between that time and eleven o'clock at night, I will write out the whole of the notes, and the preface, as I give you leave to turn the lock and key upon me. I am engaged to dine with Michael Castle, but I will not be one minute past my time. If I am, I permit you to send a note to Michael Castle requesting him to send mine home to fulfil engagements, like an honest man. S.T.C.

Well knowing that it was Mr. Coleridge's intention to do all that was right, but aware at the same time that, however prompt he might be in resolving, he had to contend, in the fulfilment, with great constitutional indecision, I had long resolved to leave the completion of his work wholly to himself, and not to urge him to a speed which would render that a toil, which was designed to be a pleasure.

While the whole of that account cannot quite be taken at the foot of the letter, it does give a fair picture of the very different characters of the young Coleridge and the young Cottle.

This was how, many years later, Cottle found out about the drug-taking:

I had often spoken to Hannah More of S.T.Coleridge, and proceeded with him, one morning, to Barley wood, her residence, eleven miles from Bristol. The interview was mutually agreeable, nor was there any lack of conversation; but I was struck with something singular in Mr. Coleridge's eye. I expressed to a friend, the next day, my concern at having beheld him, during his visit to Hannah More, so extremely paralytic, his hands shaking to an alarming degree, so that he could not take a glass of wine without spilling it, though one hand supported the other! "That", said he, "arises from the immoderate quantity of OPIUM he takes."

The letter which Cottle then wrote to Coleridge does not show him at his best. He was no doubt irritated that he had not made the discovery himself, considering himself with some justification Coleridge's oldest friend in Bristol. He was cross that he had given Coleridge money, only for it to be expended for such purpose. He probably had better motives as well. A little of it will be enough to give the letter's flavour:

> When I think of Coleridge, I wish to recall the image of him, such as he appeared in past years; now, how has the baneful use of opium thrown a dark cloud over you and your prospects. I would not say anything needlessly harsh or unkind, but I must be *faithful*. It is the irresistible voice of conscience. Others may still flatter you, and hang upon your words, but I have another, though a less gracious duty to perform. I see a brother sinning a sin unto death, and shall I not warn him? I see him perhaps on the borders of eternity, in effect, despising his Maker's law, and yet indifferent to his perilous state!

There is a great deal of it in much the same style.

Cottle had also made the acquaintance of De Quincey, whose efforts in the way of opium eating were to make Coleridge's look puny. De Quincey had gone to Cottle and asked if he might anonymously make a gift to Coleridge, who was known to be hard up. Through Cottle's agency, De Quincey gave Coleridge £300. Cottle was criticized for telling the story in his memoirs, but defended himself:

> I have been thus particular in detailing the whole of this affair, so honourable to Mr. De Quincey; and, as I was the communicating agent, I thought it right, on this occasion, to give publicity to the transaction, on the principle of doing justice to all.

He adds, less defensibly:

> Notwithstanding the prohibition, some indirect notices from myself, could have left no doubt with Mr. C of the source of this handsome gift.

De Quincey was less kind about Cottle. He declared that Cottle's contribution to life consisted of two epic poems and a new kind of blacking.

Cottle's *is* the kind of book which is liable to give offence at the time, in the same degree as it is valued by historians. It was avidly read when published, and still makes good reading. After spending so much of his life in the shadow of the giants, he cannot be blamed too much for wishing to make a stir himself before he died. The epic poems brought him no fame, so he decided to see what a bit of blacking might do. Very few of those he criticized were in a position to throw stones at him. Neither Coleridge nor De Quincey were monuments of discretion. Our knowledge of the period would be much less without Cottle, though he had his priggish side, and probably, at least in conversation, his boring side. There is much to like about him; and he did, after all, publish the early works of Wordsworth and company, and even lost money on them.

It is the first mild day of March:
Each minute sweeter than before,
The redbreast sings from the tall larch
That stands beside our door.

There is a blessing in the air,
Which seems a sense of joy to yield
To the bare trees and mountains bare,
And grass in the green field.

Written by Wordsworth at Alfoxden, 1798. Published by Joseph Cottle, bookseller, Bristol. It is not enough to say that someone was bound to have published those lines. Cottle did. And that is enough for fame.

John Skinner

The village of Camerton lies in what was once the middle of the North Somerset coalfield, on the line of the derelict Somerset coal canal. The Somerset villages hereabouts are not your thatched-cottage chocolate-box types. Few places which have lived by coal can be. Yet the countryside is pleasant enough, even if some of the cheerful grassy tumps conceal slag-heaps, and Camerton today makes a sufficiently pastoral scene. The Rectory has an air of distinction, though large and tending to dilapidation. The beech wood on the hill above is green and friendly when the sun shines. You would not know, passing by, that this had been the setting for a tragedy.

Tragedy is not the conflict of goodness with evil. It is the breaking of goodness by goodness: but it is better to be honest and stupid than dishonest and clever. Today we use the phrase "he means well" as a condemnation. But it is better to mean well than to mean badly. Othello is very irritating, but we do not seriously think Iago preferable.

John Skinner, Rector of Camerton from 1800 until his death in 1839, was an honest, stupid man. We are well informed about him from his journal. Ninety-eight volumes of it are in the British Museum, and even that is not the whole. John Skinner's handwriting was so bad that the journal had to be transcribed by his brother Russell, and because Russell died seven years before John, the later volumes are lost.

The journals are mostly composed of disquisitions on archaeology and topography. It was by these Skinner hoped his name would live, and it was these which nearly submerged it. His theories about Camerton, which he believed to be the Roman Camolodonum, if not Arthur's Camelot, were a source of amusement to fellow-antiquarians in his lifetime, though he is now held to have been a useful field archaeologist in lesser, more practical matters. But among these arid tracts of mostly second-rate scholarship, there are oases. These are his accounts of his family life, and of parochial affairs. In 1930, a selection of them was published, under the title *Journal of a Somerset Rector*, by Howard Coombs and Arthur Bax. In 1971, Howard and Peter Coombs published a revised and enlarged edition (later reissued in paperback — O.U.P., 1984). By these labours they placed us much in their debt.

Skinner had begun his career with high hopes. He was first a curate at Claverton, near Bath, and then at Brent Knoll. Railway travellers and motorists will remember Brent Knoll, sticking suddenly up from the Somerset levels, an unexpected outcrop of the Mendips, near Highbridge. He arrived at Brent Knoll on horseback, riding straight up and over the Knoll *en route*. This suggests the kind of vigour and enthusiasm a country parson needed. When his uncle bought him the comfortable living at Camerton, it seemed a situation full of promise for both villagers and priest.

Skinner's trouble was that he could not get on with people. He was meticulously honest, hard-working, conscientious in all his duties. The people of Camerton hated him for it. He had some of the bad qualities of the Methodists he so detested, and none of their compensating warmth. He could only forgive as a conscious and deliberate act of Christian charity, and his manner of doing it often roused its subject's fury. With his eldest son, Owen, he conducted an endless round of squabbles, growing increasingly bitter with the years. He compares himself to Lear, kicked and buffeted by his own. And yet he *wanted* to be loved by his son and surely he had been generous, forbearing, all that a good parent should be? This he believed to be true, and in a sense it *was* true. Owen, who in spite of the journal's strictures does not emerge as an altogether unsympathetic character, wanted to be loved by his father. But they drew apart, father regarding son as an unnatural ingrate, son regarding father as a self-righteous prig. "Everything that could be said or done to irritate me, my son employed", John Skinner once wrote:

> He said he would readily leave me if I would give the money to take his degree, but if I did not he would continue in my house, as he had a right to do, and if I used any force to expel him he would use force to force, and he broke one of the parlour chairs as a foretaste of what I was to expect! I said his conduct had shown him so complete and callous a villain that when he left my roof I should feel relieved of a heavy load. "You are a damned liar to call me a villain", he replied. "Who cares for such a father? I despise you from my heart."

They wounded each other with all the savagery which is only possible to those who know each other very well. Nothing can have hurt more than when Owen said of the beloved journal, "Everyone laughs at your folly in thinking the occurrences of your parish and your family worth reading." "The feeling I experience is not revenge, it is sorrow", wrote Skinner after one scene; but then he went on, fatally he went on, "O God: forgive him, change his mind, punish him by those chastisements which may conduce to his reformation."

He had married in 1805, and for five years was deeply happy. In 1810 a brother, a naval officer, and two sisters died of consumption. In 1811 a child, the fifth, died of the same disease, and then, soon afterwards, her mother. Skinner wrote these revealing words of his wife's death bed:

> She declares that the only wish she has to live longer is that she may continue to console me, and when she thinks how desolate I shall be, if left alone amidst the ill-disposed people of Camerton, without any friends to whom I may confide my cares,

or who may soothe my mind when too much irritated by their misconduct, she is most wretched.

She knew her husband well. Soon afterwards, he had an attack of consumption himself, but recovered — he was very fond of the open air, which must have helped. His survival was a doubtful mercy. Two more children died of the same disease. There only survived Owen, and Anna, poor girl, who did her best to keep the peace in the battle-torn Rectory.

As time goes on, Skinner's life becomes a succession of rows. Rows with Owen and even Anna. Rows with the lady of the manor — clearly a kindly person, one of the Jarrett family — over details of rectorial rights which he felt it his duty to preserve. His duty! How this dark, rigid man's life was plagued by his duty, and how it plagued those who sought to befriend him. Rows with the farmers, over compensation for the Rector's archaeological excavations. Rows with the colliers. Although he was a good Tory, and horrified by the Reform Bill, Skinner's sense of justice led him more than once to take the side of the colliers against their employers: he recognized that a reduction in pay of three shillings a week would cause some of them to "suffer beyond bearing", though he could not resist mentioning as well (probably with truth) that there were "some artful, ill-disposed fellows" among them. He never failed in his sick visiting. He was not spare in his charity. When times were hard, there was hot soup in the Rectory boiler. When the cholera came, he remained unflinching at his post (many parsons did not). He prepared his sermons with much care. But Camerton would have none of him. The people threw stones at him, wrote dirty words on his gate, tied tin cans to the tail of his dog, moved the marker in the lectern Bible so that he could not find the place, tormented him — he was so easily tormented — in a score of petty ways: and stayed away from church. "I don't even remember", he wrote after thirty-two years' ministry, "to have seen so small a congregation when the weather is fair."

He has no hesitation in comparing Camerton to Sodom and Gomorrah. "I am more and more disgusted with the people around me; such a total want of feeling prevails that there is absolutely nothing to work on." But at the same time he is doing all he can to comfort and succour the children of a poor half-witted woman who had been burnt to death as the result of the negligence of her husband. There is an odd but touching picture of another death. Mrs. Gullick had died, and:

> on arrival we found the family in a sad state...the children, seven in number, crying around their father. Finding that talking could afford but little consolation at that period, I desired one of the women to get some beer from the alehouse, of which I gave half a glass to each of the children and a glass to Gullick, and was glad to

51

perceive that it acted as a cordial, and they became more composed.

"But happy it is", he adds, "that the people in the lower ranks of life are not possessed of the same sensibility as their superiors." It is the kind of remark which makes one feel Gullick could have been forgiven had he thrown the beer back in his benefactor's face. Then there is trouble with Balne, the village constable, who, when Skinner accused him of failing in his duty, turned on his Rector and said "You are mad half your time, and do not know what you say and do." But when Balne was old and ill, and deserted by his wife, Skinner went to see him, read prayers and had "a long and serious conversation", gave him some sheets and blankets and half a crown.

His happiest times in his latter years were at meetings of his fellow clergy. He received much kindness from the Bishop of Bath and Wells, who shines through the pages as a real father in God. But even his brethren were tempted to torment him. He had conceived some freakish etymological theories, and the subject arose at a clerical meeting at the beautiful village of Mells.

> After some rather desultory conversation one of the party, of the name of Bumstead, asked me what was the etymon of his name. I did not perceive it at the time, but have every reason to believe, on account of what afterwards occurred, that it was done purposely to put me on the subject of etymology for the amusement of the company.

It is an amusing, revealing and very sad incident.

He tried to study his own faults. After an unnecessary dispute with the lady of the manor, he wrote: "I am not pleased with my feelings altogether just now. I fear indeed they are not what they ought to be; I will endeavour to correct them." On another occasion, "Oh, my God, I am the work of Thy hands: dispose of me and mine as most fitting to Thee." But as time goes on, the prayers for a calm submission to God's will seem — let us hope we are not being unfair to him — more conventional. In 1832, after another terrible family dispute, he wrote

> All these things are against me, and will bring down my grey hairs in sorrow to the grave. I am now going to bed, I cannot say to sleep. There is surely not one thing now in the world that can excite in my mind a wish to live longer in this toilsome state. But not my will, but Thine, be done, O God.

Next day the family quarrel went on just the same.

Even before the journal ends, he is often asking God to end a life so barren. The prayer was not answered. So one night in December, 1839, when he was

67 years old, John Skinner climbed the hill above his Rectory, and there, looking down on the village where he had laboured for forty years, among the bare trees of the beech wood, he shot himself.

Francis Kilvert

If poor John Skinner's life was a tragedy, there was a touch of tragedy in the life of another parson of the following generation, Francis Kilvert. But they were very different men. In Skinner's case, his suicide seemed a natural culmination to a life of growing grief. In Kilvert's, his early death was an unexpected abortion of a life of growing happiness. Both men kept voluminous diaries, which were not published until long after they had died. Their only fame was posthumous. Skinner was perhaps the more interesting man; Kilvert was by far the better writer, though his character remains in some respects shadowy. People have been known to compare Kilvert with Samuel Pepys, and it is not an extravagant comparison. He does some fine scenic set-pieces, but it is his gift for observation, for the detail and humour of country life, which makes his diary such good reading:

> My mother says that at Dursley, in Gloucestershire, when ladies and gentlemen used to go out to dinner together on dark nights, the gentlemen pulled out the tails of their shirts and walked before to show the way and light the ladies. These were called "Dursley Lanterns".

That was written in 1873. Take, from the year following, one of the many clerical reminiscences:

> The Archdeacon of Sarum on a Visitation tour came to a small upland parish. He asked the clerk how often the Holy Communion was administered in the year. The clerk stared. "What did you please to say?", he asked. "The Holy Communion", repeated the Archdeacon. "How often do you have it in the year?" The Clerk still stared open-mouthed in hopeless bewilderment. At length a suspicion of the Archdeacon's meaning began to dawn faintly upon him. "Aw", he blurted out, "Aw, we do never have he. We've got no tackling."

But it is by no means all humour:

> This afternoon I went to see Mrs. Drew and if possible to comfort her concerning the death of her child. She was filled with sorrow and remorse because when the

child had mouched from school last Monday and had wandered about all day with scarcely any food she had whipped him as soon as he came home in the evening and had sent him supperless to bed, although he had besought her almost in an agony to give him a bit of bread. "Oh Mother, oh Mother, do give me one bit of bread." Her heart smote her bitterly now that it was too late, when she remembered how the child had begged and prayed for food. The next morning soon after rising he fell down in a fit and he died at even. The mother asked me to go upstairs to see the child. He lay in his coffin looking very peaceful and natural with the flowers on his breast and the dark hair curling on his forehead.

Here is a piece of medical information:

Mrs. Vincent told me that her husband had not suffered so much lately from the pressure of water upon his heart which had been sensibly relieved by the water running out at his heels.

Here, an etymological observation:

Hannah Hood uses a curious word for "gulp". She says, "I took two or three 'glutches' of port wine".

Here is a characteristic descriptive passage:

I went out late last night to lock the white gate. The wind had dropped and all was still, save for the occasional slow dripping of the trees after the last heavy shower. Against the clean bright sky every leaf and twig stood out with marvellous distinctness, and as I approached the gate the moonlight streamed in up the avenue, dark with foliage, from the wide empty open Common, like moonlight streaming into a dark house through an open door. The ground was still wet and shining with the rain, and the gigantic shadow of the gate projected by the moonlight was cast far up the avenue in huge bars upon the shining ground.

Although that is a vivid description, you can hardly say it is over-written. The strength of Kilvert's writing, especially in such passages, is that he does not become effusive. He observes carefully, chooses his adjectives with care, prefers the short and pointed phrase. Only rarely does one feel that he is "tacking on a purple patch or two to give an effect of colour", and when he does one can usually find a sufficient reason, most probably a young lady, in the context.

He was born at Hardenhuish, still locally pronounced Harnish, near Chippenham, in 1840. He was the second child of the Rector. His mother came from a good family, the Ashes of Langley Burrell. He went to Oxford and was ordained. He became curate of Langley Burrell, where his father was now Rector. He later went to Clyro, in Radnorshire, as a curate for seven years; he tried repeatedly to obtain a living of his own, but failed, and went back to Langley Burrell, once again as curate to his father, for a further four years. At last, when he was thirty-seven years old, he obtained the living of Bredwardine, on the river Wye. Less than two years later he died.

It does not amount to much of a success story. He kept his diary for nine years, from the age of twenty-nine until shortly before his death. It has never been published in full: it would, his editor explains, run to nine volumes. The editor, Mr. William Plomer, clearly a loving and careful editor, published a selection in three volumes in 1938-1940, and made a further abridgement in one volume a few years later. If you ask for a copy of Kilvert's Diary it is this last volume you are most likely to get. There are in any case some gaps in the original, which possibly the writer himself, since the passages occur at times of stress in his affairs, when he might have considered his thoughts too delicate even for his descendants to share.

William Plomer says, modestly enough, that the diary has "come to be recognized as a minor classic", and probably even the extracts you have read will incline you to such a view. There is now a Francis Kilvert Society, which has put up memorials to him in the places he knew best — there is a beautiful plaque in the little church at Langley Burrell. A member of the society (though he is a little sardonic about it) is A.T. Le Quesne, who wrote *After Kilvert*, in which he attractively sets out his own journal in the master's footsteps, in a gracious and not dissimilar style. It is to be hoped that he and the Society will bring their efforts to bear on a publication of the entire diary. Until that is done, there remains a nagging suspicion that Kilvert has been, perhaps unwittingly, bowdlerized.

For the diary, apart from being a mine of information about country life in the west in the nineteenth century, does pose some problems about the man himself. To take the most obvious, why was his clerical career so unsuccessful? Of course livings could be bought and sold in the Church of England at that time, and Kilvert had no money to speak of; but there are plenty of examples of poor men of ability breaking through to high position in the church, and since Kilvert certainly did not lack ability, what was the trouble? He was not idle. He must have spent a long time writing, but much of the material for his writing comes from his own pastoral work. He loved the church and accepted its teachings. He cannot have been a bad preacher. What was wrong?

If Kilvert was thought of by his ecclesiastical superiors as an "unsound" man, can it possibly have been because of the girls? It is not suggested he behaved immorally, but were there times when he was a shade eccentric? He falls in love several times, perfectly properly, and fails to marry only so far as one can tell, because Victorian fathers did not approve of unbeneficed clergymen as suitors to their daughters. One of these ladies, Daisy, takes up a lot of the diary, and obviously returned his affection: she died unmarried, though whether that was because she loved no other, or her father pitched his demands too high for too long, we cannot say. But it is not Kilvert's rhapsodies about Daisy and her successors which cause us to lift an eyebrow. There are other girls in the books, of a different social status, and younger; much younger:

> At the school, Gipsy Lizzie looking arch and mischievous with her dark large beautiful eyes, and a dazzling smile showed her little white teeth, as she tossed her dark curls back.

We soon hear of her again:

> The classes and standard at the school have been rearranged and Gipsy Lizzie has been put into my reading class. How is the indescribable beauty of that most lovely face to be described — the dark soft curls parting back from the pure white transparent brow, the exquisite little mouth and pearly tiny teeth, the pure straight delicate features, the long dark fringes and white eyelids that droop over and curtain her eyes, when they are cast down and bent upon her book, and seem to rest upon the soft clear cheek, and when the eyes are raised, that clear unfathomable blue depth of wide wonder and enquiry and unsullied and unsuspecting innocence. Oh, child, child, if you did but know your own power. Oh, Gipsy, if you grow up as good as you are fair. Oh, that you might grow up good. May all God's angels guard you, sweet.

One does not need to be especially worldly to be a little startled by such a passage. Or:

> It is a pretty little lane this Bird's Nest lane, very shady and quiet, narrow and overbowered here and there with arching wyches and hazels. Sometimes my darling child Gipsy comes down to school this way, but more often she comes down Sunny Bank when the days are fine, and then over the narrow green-arched lane, and those sweet blue eyes have looked down this vista to the blue mountains and those little hands have gathered flowers along these banks. O my child if you did but know. If you only knew that this lane and this dingle and these fields are sweet to me and holy ground for your sweet sake. But you can never know, and if you should ever guess or read the secret, it will be but a dim misty suspicion of the truth. Ah Gipsy.

You notice how, while the descriptions are still vivid and careful, Kilvert's tidy English style forsakes him in such moments, and the words fall over each other with eagerness. Still, he writes with equal enthusiasm of his more orthodox passions:

> Such a happy day. Thank God for such a happy day. I have seen my love, my own, I have seen Daisy. She was so lovely and sweet and kind and the beautiful love is as fresh and strong as ever. I never saw her more happy and affectionate and her lovely Welsh eyes grew radiant whenever they met mine. She was looking prettier than ever and the East wind had freshened her pretty colour and her lovely hair was shining like gold. She wore a brown stuff dress and white ribbons to her hat.
> I wonder if Daisy and I will ever read these pages over together. I think we shall.

Perhaps it is, after all, as well they did not. Even dear Daisy might have cast a sharp eye on Gipsy Lizzie, to say nothing of this acquaintance, made at the Kington St. Michael school feast:

> As we were swinging the children under the elms that crown the Tor Hill a girl came up to me with a beseeching look in her eyes and an irresistible request for a swing. She was a perfect little beauty with a plump rosy face, dark hair, and lovely soft dark eyes melting with tenderness and a sweet little mouth as pretty as a rosebud. I lifted her into the swing and away she went. But about the sixth flight the girl suddenly slipped off the swing seat feet foremost and still keeping hold of the ropes she hung from the swing helpless. Unfortunately her clothes had got hitched upon the seat of the swing and were all pulled up round her waist and it instantly became apparent that she wore no drawers.

Stand by, Daisy, here's the bit really to set you rolling:

> A titter and then a shout of laughter ran through the crowd as the girl's plump person was seen naked hanging from the swing. O ye gods, the fall of Hebe was nothing to it. We hustled her out of the swing and her clothes into their proper place as soon as possible and perhaps she did not know what a spectacle she had presented. I believe it was partly my fault. When I lifted the girl into the swing there were many aspirants for the seat and in the struggle and confusion I suppose I set her down with her clothes rumpled up and her bare flesh (poor child) upon the board and as her flesh was plump and smooth and in excellent whipping condition and the board slippery, they managed to part company with this result. Poor child, when she begged so earnestly for a swing she scarcely contemplated the exhibition of herself for the amusement of the spectators. I shall never see the elms on the Tor Hill now without thinking of the fall of Hebe.

It is a passage, one feels, which exposes rather more than the poor child. But we must be careful not to give a wrong impression of Kilvert and his book. Although quite a long list of references to whippings and bare bottoms could be made, they are only a small part of the work. He does write, once,

Though I be tied and bound with the chain of my sin yet let the pitifulness of Thy Great mercy loose me.

— but that can have referred to anything, or be no more than the conventional kind of apostrophe one finds in many nineteenth-century diaries. His sins rarely went beyond the imagination, and perhaps it is significant that the more strenuous passages appear in his latter years, when years of abstinence might have been expected to take an increasing mental toll. The passages about the young ladies do not obtrude in the book. It is only when one tries to consider what kind of a man he was, and particularly the matter of his unsuccessful career, that they push themselves into consideration.

There is a another slight mystery about him. In the first flush of his enthusiasm for Daisy, Kilvert writes:

I do believe she likes me and cares for me. I fancy I can see it in her loving deep grey eyes. I wonder what she thinks of my poor disfigured eyes, whether she loves me better or worse for that. She must know. She must see. Perhaps she is sorry for me. And they say pity is akin to love.

He tells us no more about this disfigurement. If he felt it keenly, he suppressed it. He gives us plenty of evidence that there was nothing wrong with his sight. If it was a severe disfigurement, or if he only imagined it to be severe, it must have had some effect upon the course of his life. But we are left to guess.

Enough of Kilvert's own problems. Let us look at one or two more of his pictures:

Dame Matthews used to live at the Home Farm at Langley Burrell. She was a member of the family, but she must have lived a long time ago, as Mrs. Banks remarked, because she called cows 'kine'. The Dame used to sit up in the chimney corner and near her chair was a little window through which she could see all down the dairy. One evening she saw one of the farm men steal a pound of butter out of the dairy and put it into his hat, at the same moment clapping his hat upon his head.

"John", called the Dame, "John, come here. I want to speak to you". John came, carefully keeping his hat on his head. The Dame ordered some ale to be heated for him and bade him sit down in front of the roaring fire. John thanked his mistress and said he would have the ale another time, as he wanted to go home at once.

"No, John. Sit you down by the fire and drink some hot ale. 'Tis a cold night and I want to speak to you about the kine."

The miserable John, daring neither to take off his hat nor go without his mistress's leave, sat before the scorching fire drinking the hot ale till the melting butter in his hat began to run down all over his face. The Dame eyed him with malicious fun. "Now, John", she said, "you may go. I won't charge you anything for the butter."

An ecclesiastical misadventure concerning Mr. Pope, the curate of Cusop, at a confirmation service:

Pope had one candidate Miss Stokes a farmer's daughter and they went together by train. Pope went in a cutaway coat very short, with his dog, and took no gown. The train was very late. He came very late into church and sat down on a bench with the girl cheek by jowl. When it came to his turn to present his candidate he was told by the Rector to explain to the Bishop why he came so late. The Bishop has a new fashion of confirming only two persons at a time, kneeling at the rails. The Bishop had marked two young people come in very late and when they came up to the rails he thought from Pope's youthful appearance and from his having no gown that he was a young farmer candidate and brother of the girl. He spoke to them severely and told them to come on and kneel down for they were extremely late. Pope tried to explain that he was a clergyman and that the girl was his candidate but the Bishop either did not hear or did not attend, seeming to think he was dealing with a refractory ill-conditioned youth. "I know, I know," he said, "Come at once, kneel down, kneel down." Poor Pope resisted a long time and had a long battle with the Bishop, but at last unhappily he was overborne in the struggle, lost his head, gave way, knelt down, and was *confirmed* there and then, and no-one seems to have interfered to save him, though the whole church was in a titter. It is a most unfortunate thing and it will unhappily be a joke against Pope all his life. The Bishop was told of his mistake afterwards and apologised to Pope, rather shortly and cavalierly. He said, what was quite true, that Pope ought to have come in his gown. But there was a little fault on all sides.

But it is the casual comments that one enjoys as much as the longer set-pieces. The Dursley Lanterns. The Malmesbury Jackdaws:

Mrs. John Knight tells me that the Malmesbury people are commonly called "Jackdaws", to their intense disgust. It is a common saying among folks going to Malmesbury, "Let us go and see the Malmesbury Jackdaws." I remember hearing years ago, I think among the people of Kington St. Michael, that jackdaws are often called in these parts "The Parsons from Malmesbury Abbey." Perhaps the grey polls of the birds may have suggested the shaven polls of the monks, or the thievish habits of the jackdaws may have called to remembrance some tradition of the rapacity of the Abbot of Malmesbury.

A visit to the squire:

I found the squire and Mrs. Ashe in the upper drawing room. She was reading aloud to him. He asked whether I thought it wise to have lectures on winter evenings for mixed audiences of men and women, and to bring out the girls and their sweethearts for a moonlight walk.

There was no knowing what they might get up to. The very next entry indicates the mischief of the times:

Mrs. Hall told me of Edward Humphries, who married a young woman when he was 83 and had a son within the year. "Leastways his wife had", said Mrs. Hall.

Kilvert could laugh at himself as well as others. Here he is on a visit to Oxford, to renew acquaintance with his old college friend, Mayhew:

We met a short stout gentleman with a double chin and large umbrella, a kindly face and merry eye, who buttonholed Mayhew and began to inveigh in an aggrieved tone against the folly, perversity and bad taste of the University residents and visitors in rushing in crowds of 1200 to hear the Bishop of Derry give an ornamental rhetorical flourish by way of a Bampton Lecture in the morning, and leaving himself (Professor Pritchard, Professor of Astronomy and Select Preacher) to hold forth to empty benches in the afternoon. He thought it was a sin and a shame. He declared the Bishop's Bampton Lectures to be growing worse week by week and to be an insult to the understanding of the University. "Sir", he said, "they are barren, there is nothing in them at all. I have in my pocket", he continued, "a letter from a Manchester gentleman who is steeped to the eyes in cotton. He says that he was spending Sunday in Oxford and he heard in the University Church what he will never forget so long as he lives." At this point the Professor's merry eye twinkled and he smiled broadly. Thinking that the Manchester gentleman's remark applied to the balderdash which the Professor represented the Bishop's Bampton Lecture to have been, and taking my cue from the Professor's smile, I laughed loud and long. The Professor eyed me oddly and went on with his story, from which I was horrified to learn that the remark in the Manchester gentleman's letter applied not to the Bishop's lecture, but to the Professor's own select sermon, which touched the cotton lord to the heart and done him much spiritual good.

Here is a glimpse of him on one of his visits to Bristol:

> As I was sitting in a confectioner's shop between the Drawbridge and College Green eating a bun I saw lingering about the door a barefooted child, a little girl, with fair hair tossed and tangled wild, an arch espiegle eager little face and beautiful wild eyes, large and grey, which looked shyly into the shop at me with a wistful beseeching smile. She wore a poor faded ragged frock and her shapely limbs and tiny delicate beautiful feet were bare and stained with mud and dust. Christ seemed to be looking at me through the beautiful wistful imploring eyes of the barefooted hungry child. I took her out a bun, and I shall never forget the quick happy grateful smile which flashed over her face as she took it and began to eat. I asked her name and she told me, but amidst the roar of the street and the bustle of the crowded pavements I could not catch the accents of the childish voice. Never mind. I shall know some day.

On this same day he goes to visit the daughter of a friend at the Clergy Daughters' School in Great George Street. She gives him a "long, loving kiss", and they carve their initials on a beech tree in the garden. This leads to some adverse comment from the school authorities, and later the school secretary writes to the girl's father saying that if she continued to receive correspondence from Mr. Kilvert she must leave the school. He makes no comment on the episode except to say that he was very much annoyed.

Once he has his own parish, Kilvert's entries become briefer and less frequent, at least so far as we can judge from the printed selection. This was due not only to increasing duties, but to increasingly poor health His last entry was in March, 1879. In the following August, he married. His wife was Elizabeth Anne Rowland of Woodstock. She was aged 33. He had met her on a visit to Paris, not long before. So of all the women in Kilvert's life, Elizabeth Anne is surely the only one who is never mentioned in the diary.

His thoughts had turned more frequently to death in his last years, when sickness was often with him. He wrote this on a visit to Langley Burrell, where his father was still alive and ministering:

> I went out for a little while on the terrace this morning and walked up and down on the sunny side of the house. After how many illnesses such as this have I taken my first convalescent walk on the sunny terrace, and always at this time of year when the honeysuckle leaves were shooting green and the apricot blossoms were dawning and the daffodils to blow. But some day will come the last illness from which there will be no convalescence and after which there will be no going out to enjoy the

sweet sights and sounds of the early spring, the singing of the birds, the opening of the fruit blossoms, the budding dawn of green leaves, and the blowing of the March daffodils. May I then be prepared to enter into the everlasting spring and to walk among the birds and flowers of paradise.

He died of peritonitis, in Scotland, on his honeymoon. Elizabeth Ann returned to Woodstock and for the rest of her life devoted herself to good works. There were no children.

Charles Kingsley

The summer of 1860 was exceptionally wet. For three months it rained almost incessantly. The farmers were in despair. All over the country the clergy began using the prayer against rain. But the Rector of Eversley, in Hampshire, had different views. He preached a sermon on the text: *If ye then, being evil, know how to give good gifts unto your children, how much more shall your Father which is in heaven give good things to them that ask him?* If God sends rain, he maintained, he sends it for our good: who are we to question his purposes? Even at a period of much religious controversy, this sermon caused resentment and shock. But the Rector of Eversley was a bit of a scientist, who knew the threat of cholera in a hot summer, and he rejoiced that the rain should clean the drains and sweep away the refuse of the streets.

Did he not realise, asked one indignant correspondent, that God used plague as a national punishment for national sins? Yes, he replied:

> but that does not prevent my asserting man's power and right to abolish those natural plagues, when he had learnt how to do it. To pray against them, as long as he cannot conquer them, is natural, and not to be blamed. But when God has answered his prayer, in a deeper and fuller sense than he dreamed of, by teaching him how to protect himself against these plagues, it is very wrong and ungrateful to God, to go on praying s if God had not answered.

Then did the Rector believe that we should not pray for special things at all?

> God forbid! Only it seems to me that when we pray "Grant us this day we run into no kind of danger", we ought to lay our stress on the "run" rather than on the "danger"; to ask God, not to take away the danger by altering the course of nature; but to give us ight and guidance whereby to avoid it.

This sturdy thinking, very refreshing in an age when much of our religious life was decidedly stuffy, did not endear the Rector of Eversley to most of his fellow-clergy, but it won him the approval of the scientist. *Sir* Charles Lyell wrote congratulating him, and told him of two processions of German peasants who had set out to climb to the top of the Peter's Berg. One was composed of vine-dressers, who were intending to return thanks for sunshine and pray for its continuance; the others were from a corn district, wanting the drought to cease and the rain to fall. Each was eager to get possession of St. Peter's chapel before the other, to secure the saint's good offices, and as a result they came to blows with fists and sticks, much to the amusement of the Protestant heretics.

This story would have pleased the Rector, for he was a strong, indeed an aggressive Protestant (which commended him to Queen Victoria, to whom he had recently been appointed chaplain). He was a Devon man, born in the village of Holne, and his name was Charles Kingsley.

A friend who runs a Bristol bookshop said not long ago "I get asked for Kingsley less than any other of the nineteenth-century writers" He paused, considered, and then corrected himself. "Well, perhaps Scott is even worse. I do get asked for *The Water Babies* occasionally."

What about *Westward Ho!* he was asked, and he replied "Not in years."

This is a sorry state of affairs for a writer who won much acclaim in his own lifetime. Yet both those books have been established for a long time as English classics, and it is hard to imagine either of them going out of print. To say that no-one reads them, or reads them just for fun, is not in itself a condemnation, or there would be many fewer English classics.

Kingsley was a man of great energy and great, sometimes slightly overwhelming charm. He roused deep affections and deep antagonisms. He was a novelist, a theologian, a poet, a country parson, a cathedral canon, a Regius Professor of Modern History at Cambridge, a passionate husband, an enthusiastic sportsman, a vigorous social reformer. He liked to swim in country streams before breakfast. He was one of the first to whom the term "muscular Christian" was applied, not always kindly. He was one of the first to call himself, daringly, a "Christian Socialist". His friend Thomas Hughes, the author of *Tom Brown's Schooldays*, has left us a description of him, saying he was like

> a great fullgrown Newfoundland yearling dog out for an airing, plunging in and out of the water, and rushing against and shaking himself over ladies' silks and velvets, dandies' polished boots, or schoolboys' rough jackets; and all with a rollicking good humour which disarmed anger, and carried away the most precise persons into momentary enjoyment of the tumbling.

Kingsley's decline in appeal as a writer is partly, of course, no more than a matter a changing literary fashion. But as well, his attitudes have become unfashionable — or, at least, some of his attitudes, since like many versatile men he was full of contradictions. *Westward Ho!* shows him at his worst. Although the book has some very striking descriptive passages, most people today would find it repellant because of its aggressive nationalism and Protestantism. It is about the Elizabethan wars against Spain, and it was stimulated, partly, by the outbreak of the Crimean war. It will hardly now be disputed that the Crimean was one of the most pointless as well as one of the most inefficient wars Britain ever waged. Yet to Kingsley, it was a glorious and holy crusade. This attitude is reflected, in his book, in the difference between the wicked Spanish Catholics and the English Protestants who even if their behaviour is not always perfect, do everything for the best of causes. An occasional massacre is permissible. There was the occasion when *Sir* Walter Ralegh found it necessary to refuse quarter to several hundred Spaniards who had landed in Ireland.

> It was done. Right or wrong, it was done. The shrieks and curses had died away, and the Fort Del Oro was a red shambles, which the soldiers were trying to cover from the sight of heaven and earth, by dragging the bodies into the ditch, and covering them with the ruins of the rampart; while the Irish, who had beheld from the woods that awful warning, fled trembling into the deepest recesses of the forest. It was done; and it never needed to be done again. The hint was severe, but it was sufficient. Many years passed before a Spaniard set foot again in Ireland.

Later in the book, Kingsley puts these words into the mouth of *Sir* Richard Grenville:

> There are times in which mercy is cruelty. Not England alone, but the world, the Bible, the Gospel itself, is at stake; and we must do terrible things, lest we suffer more terrible ones.

This is precisely the doctrine of the Inquisition, which Kingsley so abhorred. He dedicated *Westward Ho!* to *Sir* James Brooke, the White Rajah of Sarawak, who had been hauled up before parliament, and not without reason, for indiscriminate slaughter of the natives of Borneo. "Sacrifice of human life?" said Kingsley, when a friend criticised Brooke's conduct, "Prove that it is human life. It is beast-life." He referred, in the dedication, to England's "ever glorious wars." The date was February, 1855, when the British army was dying before Sebastopol.

This attitude — "it's all right so long as it's us" — destroys pleasure in reading *Westward Ho!* today, despite all the vigour and colour with which it is written. It is not really surprising that it has come to be thought of as a book for boys (which was not Kingsley's intention), a kind of high class tuppenny blood. For boys do not worry much about the moral issues; they enjoy the action.

By contrast, *The Water Babies*, which was intended to be a book for children, has remained that, enchantingly so; but has also become an even better one for adults. It can be read, though apparently it rarely is, at different levels with different pleasures, and it shows a far more attractive Kingsley. One day the Kingsley family was at breakfast, and Mrs. Kingsley reminded her husband that he he had never written a book for their youngest child. Kingsley went straight to his study, locked the door, and came back half an hour later with the chapter that begins

> Once upon a time there was a little chimney-sweep, and his name was Tom. That is a short name, and you have heard it before, so you will not have much trouble in remembering it. He lived in a great town in the North country, where there were plenty of chimneys to sweep, and plenty of money for Tom to earn and his master to spend. He could not read or write, and did not care to do either; and he never washed himself, for there was no water up the court where he lived. He had never been taught to say his prayers. He had never heard of God, or of Christ, except in words which you have never heard, and which it would have been well if he had never heard. He cried half his time, and laughed the other half. He cried when he had to climb the dark flues, rubbing his poor knees and elbows raw; and when the soot got into his eyes, which it did every day in the week; and when his master beat him, which he did every day in the week; and when he had not enough to eat, which happened every day in the week likewise ....

Tom, you may remember, escapes his grim existence, and finds a magical, fantasy world under the waters. All sorts of things have been written about *The Water Babies*, including the inevitable theory that it proved how much Kingsley wanted to return to the womb. A letter in *The Times* a few years ago called it "a great eschatological parable." But it is Tom, his sufferings, and his joys, who stays in the mind.

These two books, which are the best known of the thirty-seven which Kingsley published, show us two sides of the man: at one time brutal and revengeful, at another warm and compassionate. The sufferings of the child sweep point his genuine, and informed concern, over social abuses. And it is as a social reformer, more than as a writer, that he has a claim upon our sympathies today; can indeed be called a pioneer.

Kingsley spent much of his life in the south-west. For a year, he lived in Clifton. It was perhaps the most important, most formative, year in his life. He attended a preparatory school, run by the Rev. Kohn Knight, from 1831 to 1832. He had been there only a month when the Bristol Riots broke out; they began as a protest against the rejection of the Reform Bill by the House of Lords, but degenerated into as unpleasant an incident as the city has seen. Robert Martin, in his biography of Kingsley, thus describes the experience:

> The terror of the rioting lasted three days, and much of the city was burned. Fascinated by the tumult and horror, Charles slipped away into the middle of it to watch the savage mob of looters and the patient soldiers sitting quietly on their horses, blood streaming from wounds on their heads and faces, waiting for the order to quiet the mob, which the terrified Mayor feared to give.

Kingsley always remembered this vividly, as who would not? — and later said that the sight

> ... made me for years the veriest aristocrat, full of hatred and contempt of those dangerous classes, whose existence I had for the first time discovered.

It says a good deal for him that after such an experience at such an age, he was able to take, in time, quite a different view of "those dangerous classes".

In the first half of the nineteenth century, there was intense religious activity in Britain. At the same time the industrial revolution, bringing with it the most appalling misery for several millions of people, was in full swing. And it rarely happened that the Christian pundits thought the one had anything to do with the other. The two great forces in religious conflict were the Oxford movement, the High Churchmen, and the Evangelicals. The High Church point of view was expressed by Cardinal Newman.

> The Catholic Church holds it better for the sun and moon to drop from heaven, for the earth to fail, and for all the many millions on it to die of starvation in extreme agony, as far as temporal affliction goes, than that one soul, I will not say should be lost, but commit one single venial sin, should tell one wilful untruth, or should steal one poor farthing without excuse. I think the principles here enumerated to be the mere preamble in the formal credentials of the Catholic Church, as as Act of Parliament might begin with "Whereas".

That is a passage from Newman's *Apologia Pro Vita Sua*, a book which was in the first place provoked by an argument with Kingsley. The poor were, in another of Newman's, "objects for compassion and benevolence", and that was all.

The Evangelicals included the great Lord Shaftesbury, who did as much as any man in the century for social reform; but he was hardly representative of them in this. There was also Wilberforce, who led the movement against slavery, but was less concerned with the evils on his doorstep. Indeed Wilberforce went so far as to say this:

> The peace of mind which religion offers indiscriminately to all ranks, affords more true satisfaction than all the expensive pleasures that are beyond the poor man's reach. In this view the poor have the advantage. If their superiors enjoy more abundant comforts, they are also exposed to many temptations from which the inferior classes are happily exempted.

For the Evangelicals, a pair of wings in the next world was more precious than a pair of boots in this. Furthermore, they were individualists, with strong views about a free market, and the necessary limitations that must be set upon state action in the economic field.

> The rich man in his castle,
> The poor man at his gate,
> God made them high and lowly,
> And ordered their estate

wrote Mrs. Alexander.

Into this situation came the Christian Socialist movement. It was not, of course, socialist in a Marxist sense; but it declared that Christian principles must be applied to industrial organisation; that the economy must be run on a basis of co-operation, not competition; that philanthropy was not enough. The movement was launched in 1848, and it was a brave thing in Britain that year to adopt the name "Socialist", for it was the year of revolutions, with Europe in turmoil; the year the ill-fated and bloodily suppressed National Workshops in Paris; to which the Bristol Riots had been hardly a sneeze.

The unofficial leader of the Christian Socialists was the saintly, but sometimes rather vague, F.D.Maurice. Kingsley, though not then known as much more that a lively country Rector, became their chief spokesman. The group started a weekly paper called *Politics for the People*. The first leading article struck a note very different from that either of Newman or Wilberforce.

> Politics have been separated from Christianity. Religious men have supposed their only business is with the world to come; political men have declared that the present world is governed on entirely different principles from that. But Politics for the People cannot be separated from Religion. The world is governed by God. This is the rich man's warning. This is the poor man's comfort.

Kingsley's most famous contribution to the Christian Socialist cause was a pamphlet, one of the memorable pamphlets of British history. It was an exposure, delivered with great pungency and force, of sweated labour in the clothing industry. It was called "Cheap Clothes and Nasty".

> King Ryence, says the legend of Prince Arthur, wore a paletot trimmed with king's beards. In the first French Revolution there were at Meudon tanneries of human skins. Mammon, at once tyrant and revolutionary, follows both these noble examples — in a more respectable way, doubtless, for Mammon hates cruelty; bodily pain is his devil — the worst evil which he, in his effeminacy, can conceive. So he shrieks benevolently when a drunken soldier is flogged; but he trims his paletots, and he adorns his legs, with the flesh of men and the skins of women, with degradation, pestilence, heathendom and despair; and then chuckles complacently over the smallness of his tailors' bills. Hypocrite! straining at a gnat and swallowing a camel! What is flogging, or hanging, King Ryence's paletot or the tanneries of Meudon, to the slavery, starvation, waste of life, year-long imprisonment in dungeons narrower and fouler than those of the Inquisition, which goes on among thousands of free English clothes-makers at this day?

Fiery polemical stuff: but there was more to it than polemic. The pamphlet was crammed with grim facts about working conditions, caused a great stir, and may even be said, in the end, to have done something for the poor tailormen.

The movement had some successes. In March, 1851, the Southampton Tailors' Association was founded — the first venture of this kind outside London. A number of local journeymen had set about raising the necessary capital themselves, in five-shilling shares, and asked the support of the Society for Promoting Working Men's Associations, which was the title under which the Christian Socialists operated for the kind of activity. The support was readily given, and F.D.Maurice came to Southampton to speak when the Association was formally constituted. The idea was that these men, with help, should raise the money needed to start, run their own affairs, and share such profits as came along, spreading among themselves the benefits of the good times and hardships of the bad.

Before they began, they ran into trouble with a local sweatshop owner, who published handbills announcing the formation of his own Working Tailors' Association, and soliciting help. They exposed him without too much difficulty, and indeed benefited from the publicity. They then proceeded to produce good work, which they sold cheaply yet still at a better profit than if they had been working for somebody else. They repaid the initial loans and even contemplated opening a co-operative store. For more than a year everything went well. But they ran into trouble, as early Christian Socialist enterprises so often did, over personalities. The manager quarrelled with his fellows, resigned and started a rival concern. Possibly they were happily absorbed into another organisation as the co-operative moevement began to grow in strength.

It is easy to mock the Christian Socialists. The movement never amounted to much. The journal failed, and so did two successors. The model co-operative workshops which they tried to establish also failed. They were innocents in business affairs, and often diddled by those they sought to befriend. The leaders gradually drifted apart. There was not much to show for it all, except — certainly a substantial exception — the London Working Men's College. Yet, they were pioneers. This is to be taken less in the socialist sense, because even then there were lots of socialists about, of one sort and another, than in the Christian one.

In recent years the Christian church in Britain has had a good record on social problems. This was far from being the case in the first half of the nineteenth century, when the most modest reform raised hands of horror on the bench of bishops, and corresponding reactions down the scale, Catholic and Evangelical alike. To recall the church, then, to its concern for suffering in this world, to reject the idea that we can with an easy conscience leave the readjustment of misfortune to the next: this was not only marking the path for those to come, but was in the true spirit of the Gospels. Let it not be forgotten.

We have said nothing about Kingsley the poet, and perhaps there is not a great deal to say. He was not really a very good poet — "too coarse-grained", said someone unkindly but shrewdly — but he left some lines which cling to memory. Many of you will remember "I once had a sweet little doll, dear"; or "When all the world is young, lad"; or "O Mary, go and call the cattle home"; or "For men must work, and women must weep," But did you know that Kingsley wrote the line, "Be good, sweet maid, and let who can be clever"? And do you remember the next line?

Do noble things, not dream them, all day long.

Not all the things Kingsley did were noble. But he tried. Very hard, he tried.

George Muller

The first time I went to Bristol county cricket ground was in 1948. I was with a friend, also a newcomer, and wondered what were the large grey forbidding buildings along two sides of the ground. A hospital? A prison? "Certainly it looks like something you can't get out of", said my friend. It was, of course, Muller's orphanage. Though no longer an orphanage, it remains an unfavourite building in Bristol. Yet one of the orphans who was brought up there once wrote that "no place ever seemed so dear", and in the last century, before that part of the city had been built up, a resident of Horfield said,

> Whenever I feel doubts about the Living God creeping into my mind, I get up and look through the night at the many windows lit up on Ashley Down, and they gleam through the darkness as stars in the sky.

George Muller was born in 1805 in Germany, near Halberstadt, though he subsequently became a naturalized British subject. He came to England in his twenties, to work for a society for promoting Christianity among the Jews. He did not feel that this was the right path for him, and became a minister of a small congregation at Teignmouth. After only a couple of years there, he moved to Bristol, which was his home for the rest of his long life. He was drawn to make the care of orphans his principal life's work, beginning with just a few in his personal charge, but expanding the work until there were more than two thousand of them in the five large buildings on Ashley Down. That is his life in outline. When he was past seventy he began a preaching mission which took him all over the world, and lasted for years.

He had become a famous man, not just in Bristol, and not just because of the orphanage. There were many philanthropists in nineteenth-century England, and many were needed. Muller was not an influential man, like Shaftesbury, nor a zealous campaigner, like Wilberforce. What took the public imagination was that he did not ask for money. Never in his life, he would say, had he asked for a penny for the orphanage: he left it to God to look after all that. When he felt anything was necessary, he prayed for it.

There have been many Christians, especially of the evangelical variety, who have made claims of this sort, claims which often do not bear examination. Critics of Muller have pointed out that, even if he did not directly appeal for money, he let it be known that he was praying for it, not least by publishing a book, called *A Narrative of Some of the Lord's Dealings with George Muller*. Yet the impression we get of him, notably in Roger Steer's book, *George Muller: Delighted in God*, is certainly that of a man of deep belief: mistaken, you may think, even self-deluded, but not as fraud. Indeed, his driving force seems to have been less compassion for the orphans, than an anxiety, through his work, to demonstrate the power of prayer. Here are his own words:

> I certainly did from my heart desire to be used by God to benefit the bodies of poor children, bereaved of both parents, and seek, in other respects, with the help of God, to do them good for this life; I also particularly longed to be used by God in getting the dear orphans trained up to the fear of God; but still, the first and primary object of the work was that God might be magnified by the fact, that the orphans under my care are provided, with all they need, only by prayer and faith, without anyone being asked by me or my fellow-labourers, whereby it may be seen, that God is FAITHFUL STILL, and HEARS PRAYER STILL.

Steer, in his book, compares Muller with Mother Teresa of Calcutta, of whom Malcolm Muggeridge recently wrote,

> In true evangelical style, she goes to God with her needs and difficulties, and is always marvelling at the magnificent response in meeting her every requirement, great and small. Those of us who cannot participate in such particular requests are not so much sophisticated as less gifted with faith.

Yet Muller denied that he had been granted a special gift of faith.

The book gives us a vivid picture of a remarkable man, contains a lot of research, and is easy to read. It is, however, uneven. There are times when it seems that the author cannot make up his mind whether he is writing a serious biography or an evangelical tract, and finds it difficult to harmonize the two approaches. The difficulties show in his style, which varies between the academic and the journalistic. But this must always be a problem in writing of such a man. There is a particularly interesting chapter given to the recollections of some of the orphans, describing what life was like within those grey walls. Some of the tributes are touching. We could have done with a few on the other side to balance them, but in the nature of things they cannot have been easy to find. Many of the children had been the poorest of the poor. William Ready, for instance, was born in 1860 in a London workhouse, and by the time he was twelve was a waif, sleeping in dustbins or under the railway arches.

> I was not happy I can assure you, when I found myself inside the block, with the great iron gates closing behind me. I did not look upon those as my friends who had interfered with my liberty of the streets... I was as a bird in a cage and if anyone had said to me "You may go back", I should have said, "Thank you, sir! You are my friend."

He was given a bath, put into uniform — corduroy trousers, blue vest and coat, white collar, and shown into the dining hall.

The boys gathered around me like flies round a sugar basin and they began to pinch and pull my hair. The bell rang and we passed to our places. For the first time in my life I was not feeling hungry. Oh! to go back to my old haunts, to the rush of cabs and buses! Two slices of bread and treacle were set before me on a little place but I could not touch them...The boys on either side of me soon finished my share.

But he had recovered his appetite by breakfast-time, and looked back happily on his years there. He became a Nonconformist minister and a popular preacher in New Zealand. Muller gave his children a good all-round education. It is true that most of the boys were apprenticed to trades, and most of the girls went into domestic service, but he did not share the view, common at the time, that the lower classes should be able to read their Bibles, add up a column of figures, and sign their names, and that anything more than that was not only unnecessary but dangerous. Discipline was strict, but so it was in practically all schools of the time, of any kind. When Muller had to expel a child, which was a rare occurrence, he would do so publicly with prayer. This sounds rather unpleasantly sanctimonious, but after all at one of our grand old public schools the child would more probably have been despatched publicly with a flogging.

It is difficult to disagree with Mr. Steer's judgment:

Nowadays, of course, it is no longer considered proper to house children in such large buildings as those Muller built in Ashley Down. Indeed, the Muller Homes today have long since felt it right to come into line with current official policy, which is to house children in small house groups so that life should conform as closely as possible to a normal home atmosphere. However, by nineteenth century standards, George Muller must be considered both a pioneer and a radical. He, alone, offered modern homes to thousands of children who would otherwise have been either homeless, or sent to a workhouse or debtors' prison, or grudgingly offered a corner in the overcrowded home of a relative. And there were no barriers to entry at Muller's Homes on the grounds of poverty, class or creed... Admittance to other orphanages.. was normally gained, not according to the relative needs of the child, but upon personal recommendation or by a majority of votes at the meetings of subscribers.

Muller never held a subscribers' meeting, nor made public the names of subscribers. Dickens once visited Ashley Down: he heard rumours that the children did not get enough to eat. Muller sent for an assistant, gave him the keys, and instructed that Mr. Dickens was free to go wherever he wished. Dickens was entirely reassured. The food was monotonous, certainly (bread was known as "toke", from the grace referring to "these tokens of thy love") but there was meat three times a week and meat broth twice, and a lot of fruit, because of Bristol's situation as a port. And there were regular great occasions: Muller knew how children like a special treat — the summer outing, his birthday (always cake and apple dumplings) and of course Christmas. Muller's journal for 1884 records some of the gifts sent for Christmas.

> From a Bristol wholesale house 8 barrels of flour, 1 barrel of currants, and 16 quarter boxes of Valencias, for the children's Christmas puddings... From Clifton we received for the children a number of dolls, some fancy boxes, albums, games, balls, tops and a great variety of other playthings. From Durdham Down...dressdolls, boxes and packets of chocolates and sweets, some drums, tops, balls, marbles, whips and guns, boxes of toys, books, fancy cards, paint boxes, transparent slates, pocket handkerchiefs, wool ties and ruffs, pencils, trumpets... From a Bristol wholesale house, 15 boxes of fruit, 10 boxes of oranges, 10 boxes of figs, and a sack of nuts..

One Christmas, 150 pheasants arrived from Cornwall. We wonder what the children made of them.

One child wrote to the orphanage in later life,

> Well do I remember the happy Christmases spent at No. 4; the start of the preparation for the decorations; the arrival of the great, big Christmas tree, nothing on it, but I knew before Christmas it would be loaded with toys and presents, and somewhere amongst the many there would be one for me... I expect the times are just as exciting as when I was there, imagine the decorations being got ready, and the secrecy of it all, and then learning the lovely carols, and the Christmas Shop! I would love to peep in, to see if it is really like it used to be. I don't think it could possibly be better.

A great man, George Muller. *He* would say, do not speak of George Muller; speak only of George Muller's heavenly Father.

Arnold Thomas

Not very many people in Bristol will recall Arnold Thomas. He died in 1924, and his name strikes few chords now. This would not have worried him in the least, for he was the most modest of men. A congregational minister who, while distinguished in his profession, did not scale the peaks of fame, and yet was loved and valued by all those who knew him.

He was received into membership of Highbury Chapel, Bristol, in 1867. Nine years later he became its minister, and he held that post until a month or two before his death. Highbury and the city of Bristol was his life though he was occasionally pressed into wider service. In 1899, for instance, he was Chairman of the Congregational Union, and when the annual meetings were held in Bristol he reminded his audience, a little wistfully, that when his father had held that office three barrels of beer were provided at the back of the hall for the assembly, and a side of beef. He said of Bristol:

> A man ought to care for his own city. He ought to take some pride in it; he ought to be willing to serve it. He ought to be prepared to make sacrifices for the sake of it. Bristol is not, perhaps, one of the most famous cities of the world. It is not Rome or Athens or Jerusalem. And yet it is no mean city. Have you never come home from your summer holiday and strolled across the down on an autumn evening, when the tide has been high, and the setting sun has glorified the river and the distant channel and the Welsh hills, and said to yourself, "We have seen nothing, after all, to beat this in all our travels"?

The strict answer, for most of us, would probably be "Candidly, no. I have not ever felt like that." But it is a finely spoken tribute, and tells you something about the man as well as the city.

After his death, a memoir of Arnold Thomas was written by Nathaniel Micklem, with some of his collected papers and addresses. Reading them now, one is struck by his thoughts on Christian unity, which are very relevant today. There was nothing shamefaced about his Congregationalism. He did not much like the word "Nonconformist", which, he held, "is but an accident, and is by no means of our essence", but his Nonconformity did not lack courage, nor, for that matter, courtesy. When the Bishop of Bristol was present at a meeting of the Congregational Union in Bristol, etiquette required that he should be asked to pronounce the benediction. Stout Congregational principle could not see why. Arnold Thomas solved the problem by inviting the Bishop to pronounce the blessing — "as the youngest bishop present." He enjoyed, too, telling the story of his visit to St. Paul's

Cathedral. He remarked to one of the vergers, "I suppose it is an excellent position you have here"; and the verger replied, "Yes, yes — there is only one drawback; I can never get to a place of worship!"

More seriously, early in this century the Education Act of 1902 brought relations between Nonconformists and other Christians to their bitterest state for many years. Thomas, like many others, felt is necessary to refuse to pay the education rate, and in consequence his goods were distrained upon. "This afternoon", he wrote, "my worldly goods — some of them — are to be sold in a neighbouring coach-house. It seems rather farcical, but I suppose this kind of thing has to be done." There was nothing of the fanatic about him, but there was nothing of the theological weakling either.

Yet it was Arnold Thomas who, perhaps more than any other man except Dean Burroughs, brought about the happy relationship between the Church of England and the Free Churches in Bristol which in the last half century has enabled the city to take a leading part in the modern ecumenical movement. In 1918, he had been asked to offer the consecration prayer in the cathedral, which he always regarded as the city's mother church. This caused 33 Anglican clergy to sign an indignant protest; but 108 others wrote a letter of approval. On Christmas Eve, 1922, he preached in the cathedral. When he died, the Bishop of Bristol spoke at his funeral in Highbury Chapel. Such events seem commonplace today. That was because men such as Thomas and Burroughs led the way.

In particular, it is interesting to see how Arnold Thomas saw the way ahead. When what was known as the "Lambeth appeal" was made, he said,

The spirit of the Bishops' appeal leaves nothing to be desired, and should have the honest and sympathetic consideration of all whom it concerns. I believe much may come of it if the same spirit continues to prevail. I have never seen any essential difference between Episcopacy "exercised in a representative and constitutional manner" and the kind of Episcopacy which is commonly exercised, under other names, in most religious communions today. I should not feel much difficulty, therefore, on this score. Nor do I think our ministers need hesitate to accept a "form of commission or recognition" which would commend their ministry to Anglican congregations. As to ordination, much depends on the meaning to be attached to the word. If it means only authority to minister in the Anglican Communion, no Free Church minister need scruple to accept it. But if its meaning must be defined by the terms of the present ordination service, I do not see any hope of its being generally accepted. I venture to think, therefore, that some modification of the existing service will be needed or an alternative service, to be used in the case of those who are accredited ministers in other communions.

Those words bear re-reading and consideration.

There was another aspect of Arnold Thomas's Bristol work which continues to bear fruit. Whatever the doctrinal difficulties between the churches, he was very anxious that they should work together socially, and it was greatly thanks to him that they did and do. He wanted better schools, better houses, municipal buildings, picture galleries, a museum, music. "Do you ask", he said in a sermon, "what these things have to do with religion?" And he answered, "A great deal. For when a man gets Christ's religion he becomes, necessarily, a public man....He has passed from death into life, and the proof of it is that he loves the brethren, and will do all that is in his power for the promotion of their happiness."

Highbury Chapel still stands at the top of Tyndalls Park Road. The architect was Butterfield, and it is a distinguished building. It is one of the few Free Churches Butterfield built, though of more of an Anglican than a Nonconformist stamp. It has now ceased to belong to the Congregational (or United Reformed) church. The Congregationalists are well equipped in that area, and it was happily handed over to become Cotham Parish Church. This would surely have pleased Thomas. At his funeral the Bishop of Bristol said: "Arnold Thomas was not yours alone; he was ours." He was certainly Bristol's, and it is impossible to read of and about him without the sense of a torch handed on to us."

Hugh Redwood

In the 1930's our father/grandfather was a minister in East London. One Sunday Hugh Redwood came to preach in his church. Hugh Redwood was a great name at that time. He was a leading journalist, deputy editor of the *News Chronicle*, the author of a book, *God in the Slums*, which was a bestseller. Some readers may still remember the stir which that book caused: slums were very much on the country's mind and conscience in the 'thirties. He was now making a new reputation as an evangelistic preacher, with a powerful and unconventional style.

Alan Gibson was then aged about ten, and attended the big elementary school at the end of the road, Farmer Road. He edited a class magazine, called *The Farmer Weekly*, and every week-end would type it out on his father's typewriter, frequently mangling the ribbons in the process. He was engaged on this task the week-end Hugh Redwood came to stay. A few days later Redwood sent an unsolicited contribution. It began, "Some copies of your excellent periodical have recently come into my hands", and he referred to the staff as "fellow-journalists". You can imagine what pride and pleasure this gave.

There is a good deal of autobiographical material in *God in the Slums*, and its successor, *God in the Shadows*, which was very nearly as successful. But his full-scale biography did not come out until 1948. It was called *Bristol Fashion*, for he was a Bristol man, and proud of it. This is the book from which we shall, principally, quote in this article. In the frontispiece he looks much as a boy remembered, and astonishingly like Ernest Bevin — the same build, the same square jaw, the same horn-rimmed spectacles. He and Bevin were born within a year of each other, and must often have met. Indeed, they had many qualities in common. Redwood's sympathies were always with the left, but increasingly the main emphasis in his life was religious, whereas Bevin's was economic. But they were both men of drive, and sometimes hidden compassion, and humour, and gusto.

It was his religious work which Redwood came to regard as his most important, though he remained a professional journalist. He was fortunate that he was able to harmonize his vocation and his profession. For instance, the series of "One Minute Sermons" which he wrote in the *News Chronicle* for many years were outstanding in the journalism of the period.

But to start in Bristol. Redwood begins by recalling the arrival there, twelve years before the death of Queen Victoria, of a Scotsman from the Firth of Clyde who planned to invade new waters:

Take a man or a maid from Bristol, set them free for a time from the sordid business of earning a living, whether in its boot-and-shoe, chocolate, tobacco or clothing factories; its markets, shops and professional chamber, or, for that matter, its newspaper offices — observe the ingenuity with which we have worked ourselves into this preamble — put them on a steamer at Hotwells, and, even though the tide below and the Avon mud at its smelliest, you have already begun to transport them into the atmosphere of romance. Ilfracombe, that is their destination, and it is a name and place to conjure with, as Alexander Campbell knew instinctively. Perhaps this is less true now than in his time. Today you can do the journey by motor-coach. You will then be independent of tides, and we can at least hope that you will not be sick; but you will know nothing of the old magic. You will miss the slow change of the sea from ochreous brown to white-flecked translucent green, coincident with a change in your own inmost being, a refreshment, a purification. And missing that inner change, you will be unprepared for that which Ilfracombe can still do for you, but could do better in the days before talkies and Technicolour, when the band on the Capstone, without the help of a single saxophone, played gavottes and valses, and when the only coaches the little town knew were the four-in-hands of Tom Copp and Tom Colwill.

A day trip to Ilfracombe could be a thing of wonder and beauty that no roaring excursion by road could equal, especially if the tides were late and the sun near setting when the hawsers were dropped from the pier-end bollards and the paddles began to revolve for the homeward run. In the gathering dusk one did not notice, or want to notice, that the water was turning brown again: away to the west it was pearly still, and abeam and ahead there were twinkling lights like strings of beads to mark where Minehead and Barry lay and presently Weston and Clevedon: until we are in Bristol river again, and over our heads, with their upturned faces, a dark line is drawn for a moment across the starlight as we pass under Clifton Suspension Bridge. Had we the means of knowing it, the number of people who committed matrimony with the aid of Ilfracombe and the Campbell steamers would probably set us gasping. I speak with feeling, as one of them.

Alexander Campbell became a close friend of the Redwood family and this was not the only way he had a strong influence on Hugh's life. Hugh's father, of whom a lively and touching picture is drawn in the book, was chief reporter of the *Western Daily Press*. But all the boy's early thoughts were of the sea. He spent many hours "being a ship" on Durdham Down, using the depressions and the paths as reefs and channels, the furze clumps and hawthorn trees as an archipelago.

I paced out distances until, by attention to angles of take-off and number of steps taken, I could find my way to any given spot on the Downs even in total darkness and fog. By night an unwary walker might break his neck with ease among the "reefs", but I never fell. I could start from the far side and cross to the Zoo gates, which meant threading my way through the "archipelago", without so much as tripping over a tree root. Long after I had left school and was a cub reporter, I sometimes profited by a fog to go up to Durdham Down and see if the knack was still with me. It was, and I think it may be even today.

The Redwoods were an orthodox Anglican family, quite strict by modern standards, but suspicious of more evangelical religious varieties. They had a maid, partly a nursemaid, called Annie Tye, and Annie was "chapel". So was Miss Dyson next door, who played Moody and Sankey hymns on her American organ. Mrs. Redwood would counter the distant strains of Sankey by striking up "The Church's One Foundation" on the pianoforte, and would sometimes even go so far as to add a tincture of Rome with the celebrated piano solo, "The Bells of the Monastery".

Sometimes, however, the youthful Hugh was allowed to accompany Annie to her home, where he willingly risked a tinge of heresy, since Annie's husband was a sailor:

The peculiar pride of the Tye household was an organ of the barrel type, housed in a tiny room at the back of a greengrocer's shop. Here I would clamber in to a bench behind a table covered with glossy American cloth, and Mr. Tye would deposit the organ before me, so that I might turn the handle thereof and take it through its repertory. The organ was a delight to me: I marvelled at its ingenious mechanism, and the way in which the tunes it played were disposed around brass cylinders in the shape of hundreds of tiny pins. But what I liked best about it was that every hymn on the programme (the Tye organ played nothing but hymns on Sundays) had a pungently nautical flavour. You can imagine how I approved of Mr. Tye's choice, and with what zest I provided the music for the Gospel lyrics we all joined in singing, "We are out on the ocean sailing", "Let the lower lights be burning", and most especially "Pull for the shore, sailor". He could draw on a rich fund of stories to point these hymns and choruses, and in his then employment as night watchman for a line of coasting steamers, he made me all manner of wonderful promises, contingent upon my undertaking always to be a good boy and do what my mother and Annie told me, which, it seemed, would be tantamount to keeping my lower lights burning, sailing the ocean and pulling for the shore, all at one and same time.

Some of you will still remember those hymns, if they really can be called hymns.

Brightly beams our Father's mercy,
From his lighthouse evermore;
But to us he gives the keeping
Of the lights along the shore.

Trim your feeble lamp, my brother;
Some poor seaman, tempest-tost,
Trying now to make the harbour,
In the darkness *may be lost.*

The words "may be lost" are italicized even in the hymn-book. And then the chorus:

Let the lower lights be burning!
Send a gleam across the wave!
Some poor fainting, struggling seaman
You may rescue! You may save!

Although he was too literate a man to regard these lines as particularly good verse, the image they portrayed, perhaps fixed in his mind by looking out from

79

the Sea Walls on the Downs on foggy nights, stayed with Hugh Redwood throughout his life.

However, Mr. Tye's evangelicalism had its limits, for soon he gave up being a night watchman and became, O horror, the licensee of a pub. The name of the pub was the British Queen. We do not know where it was — indeed it may still exist. All Redwood tells us about it is that it was much favoured by boot-and-shoe operatives:

> I forget how I came to track him there, for Annie had left us by now, but I know that I walked in on him one afternoon after school, and was given a royal welcome. Business was slack, and I sat alone at a table in the bar to which he brought me a glass of shandy gaff. The table was covered with American Cloth and remarkably like the one which used to stand in his organ chamber, but somehow we didn't talk of the organ. He recognized no doubt, that it belonged to the days of my infancy; and it may have occurred to him that the novel spectacle of a schoolboy, and a Cathedral schoolboy at that, sitting there with his homework books on the table drinking lemon with a strong dash of bitter, was a warning to both parties that the lower lights had gone out. I saw no harm in it, however, and mentioned the visit when I got home — with results that surprised and pained me deeply.

Well, Hugh Redwood turned his back upon the sea, though he always loved it, and followed in father's footsteps, becoming a junior reporter on the *Western Daily Press* at a salary of ten shillings a week. It was impressed upon him that he only got so much because he was his father's son. Otherwise the proprietor would have demanded a premium for the priceless experience. So he did the weddings and funerals, and gradually was allowed to extend his activities — a little musical and dramatic criticism, the occasional book review; the Empire Variety Theatre every Monday evening, the Clifton Rugby Football Club. But he was not allowed to expand too quickly, nor to express himself too freely. The following incident illustrates the way in which young reporters were, in those days, and for better or worse, kept in their place. He was constantly reporting inquests,

> — and always one had to begin in the same old way. "The City Coroner Mr. H.G.Doggett — or the Deputy-Coroner, Mr. A.E. Barker — held an inquest at such-and-such a place yesterday, touching the death of so-and-so." In the eyes of Mr. Doggett himself, a stickler for order and custom, any departure from this ancient gambit would, I believe, have furnished the corpse for another inquest. On the other hand, I have an idea that Mr. Barker, who had a delightfully twisted nose and looked down it, at times, on established ways, was often tempted to break new ground. There came a day when he and I broke it together. An inquest was held at a local workhouse, and certain of the workhouse officials came in for a slating

from the Deputy-Coroner which made their ears tingle. I decided that the occasion was historic, so I began my report in this fashion: Some pertinent remarks were made, at an inquest at Blank Workhouse yesterday, by the Deputy-Coroner, Mr. A.E.Barker.

It looked pretty daring when I had written it, and for a moment or two I hesitated. Then I took my copy across the corridor and dropped it into the basket. I went back to my desk in the empty reporters' room and waited. For a while nothing happened. Over the way I could hear a murmuring, as of high minds in conference, and presently somebody came out of the sub-editors' room and walked to the end of the corridor, where the Editor had his sanctum. Five minutes later: "The Editor wants to see you, Redwood." "The Editor", mind, not "Hicks", or even "Mr. Hicks", I knew I was for it.

The Editor's manner was brief and devastating. My copy lay before him on a desk graced by a bowl of home-grown roses. But there were no roses for me. To refresh my memory he read me my opening sentence, and then looked at me over the top of his glasses. "Kindly remember in future", he said "that you are a reporter, and not a leader-writer."

After seven years on the *Press* in Bristol, during which his salary rose dizzily to 35s.a week, Hugh Redwood went to London, first for the *Central News*, the agency, and later to the *Daily News* which became in due course the *News Chronicle*. We will not follow him through his successive Fleet Street jobs. He did well in all of them, though no doubt he did sometimes forget that he was a reporter, and not a leader-writer. He very much enjoyed his spell as a foreign correspondent, travelling Europe and mixing with the mighty. He relished his eminence, but never became conceited about it. He spent some time as a sub-editor, and he has written this passage about the relations of sub-editors and reporters, which everyone who has had anything to do with journalism will recognize as true, as true now as when it was written.

I have been young and now am old, yet have I not seen the reporter who loved the sub-editor, or the sub-editor prepared to admit that, without him, the reporter could earn his bread.

The sub-editor is at this disadvantage, that the newspaper public knows nothing about him, and has no conscious reason to care. If it should ever hear him mentioned, it assumes that, as his name suggests, he is some kind of secondary or assistant editor, a little, but only a very little, lower than the angels. Sub-editors have been known to labour under this misapprehension themselves. The truth is, of course, that they are the diamond-cutters of journalism. The reporter will tell you that they are ghouls, whose obscene joy is to savage and disembowel his copy, seizing with devilish instinct upon those passages in which he has taken most pride and tearing them out with blue pencils. In cold fact the sub-editor seldom or never uses a blue pencil. He cuts for two reasons, and the love of cutting is not one of them. He cuts because he has to, because his problem all the time is space. He also cuts because he is a craftsman, and has learned by long experience how to bring out the best in a story.

This — we cannot keep out of it, because we have sometimes been reporters ourselves — this, we are bound to say, is a characteristically arrogant sub-editorial view. However, he does go on:

> When the sub-editor encounters copy that needs no cutting, copy correct in spelling and grammar, the output of a balanced mind which knows the number of words to a column, he ponders it for a moment in silence and then says, "This man is too good to be a reporter."

It is an ancient argument with a richly repetitive future before it. And before we move to the culminating phase of Hugh Redwood's career, let us give you another of his Fleet Street reminiscences. At least, its origins were in Fleet Street. Henry Cadbury, the proprietor of the *Daily News*, of which Redwood was foreign editor, decided suddenly to go to America — it was the time of the Naval Conference at Washington — and thought Redwood had better go too. Apart from helping with the reports, he was to find a new correspondent for the paper in New York. Redwood was very pleased, sailed for New York, and made the cable and wireless arrangements expeditiously. He had arrived on a Saturday morning, and fixed an interview with a potential correspondent for the Monday. Everything going well. Henry Cadbury arrived for breakfast on Sunday, and wasted less time.

> He asked me to show him the sights of New York — on foot, and we didn't miss any of them. He departed for Philadelphia after lunch, at my urgent suggestion; and before my feet were ready for service again, had shaken the dust of the Quaker City from his own, to hit the trail for Washington. On Monday evening he wired me to say he found it necessary to return to England on Tuesday and would breakfast with me at 7 am.

Henry Cadbury was clearly, at this time of his life, trying to live up to the new newspaper-proprietor image made fashionable by Northcliffe and Beaverbrook. Redwood, in some awe and alarm awaited his return.

> In the meantime, I had interviewed and appointed my man, who had thereupon taken me to dinner and afterwards to the Winter Garden. We emerged from that

place of entertainment to encounter, on its very doorstep, the press agent of the Hippodrome, who was grieved at our choice, since the Hippodrome, as he pointed out, could have shown us the dandiest troop of performing elephants ever. But even now it was not too late. He insisted that we should accompany him to the elephants' quarters forthwith in order to witness a performance solely for our benefit. They lived in a very forbidding part of Manhattan, six or eight of them — one is not always certain about the numbers of elephants one meets in New York after midnight — in a gloomy and cavernous building, apparently some sort of warehouse, where the largest of them wound up a fantastic programme by seizing our newly appointed correspondent in his trunk, and waving him high in the air. It was unfortunate that he had, as it proved, a weak stomach; but, as our guide observed, he would feel all the better for it afterwards, especially if he now brought me along to the club for a demi-tasse. At the club we met the press-agent's wife, who was a very charming opera-singer, and defied the prohibition laws then in force by drinking extremely bad burgundy served in small cups as black coffee. Wine, women and elephants make a heady mixture, and it jolted me rather severely when, at four o'clock in the morning, I returned to my hotel and was presented with Henry Cadbury's telegram. It seemed unwise to go to bed, so I dozed in a chair in my room until six, when a cold bath gave me an air of such freshness that my tireless principal, over the breakfast table, was led to suggest some more sightseeing. He also thought, though I doubted it, that he would like to see our new representative. So we mounted to the summits of the Woolworth and Equitable skyscrapers in the company of a brave but unhappy man whose stomach, only a few hours before, had been badly unsettled by elephants. And even the strongest stomach is not always proof against the swiftly descending Woolworth non-stop elevators. Sic transit...

The turning-point in Redwood's life came in 1928, when he was forty-seven years old. The word "turning-point" seems appropriate because it is less emotional than "conversion", the word he preferred himself. One feels, after reading the autobiography, that the turning-point, or the conversion, existed chiefly in his own mind. It was a change of direction, a change of emphasis; it was not a change of character. Everything he tells us about himself, and which others have told of him, indicates clearly that he was no brand plucked from the burning. Although he likes occasionally to picture himself as a bit of a dasher, as in the story of the elephants in New York, he had obviously always been a good man: a warm, friendly man, with orthodox Anglican religious views which he did not allow to trouble him unduly, probably because he did not need to. After his conversion, he was much the same kind of man: an extra zeal in good works, partly counter-balanced by a little extra intolerance towards those who saw things differently. This is often all that "conversion" means, at least among those who have a natural inclination towards goodness.

Conversion can take away a blessing for every one it confers. But these are arguable matters. Let him get on with the story himself.

Early in the morning of January 7th, 1928, there were severe floods at Westminster, where the Thames broke its banks. It was a big story, and the *Daily News*, of which Redwood was then night editor, had an exclusive scoop, by a lucky chance or two. He was so pleased by this that he actually read what the reporters had written about it; and he was so moved by what they wrote about it that he went down to the badly flooded area, not in search of a story — for it was Saturday — but just to ask if there was anything he could do to help. Thus he was introduced to the Slums Department of the Salvation Army.

If you ask people today what they remember of Hugh Redwood, you tend to get the answer, "Ah, yes — the journalist who joined the Salvation Army", or words to that effect. In fact he never became technically a member. He remained a member of the Church of England. But it was through the Army that his activities broadened and changed. He worked with them closely for many years, helping the Slums Department in a kind of "big-brother" capacity — the phrase then did not have the sinister implications of 1984. Because of his work with them he wrote *God in the Slums*, and because of the tremendous success of *God in the Slums*, he became an evangelist. In his autobiography there is a picture of him, still looking like Ernest Bevin, addressing an audience of twelve and a half thousand at a United Service of Witness in Toronto, the Primate of Canada on his right. He preached from a text in Jeremiah, "Old cast clouts and old rotten rags", which were the means, you may remember, by which the prophet was rescued from prison. It was a characteristic text, and if memory is right he preached on the same theme at Leyton.

Tom Clarke, the editor of the *News Chronicle*, decided to get "a touch of God into the paper", and so Redwood became religious editor, a specially created post to which he was obviously well suited. He was able to combine it with his evangelistic activities, but he did not take his responsibilities lightly. Indeed he used his contacts to produce at least one more scoop, when the *Chronicle*, alone among the papers, announced the news that the Salvation Army was appointing its first woman General, Evangeline Booth.

Nor did he lose a scrap of his sense of humour. In fact he thought most religious people a great deal too solemn:

I believe that to speak in the name of Christ is to speak in His presence; and though it is only by faith that I can catch His encouraging eye, is my faith so dim that I can never discern a twinkle in it? A twinkle, surely, at the introductory remark of the chairman of a meeting at Newport, at which I was the last of six speakers: "Ladies and gentlemen, we have had a feast of fat things, and now..." But at this point he lost control of his audience, for it is not disputed that, physically at any rate, I can fill a pulpit as well as most men. Then there was the Portsmouth chairman who, convinced that it was needless to introduce one "with whose name we are all so familiar", called, without more ado, on Mr. Huge Redmond. Once at Pontypridd I was told in the vestry before the service that the choir was going to sing twice, and that they had been careful to choose appropriate music. Immediately before I rose to speak they sang the anthem "Be not afraid", and they followed it up as soon as I finished by singing the anthem "Thanks be to God". Now I should hardly have thought this could happen a second time, but a Bristol choir did exactly the same thing two or three years ago. When, before my address, the choir-master came forward to announce the first of two excerpts from Elijah there stole upon me a strange "I've-been-here-before" feeling. I made some play with it when I spoke. I had been right with the first anthem: I told them what their second would be. In due course, the choir-master came to the front again. "As I explained", he said, "We chose our numbers from Elijah. And as you have heard, we shall now sing "Thanks be to God". But we might have decided on "It is enough".

Hugh Redwood in his youth appears to have had some slight difficulty in making up his mind which of two girls to marry. He was married long and happily to the first, and when she died, he married the second, equally happily. So the Campbell steamers served him well. By the first marriage he had a daughter, crippled by illness, a woman of great courage who also did remarkable work in her own right. He lived into his eighties and died in 1963.

We will not attempt any assessment of his work. We do not know how his style would be accepted today. He was certainly responsible for innumerable acts of goodwill to the destitute, through a fund which he set up and which his readers kept going. He had the true charity which knows the risk of being imposed upon, but accepts the risk rather than let pass the chance of doing good — which is not to say he did not come to have a quick eye for the frauds. He saw the signs of a mighty spiritual revival in the slums, and he does not seem to have been right about that. But goodwill is always true currency. After all, an organisation such as "Shelter", although it seems worlds away from Hugh Redwood and the Salvation Army soup kitchens and bread and treacle, still works on the principle that if you cannot solve the problem all at once, that is no excuse for not housing the next family.

But the rightness of his views, and the amount of his achievements are not our chief concern. He should be remembered as a jovial, witty, hardworking, exceptionally talented and good-hearted Bristolian. He concludes his autobiography with this passage:

One of my favourite Old Testament chapters is the eighth chapter of Nehemiah,

85

which tells how Ezra the scribe recited the law to the people at Jerusalem. They erected for him a pulpit of wood, "in the street that was before the water gate", and there, from daybreak to noon, he read to a "congregation of both men and women and all that could hear with understanding."

They were moved at first to grief and tears, for when the law was explained to them they perceived how far they had strayed from the paths which the Lord their God had laid down for them. But Nehemiah, the governor, told them to hold their peace. This was a great and holy day, a day in which to rejoice and be glad, and discover the joy of the Lord as their strength. They were still the people of God, and had by Him been given a new deliverance. At that, we read, they made "great mirth, because they had understood."

Well, I too, am a scribe of sorts, with a pulpit of wood-pulp, if not of wood, in the street of the old Fleet river, before the Gate of Lud. Like Ezra, as I realise, I have been talking for an unconscionable time. But if, in these somewhat intimate pages, I have been able to show the law at work, with something of the adventure resultant from making one's calling one's Christian Vocation, I hope that some of my readers may find the gladness of understanding.

Let me return to my first metaphor. My boat has been long in the building, but it is ready for launching at last. I tap the last keys, drive the last rivets, knock away the shores and send her down the ways. "All ship-shape and Bristol fashion": so may she start on her voyaging, that perhaps, in God's goodness, some voyager may have cause to declare her "well-found".

VICTUALS

Various sovereign remedies have been proposed for those who seek athletic success, some of doubtful legality. A few years ago we heard all about the slow sodium pill, without which it appeared that no sporting Englishman's equipment in the tropics would henceforth be complete. Each year brings its fresh medical miracle. Sceptics may remember what happened when Bill Neat of Bristol fought Tom Hickman, the Gas Man, in 1821. After the Gas Man, had been knocked out, spurting blood in all directions, the first act of his doctors was to bleed him. They could not even wait until he was taken to bed, but set to on the field of battle itself, to carry on the work which Neat had so heartily begun. Nevertheless, the Gas Man survived, and the swift action of the doctors was much admired.

When Wolverhampton Wanderers were roaring favourites for the F.A. Cup in 1939, against Portsmouth in the final, their success was attributed to some secret glandular process. Glands were all the rage at this time. Portsmouth disdained medicine, put their faith in magic (in the form of Mr. Jack Tinn's lucky spats) and won 4-1.

The homelier kind of medical advice, while probably no more accurate than that of the experts, usually lasts longer, perhaps because it is harder to disprove. An apple a day keeps the doctor away. Cast not a clout till May be out. Of this kind is the belief (which could certainly produce stout evidence in its favour) that the best fast bowlers train on beer. Or that selectors should develop their brains, as Jeeves did, by a diet of fish. Or that, if you wish to put a visiting cricket eleven off its game, you should provide duck and custard for lunch.

In 1829 the Lansdown club were playing Kingscote at Bath, and it was reckoned a big match. The famous John Sparks was the Lansdown coach, umpire, groundsman and caterer. James Pycroft, then a boy of 16, was playing his first game for Lansdown, and at the end of the first day asked Sparks what he thought the chances were.

"I should say", said Sparks, "the side that lives nearest home has the best chance."

"Why so?"

"You see, sir, many things go to spoil your chance at cricket. First there's the dinner..."

"What! do men drink too much? these men are not the sort of characters to get drunk."

"No sir, but sometimes they eats too much. Now duck and custard is particularly a bad thing to play upon. I had my dinner at the side table, and saw what was going on. So I said to Harry, the waiter, 'Hand these custards to that gentleman (pointing to Protheroe who was going on to bowl); and after that hand him some bottle beer, and be sure to recommend the salad with his cheese'."

"Well, and what then?"

"What then! Why, didn't you see how Mr. Broadley hit him all over the ground? Didn't he bowl him long hops and tosses until he was quite hit off? My duck and custard, shaken up with bottled beer into a nice state of fermentation, did all that — ha ha!"

The Lansdown Cricket Club was in the middle of the nineteenth century a kind of M.C.C. of the west, a centre where all the best players went to get a game: whether it was for the club or against them did not seem to matter much. Thus W.G.Grace played in 23 matches for them, and 41 against them, over a period of 35 years. The first time he played for them, he went in at No 15 (out of 22) and scored 0 and 0. But he was only 15 years old at the time, and his elder brother, E.M. scored 73 and 9. W.G. and E.M. later opened the innings for Lansdown, in 1880, the same year when they opened for England against Australia, in the first Test match ever played in England.

Henry Daubeney, of Lansdown, claimed to be the inventor of the leg greave, or pad (Robert Robinson of Hambledon had tried wooden greaves much earlier, but had been laughed out of them). "By this device", Pycroft wrote, "Daubeney used to stand up to leg balls far more boldly than he otherwise could have done." Pycroft saw Daubeney hit a 7 in a match at Stonehenge, a remote place for a cricket field in those days. Indeed, Stonehenge gave up the match on the second day, "being unable to bring their men to the ground."

It was not uncommon, in the first half of the nineteenth century, for matches to be conceded for this reason, or even (as in Pickwick) because it was felt one side had achieved an unassailable superiority. As late as 1850, Teignbridge "declined further play" against Lansdown, needing 48 runs with 2 wickets to fall. No doubt on some of these occasions the refreshments were a temptation. Why waste time when there is only an hour left before the inexorable train goes? Lansdown's hospitality was famous, though once when they played the Purton club at Purton, they found half their side out of action through the effects of a crab provided by the genial Vicar; conceivably a revenge for the duck and custard.

The two — mostly professional — touring organisations of the day were the All England XI and the United England XI. Between 1852 and 1865 Lansdown played seven matches against the All England and one against the United. They beat the All England twice and the United once, all matches played with odds. The most famous victory was in 1865, when Eighteen of Lansdown beat the United by an innings and 113 runs. E.M.Grace scored 121, and with two brothers — W.G. and Henry — took all the England wickets in both innings. Three years earlier there had been an even bigger sensation on the Lansdown ground (their first ground, up on the down itself). M.C.C. sent a team to play Western Counties. Alfred Mynn of Kent and Fuller Pilch of Norfolk were "given men" for Western Counties, no names then more renowned. Pilch scored a century, and Mynn took 6 wickets in the first Marylebone innings. He had taken two more in the second, when the Sheriff's Officer appeared with a warrant for his arrest: he owed a debt of £130. The *Bath Chronicle* scooped the world with the story:

> It was arranged that Mr. Mynn should not be disturbed till the conclusion of the game, but that he should surrender himself. When the last wicket was drawn the players returned to their cottage, Mr. Mynn being followed closely by the officers who kept their man in view. However, Mr. Mynn got into the cottage and a number of his friends placed themselves in the doorway and effectually prevented the officers from entering. The upshot of the matter was that one of Mr. Mynn's friends undertook to pay the money or to deliver Mr. Mynn to the Sherriff's Officer.

Mynn was less subtle than another cricketer of the same period, a notable bowler, who was often engaged by local twenty-twos to oppose the England sides. He was pressed to pay a debt of £12, and made an arrangement with his creditor to be arrested just before the start of a match. He showed suitable astonishment when arrested, and the local cricketing authorities, alarmed at the prospect of losing their star bowler, promptly sent round the hat and paid the debt, which was what both debtor and creditor had calculated would happen.

When Lansdown moved to the Combe Park ground, where they still play, they maintained their reputation for lavish fare. Luncheons were sent up from Fisher's restaurant in Northgate Street, one of the celebrated Bath restaurants of the period, with champagne at 4/- a bottle. Even so a young medical student, F.J.Poynton, found it more than his pocket could face, and used to slip off to the nearest inn, for beer and bread and cheese. Poynton (later a Harley Street surgeon) played for Somerset in their first ever match against Surrey at the Oval. They were beaten by an innings and 375 runs. As Poynton was walking sadly back to the pavilion, a "pale and weedy reporter" (his own phrase) asked him if Somerset were really a first class county. This may have been no more than an innocent request for information, but Poynton saw it otherwise, and was about to crack his bat on the pale and weedy head, when his team-mate, the Rev A.P.Wickham, intervened and led him away.

This was in 1891, when Somerset were officially given first-class status. But ten years before then, the first county week had been held at Combe Park. Without the existence of the Lansdown club, the county club might never have come into existence. When it did, Lansdown was awarded an automatic seat on the committee. The list of Lansdown players includes Walter Long, who became the First Lord of the Admiralty; John Simon, who became Lord Chancellor; and Martin Hawke, who became captain of Yorkshire, the only one of the three whose career can be said to have been an unqualified success. Lansdown proudly possess a photograph of George V at Lord's, flanked by Hawke and Long.

Pycroft, who had played his first big match for Lansdown against Kingscote, also played his last — many years later. The old man finished with custard, not duck. He scored 39 not out. His eye was not what it had been. The ball kept just missing the stumps, while the fielders whistled and cast their eyes to heaven, as fielders in such circumstances do. This produced from Pycroft a fitting farewell aphorism, a sound piece of advice for all batsmen ever since: "I'll tell you what, gentlemen; I am here to guard three stumps, not five, and claim to play accordingly."

Somerset and Dorset bear many resemblances, especially in their hinterlands. The Piddle valley in Dorset is just such a part of Dorset as could be transplanted over the border. In the years after the war, the West of England Home Service used to run a series of radio programmes called "Village on the Air". They were delightful programmes for a young man to do. The task was to spend over several days there, and in the programme you talked about the village and its history, and interviewed some of the local inhabitants. One of the villages chosen was Briantspiddle, discretely altered by the *Radio Times* to Briantspuddle. In this it followed the usage of many Victorian signposts, and even, sadly, of the Trades Unions who were anxious lest their martyrs should be demeaned. The names of the seven Piddle villages are Tolpiddle, Affpiddle, Briantspiddle, Turnerspiddle, Piddletrenthide, Piddlehinton, and Piddle-town. They are all in the valley of the river Piddle, which got its name, it is averred, because the giant of Cerne Abbas, in a rainy season, released himself with exceptional vigour and created the river. There is also a hill nearby, called Site Hill; but on the old maps it is spelt slightly differently, and this is where the giant (whom you may still see, rudely carved, on the flank of the downs) performed the major operation.

The chief interest in Briantspiddle then, as memory serves, was because it was the home of a bold effort in rural reconstruction, a kind of miniature Dartington Hall. How it ultimately fared we do not know, but the next Piddle village to engage our attention was Piddlethrenthide, partly because of the efforts of its Vicar, Derek Parry, obviously a man of wit and resource. He gathered together the recipes, some old, some new, of the cooks of the valley — nothing too obscure, but giving some indication of what the stalwart people of those parts like to eat, and published *The Piddle Valley Cookbook*, all profits to go to the Piddletrenthide Church Restoration Fund. This is a beautiful medieval church, but inevitably needs upkeep. Ralph Wightman, an old and dear friend, who was always proud of being the Piddletrenthide butcher's son, is buried in the churchyard.

At the beginning there is a heartfelt poem, written by four pupils of Piddletrenthide School:

> At school we have mash, which tastes just like Flash,
> But we're told it is good for our tummies.
> We don't doubt their word, but the mash is absurd,
> And we'd rather have something more yummies.

At the end, there is a poem by the Vicar's wife: but before that occurs the last recipe, called "Vicarage Cold Pot":

> Take one Vicar (not too stale), mix with one wife, marinated in paint and wallpaper, season with two sons, to add spice and variety, stir together and place in one large, draughty vicarage with a sprinkling of mice (the church variety) and a teaspoonful of friendly ghosts. Cook for any length of time and enjoy the result throughout the year.

And then the little poem:

> In order to forestall a riot,
> And keep the whole family quiet,
> I have said I will cook
> All the things in this book,
> And then we'll all go on a diet.

As for the recipes themselves, we cannot judge, but can at least enjoy their names, very few of which are in French or other fancy languages. "Piddle Potage" sounds good. "Dot's Curried Vegetable Soup" is all right for those who enjoy the strange taste of curries. "Portland-style Mackerel" involves mixing mackerel with gooseberries. "Poacher's Pie", provided by Peggy Cake from Plush (another village in the valley) echoes Mrs. Beeton with its opening sentence; "First catch your rabbits." An underestimated dish, probably, poacher's pie, with a long history. "Friday Pie" sounds very good, mostly bacon and cheese. So does "Abbot's Ford Tongue", though "Purbeck Meat Balls" might tax the digestion. Some of these names are newly invented, but other recipes do give a real indication of what country people of the west used to have for celebrations in feast days — they could not afford such luxuries all the time. One particularly pleasing name is The Adaptable Pudding, which reflects the times when you never knew when the man was going to be home for his supper, because it was harvest, or the farmer was being awkward, or there might have been a pal in the pub.

We trust this book is still in print, and that you will buy it. Any man who likes his grub and is loved by his wife would find it a worthy investment. Besides, you can take her out for an afternoon out down the Piddle valley, and as you see Piddletrenthide Church proudly on the way to restoration, can say you have made your contribution to it.

Call in at Bridport in the early nineteenth century, take a cup of tea with Mr. H.B.Way, and try a slice of his home-made potato bread. He is so proud of it that he has sent a sample, and the recipe, to the Society of Arts.

The idea of mixing potatoes with the flour had at first been received with scorn by Mr. Way's family, his neighbours, and, most importantly of all his cook, Hannah Peters. But before long they were all, he claimed, convinced, even Miss Peters. They actually *preferred* the new mixture, and "I assure you", he says, "that it is a matter of regret to my whole family, when, from the scarcity of potatoes, we recommence the use of bread made wholly from wheat."

The Society of Arts went some way to confirming Mr. Way's claims. They kept his loaf for a fortnight, during which time most of the members sampled it. They reported that what remained "had every appearance of bread made wholly from wheaten flour well fermented, and well tasted, without being in the least mouldy or stale, though it had been baked fourteen days. It appeared to the committee", the report goes on, "a very successful mode of making bread, and that it might tend to lessen the consumption of flour; an object of considerable national importance" — there was, of course, a war on. Mr. Way himself produced statistics to prove that the bread not only tasted better, not only lasted longer, but was also cheaper.

Here is the recipe for this miraculous product, as he gives it. Unfortunately the quantities are rather large, but you can work them out proportionately. Sixteen pounds of potatoes were washed, peeled and boiled, after which they weighed thirteen pounds. They were then mixed, while warm, with twice the amount — twenty-six pounds — of flour. The potatoes were bruised as fine as possible, and half a pound of yeast added. Four quarts of warm water were added to the mixture, and the whole well kneaded together, and left two hours to rise. This amount provided what Mr. Way calls "six loaves and two cakes"; the baking, in his iron oven, took two hours.

Now was this recipe, of which Mr. Way was so proud, and of which the learned Society so approved, really a cooking discovery of some significance?

Or was it merely another version of our old and esteemed friend, the potato cake?

A Cornish pasty is a most excellent dish if you know where to buy it, or can have faith in the cook. You used to be able to get really good pasties at the Norway Inn, Devoran, on the road between Truro and Falmouth. We use the past tense simply because we have not been there lately to check. About 1950 the Norway was almost the only place in West Penwith where you could take a visitor to show him what a pasty should really be. Mind, you had to pay for them. In the average pub or shop in those days a pasty cost sixpence or so, pastry and a mixture of potato and turnip with a fringe of tasteless meat. At the Norway they were half a crown, and true value for money. Someone had told Bon Viveur about them, and his/her rapturous cutting from the *The Daily Telegraph* was pinned up proudly on the wall.

The association of Cornwall with pasties is usually thought to be to do with the mines. It is true that the tin miners used to fit them into their large flat thigh pockets as they went down the shafts — in the earlier days, by ladders. This is one of the ways in which you may test how much claim to be "Cornish" a pasty has: is the crust firm? There was once a miner who had a week's holiday in London, met a Cockney girl, whom he married. She had been a cook, and was very proud of her light, flaky pastry. When they were back in Cornwall after the honeymoon, she sent him off with the usual pasty for his snap. She waited eagerly afterwards for his comments. He said nothing rude, for he was very much in love. He said nothing at all. After a week or two of this invariable treatment she plucked up her courage and asked him how the pasties were suiting him. "Ah", he said, "Handsome, maid, handsome." And then a pause, and out it came: "Mind", he said, "what us do call a pasty down here...well, see, take Jan Pascoe's wife. Once he dropped one of pasties down shaft, and when us got to bottom 'twas all in one piece."

The proper *content* of a pasty is more arguable. The reason why the Cornish are so well behaved is that the devil is scared to cross the Tamar lest a housewife should seize him and clap him in a pasty. If baked Beelzebub could be an acceptable filling, there is plenty of scope. Meat is normal, but not essential. Fish pasties were common in ports such as Newlyn and Looe. Apple pasties were more frequently found in Devon. We have known, though fortunately not tasted, a pasty which had cream and jam at one end, and meat at the other. This traditional Cornish feast was invented entirely for the gullible tourist. Indeed in many cases the addition of the term "Cornish" to a title means nothing but an attempt at a tourist sales plug. There was a shop in Hayle which had the nerve to sell bags of "gull food", which consisted simply of lumps of stale bread. We thought this pretty cool until we saw a similar product on sale at St. Ives, charging a penny more, presumably because it was now called "Cornish Gull Food". Not all the "Cornish" appellations are spurious. There is a genuine recipe for Cornish ice cream, although it is not always observed as advertised, and Furniss of Truro make a very pleasing ginger biscuit called a "Cornish fairing".

The term "pasty" has in recent years been challenged by "tiddy oggie", or briefly "oggie". It is not, we think, a true West Country phrase. A Mrs. Burch, a redoubtable old lady, used for years to keep an oggie stall at the Devonport end of the Torpoint car ferry, and very pleasing they were to consume on your leisurely crossing. "Oggie" was originally naval slang, and commonly heard in Portsmouth. It became a kind of generalized West of England warcry. The rugby team of St. Luke's College, Exeter, used it — thriced repeated — as a rallying call. A learned derivation from "ogee", a church architectural term supposedly passed on by the sport-loving stonemasons of Exeter Cathedral, was once aired in *The Times*, but has failed, to its author's regret, to carry general conviction.

In thinking of Cornish victuals, we ought not to forget the treacle mines. They still pop up in the news when the silly season comes round. The story is a familiar one: how in the last century the discovery of large deposits of easily-accessible surface treacle in Bolivia made deep-lode working in this country economically impossible. Although a Lord Lieutenant of Cornwall sought to rally public opinion with his famous message that the industry had faced many a sticky prospect before and won through, the mines in Cornwall (and there were some in Devon too) went into a rapid decline. In some ways, of course, the industry's public relations were already bad. When Lewis Carroll wrote in *Alice in Wonderland*, linking treacle with his underground heroine, it was recognized as a powerful and deserved protest against the use of child labour in the mines.

There have been many recent rumours of revival. When the great new derricks were built, first on North Hessary Tor and then on Caradon Hill, it was widely believed hat these were part of new treacle mine workings, and much disappointment when it was realized that all they helped to provide was an admittedly copious supply of soothing syrup.

Well, well: it is an old joke which can be laboured too far. There are various theories of how it began. Mr. A.K.Hamilton Jenkins says that the original (fictional) treacle mine was in Tredavoe, near Penzance, and that innocents would be asked to have a look at it on All Fools' Day. But this claim has been fiercely disputed, because as time went on nearly every mining area began to claim its own, most of them believed in the locality to have been the original, if not the only example. Oddly enough, the custom never seems to have spread to another derelict industrial area, the North Somerset coalfield.

There is another theory that a "treacle mine" was simply a rich mine, a mine doing exceptionally well. Another, that they are in some way connected with the remarkable figure who constantly crops up in Cornish folklore, the unjust steward, Jan Tregeagle. It is true that Tregeagle is usually pronounced "Tregeagle", which makes the assonance less striking, but then the Cornish might often have spoken of "traycle". There was a real Tregeagle mine — that was its name — at St. Neot in this century; possibly others.

Treacle was not the only usual substance mined by fancy. There were strawberry mines, gooseberry mines, currant mines, lemon mines, junket mines. Not, so far as is known, pasty mines. This is a little surprising, for though pasties are not in fact hewn from the living rock, Mrs. Jan Pascoe was not the only cook who could give you that impression.

On Twelfth Night — or sometimes, less commonly, on Christmas Eve — it was the custom to wassail the apple trees. It happened in various places all over England, but it may well have had its origin in the classic cider country of Devon and Somerset, and it lasted there longer than anywhere else — indeed, well into the present century.

There were many local variations in the practice, as there always are with this kind of old custom, but this was a typical version.

On Twelfth Night, the farmer and his labourers would go to the orchard, carrying their guns and a large can of cider. They danced round the best bearing apple tree, singing three times over, such lines as these:

Here's to thee
Old apple-tree,
Whence thou may'st bud,
And whence thou may'st blow,
And whence thou may'st bear
Apples enow!
Hats full!
Caps full!
Bushel bushel sacks full!
And my pockets full too.

(The tune, incidentally, seems to be unknown. We heard what claimed to be a version of it a year or two ago, but had no difficulty in recognising it as one specially composed by Cecil Cope for a radio programme in 1949).

After the singing, the men cheered, fired their guns, and returned to the farmhouse. The women bolted the door against them until someone had managed to guess what was roasting on the spit inside. Then the successful guesser was given the roast — which might be edible, but might again be an old boot.

If this custom was neglected, then the apple crop was sure to be a poor one.

In Cornwall, after everyone had had a drink of the cider, the rest was poured on the trunk of the tree, and sometimes hot cakes were placed on its branches. Sometimes, instead of cider, the drink called lambswool was used. To make this, apples were suspended above a can of hot, spiced ale and roasted until they fell in. Herrick writes about it:

> Wassail the trees, that they may beare
> You many a plum, and many a peare;
> For more or lesse fruits they may bring
> An you do give them wassailing.

And there is a reference to lambswool in *The Midsummer Night's Dream* ("crab" means, of course, crabapple):

> Sometimes lurk I in a gossip's bowl,
> In very likeness of a roasted crab;
> And when she drinks, against her lips I bob,
> And on her wither'd dew-lap pour the ale.

"Crying the neck" is a custom that has gone, though it was still carried out nearly everywhere in the western countryside not much more than a hundred years ago. Violet Alford, in her *Introduction to English Folklore*, published in 1952, describes how, when the custom was incorporated in a pageant near Barnstaple, "everybody remembered it and knew how to carry it out." The latest recorded date we have found is 1899.

The "neck" was the last sheaf of wheat to be cut, and it was cut by the oldest reaper. He cried out "I hav'et! I hav'et I hav'et!" The rest replied, "What hav'ee? What hav'ee? What hav'ee?" "A neck! A neck! A neck!" And they would bind it with ribbons and decorate it with flowers, and carry it back to the farmhouse in triumph, with much cheering and the singing of a song:

> A neck! A neck! A neck!
> Whose neck?
> Varmer Ferris's, Varmer Ferris's.
> It's all a-cut
> And all abound,
> And all a-taken from the ground!

This was the version sung in the Torbay area.

In Cornwall, the one who cut the neck was not usually the oldest inhabitant, but a strong young man, who would run as fast as he could with it back to the farmhouse, where the dairymaid was waiting with a pail of water. If he could dodge into the house, by door or window, without getting any of the water thrown over him, he could kiss the dairymaid. Otherwise, he was due for a proper sousing. This has been described by mythologists as a relic of an ancient fertility rite, though possibly, as with many research students, they are inclined to find what they are looking for.

But the pail of water does show the connection between crying the neck and the tradition of the Corn Baby. There were certainly corn babies in the west, as there had been in the Egypt of the Pharaohs. The Corn Baby was a small figure made from either the first or the last corn to be cut, dressed in a child's clothes. Again there was the run to the farmhouse, with all those standing by trying to throw water on the baby: but perhaps they did not try too hard, because the drier the Corn Baby remained, the better the next year's harvest would be. Once safely in the farmhouse, the baby would sit on the mantelpiece till harvest came again.

Crying the neck had, in its latter days, ceased to have any mystical significance. The songs and shouts would go up chiefly to inform neighbouring farmers that *our* harvest was done, while *you* are still struggling. The philosophical work which would penetrate most nearly to its latter meaning is not *The Golden Bough*, by the learned Mr. Fraser, but *One-upmanship*, by our hero of Station Road, Yeovil, Mr. Stephen Potter.

Corn babies would sometimes put in an appearance at Christian harvest festivals. This was a comparatively late addition to the church's calendar, and the man chiefly responsible was the Rev R.S.Hawker, Vicar of Morwenstow, in Cornwall. He was not in fact a Cornishman — his father had been vicar of the parish of Charles, in Plymouth. Nor, despite his conscientious charitableness, does he seem to have liked the Cornish too much. He felt that they had been debased by the Wesleys. He was one of the leaders of the ritualist movement, with passionate affection for the medieval world, Cornish saints, and cats. He took the cats with him to church, and on one occasion regretfully excommunicated one of them for killing a mouse on consecrated ground. He was a writer of considerable ability, and was responsible for the greater part of "And shall Trelawney die?" which has almost become the Cornish anthem. He went about his duties wearing a long claret-coloured kind of cassock, opening over a blue fisherman's jersey, with a red cross worked upon it; a claret-coloured wideawake hat, fisherman's boots, and crimson gloves. He had a remarkable record of saving life from wrecks on the terrible coast of North Cornwall. He was devoted to his wife, whom he married when he was twenty and she more than twice his age. He would not smoke because she found the smell offensive. He had a roaring temper and an instinctive generosity of spirit. All in all, he was an eccentric, consciously so, but to say that is to leave out most of the important things about him. There is a story of how, one day, he was taking his wife to the summer-house he built for her on the cliffs, and was furious to find there a man with long hair and a beard, a cloak and sombrero, puffing out clouds of smoke. "Who are you, sir?" demanded Hawker. "Sir", came the reply, "my name is Alfred Tennyson." After that unpropitious start they got on better, because they had much in common, including a devotion to the Arthurian legends. In fact, it has been said that the connection between Tintagel and Arthur really began with Hawker: not all that much of an overstatement.

Harvest Festivals seem an improbable enthusiasm for a High Churchman, but Hawker was much concerned with agricultural distress. Morwenstow was one of the worst sufferers from the truck system of payment. The rate of wages was eight shillings a week, but seven shillings worth was paid in corn, nine gallons for a week irrespective of the market price. This left a shilling to pay the rent. It left, Hawker explained, for fuel, for shoes, for clothing, for groceries, for tools, for club...nil; no pounds, no shillings, and nothing. He launched an appeal for the sufferers and had some success, and made himself unpopular with the farmers by his attacks on the truck system, though it was to linger on in the west for many years. He could even be kind to those who disagreed with him theologically. Once at his table a Roman Catholic, an Anglican, a Nothingarian and an Independent minister were lunching. "Clean and unclean beasts feeding together in the Ark", he explained. "But how odd", said a friend, "that you should get them to meet!" "Well, I thought it best: they never will meet in the next world." Although he said such outrageous things, he was clearly a difficult man to dislike. "If all gentlemen were like our Vicar", they said in the village, "the world would have no wrongs in it".

Harvest Festivals are still very popular in Cornwall, and many churches, especially the Methodists, look to them for the biggest congregations of the year ("Bain't nuthin' like a Bible Christin 'arrvest" was a phrase one often used to hear). The "harvest homes" of the Somerset villages fall, however, into a rather different category — more a combination of a religious ceremony and village revel. The one at East Brent dates back to 1857. The original motive of the good parson who founded it was perhaps no higher than to see that the underpaid agricultural labourers and their families had at least one square meal a year. The Brent harvest home has now become famous — perhaps too famous — and draws visitors from long distances. Others are more modest and more pleasingly domestic. We went not long ago to East Huntspill, not more than a few miles from Brent, and nearly all the 450 people who sat down at lunchtime to consume 340 lbs. of beef and ham were local, or as near as makes no difference.

It was a splendid day, made all the better because the sun was shining — which at East Huntspill on this day is regarded as a minor miracle in itself. The scene in the big marquee was noble: the brawny, shirt-sleeved carvers in their central enclave, the lady hurrying from table to table with second, third, fourth helpings of meat, and yet with a hush over the multitude, as they forswore the trivial pleasures of conversation for the solid attractions of food. They took the meal seriously and it deserved to be taken seriously. They took the evening procession seriously too. Weeks of work and centuries of craftsmanship had gone into the preparations of the harvest wagons with their intricate and beautiful decorations. The villagers do it for nothing but the satisfaction of a job well done.

Jollification and thanksgiving are the two parts of harvest, and perhaps at East Huntspill old Robert Hawker might have felt that the jollification was a little overdone. At the service which began the day's proceedings the pretty little church was only half full, and the Vicar of West Monkton was right to remind us in his address that we *have* much to be thankful for, and to ask us whether we are doing enough for the one third of the world's population still living below subsistence level. Of course we sang

All is safely gathered in
Ere the winter storms begin.

But there is another way in which harvest can be seen: it can be regarded as a parable of life and death — as ye sow, so shall ye reap. And the hymn, you remember, looks to another harvest when it goes on

Gather Thou thy people in
Free from sorrow, free from sin.

So we hoped that East Huntspill harvest home makes a whacking profit, some of which will go to the Freedom from Hunger campaign.

Another custom which we would like to see revived, and which could be done without much trouble, is the ringing of the pancake bell. The original intention of the bell was to summon the people to confessions before Lent, but the association with pancakes was a natural one and goes back a long way. In *Poor Robin's Almanack* for 1684 are the lines,

Hark, I hear the Pancake Bell

VICTUALS

And fritters make a gallant smell!

Since Lent meant an abstinence from meat for forty days, all the dripping and lard was used up the day before. This is usually held to be the origin of pancakes on Shrove Tuesday. The ringing of the bell at eleven or twelve in the morning summoned all the apprentice-boys, and any others who were hungry and could put up a claim, to their pancakes. It is a long time since churches have done much cooking, so the custom must date back to the time of church houses, and very likely before then to the monasteries.

The Rev H.G.S.Atchley, who was Vicar or All Saints, Oakhill, in Somerset, in the early years of this century, and an authority on church bells, made a list of places where the pancake bell was still rung. His list, in manuscript, was dated about 1920, and seems to depend a good deal on the *Victoria County History of England*, which was then gradually being produced. He gives more than eighty churches and one town hall, Shrewsbury. In some cases there was special bell, used only on that occasion, perhaps shaped like a pancake, a gong rather than a bell. In others one or two of the ordinary ring were used. At Daventry for some reason the bells were rung muffled, and there are other oddities. Most of Mr. Atchley's churches are in the Midlands, the area he knew best, but in the west he mentions Cirencester, Ilminster and Portishead.

There are also traditions of pancake bells in Cornwall, notably at St. Ives. Shrove Tuesday used to be great day at St. Ives, The boys would tie stones to cords, and parade the town, slinging the stones against the doors, and shouting

Give me a pancake now now now
Or I'll souse un your door with a row tow tow.

This has something of a modern ring to it, but in 1864 a correspondent assured Professor Robert Hunt that the custom was observed "in the lower parts of the town only."

But pancake bells. Are there any left? Are there, perhaps, any churches where one might hope to get a free pancake? There are certainly pancake races in several places, jovial occasions when the housewives compete, when the route is marked out with tossing positions.

This chapter has been full of feasting, so let us end with a rather sad and hungry story. It concerns the Devon painter Benjamin Haydon, a man of considerable abilities who was justly renowned in his day, but whose life ended, partly through ill luck and partly through temperamental failings of his own, in disappointment, disillusion and suicide.

Haydon was an indefatigable diarist. From this we learn that in 1813, when he was 27, his chief preoccupation for the whole year, was an enormous painting of "Solomon", one of those wall-sized affairs which, unwisely, he liked best to paint. He finished it early in 1814, and actually sold it for 600 guineas, a sum which was still not enough to pay off all his debts. He had been living the traditional artist's life, half starved in a garret, though one has to remember that his descriptions certainly do not minimize his sufferings. But among his friends were some of the most distinguished men of the day, John and Leigh Hunt (whom he enjoyed visiting in Newgate when they were sent there for being rude about the Prince of Wales), Hazlitt and Lamb, Barnes of *The Times*, and a promising pupil, a fellow-Devonian called Eastlake. He was also much captivated by a charming young gipsy girl whom he was later to paint as Gavin's daughter.

One day, to Haydon's delight, Hazlitt invited him to a christening party for his son. Here, at least, was the certainty of a square meal. Haydon arrived punctually at four. Hazlitt was out. "I walked up and found his wife ill by the fire in a bedgown — nothing ready for guests and everything wearing the appearance of neglect and indifference. I said 'Where is Hazlitt?' 'Oh dear, William has gone to look for a parson'. 'A parson; why, has he not thought of that before?' 'No, he didn't'." So Haydon went out into the park through Queen's Square and met Hazlitt in a rage coming home.

"'Have ye got a parson?' 'No, sir', said he, 'these fellows are all out.' 'What will you do?' 'Nothing'. So in we walked, Hazlitt growling at all the parsons and the church. When we came in we sat down — nobody was come — no table laid — no appearance of dinner. On my life there is nothing so heartless as going out to dinner and finding no dinner ready."

Haydon's wrath continued to mount. He was a man who liked his victuals. After he had been sitting down expectantly for sometime, the other guests began to drop in. Ultimately a maid appeared and deposited a heap of knives and forks. Then a dish of potatoes, which the painter disgustedly describes as "cold, waxy and yellow", and then "a great bit of beef with a bone like a battering-ram, toppling on all its corners. Neither Hazlitt nor Lamb seemed at all disturbed, but set to work helping each other."

Poor Haydon! (One suspects that to some extent they were deliberately, and perhaps rather cruelly, teasing him). His last comment on the fiasco sums up the character of this talented, pompous, unhappy man.

Even Lamb's wit and Hazlitt's disquisitions, in a large room, wainscotted and ancient, where Milton had mediated, could not reconcile me to such violation of all the decencies of life. I returned weary, and placing on the floor of my room soon recovered under the imposing look of my picture.

INNS

Although we have often visited inns together, naturally we have often done so separately. Hence our recollections of them and experiences of them are different. In this section, therefore, the personal element — which is obviously important — has involved the use of the first personal singular occasionally. We hope this does not involve confusion.

We doubt if it is possible, or ever will be, to establish the identity of the oldest English inn. What constituted an inn? A place where you could stay, or a place where you could only obtain refreshment? Solid as well as liquid refreshment? The earliest English licensing laws created "licensed *victuallers*": the intention was quite clearly to provide a social service other than simply the sale of alcoholic drinks. Although the term "licensed victualler" is still with us, as early as the seventeenth century there were complaints that it was not strictly interpreted, and that the supposed victuallers were nothing more than dram-sellers, as they were called. The saying "good wine needs no bush" derives from the time when a bush, or a representation of one, was hung in the door or window to indicate that drink was available.

The George, at Norton St. Philip, in Somerset, claims to be the oldest licensed house in England, and so far as we know this claim has not been seriously disputed. Its ancestry goes back at least to 1398. It is a beautiful old building and still a very good inn. The Society for the Preservation of Drinking Beers from the Wood (predecessor of the Campaign for Real Ale) used to hold its annual dinners there for many years, and notable occasions they were, with roast beef and Yorkshire pudding. The George very nearly made a dramatic appearance in history: the Duke of Monmouth was dressing at one of its windows, watching a preliminary skirmish on the morning of Sedgemoor, when a sniper's bullet narrowly missed him. It was not, it transpired, a fortunate escape for the Duke.

But to be the earliest licensed house still in existence is not necessarily to be the oldest inn, since inns existed long before any legal definitions of them. The Fighting Cocks at St. Albans claims an ancestry going back to the eighth century. The Fountain at Canterbury and the Bell at Finedon claim an eleventh century origin. The Trip to Jerusalem, at Nottingham, which most people probably think of as our oldest inn, is supposed to date from 1189. But no-one really knows these things for certain, or whether these houses have been in any real sense inns through the whole of their history. The claim of the George at Norton St. Philip, while less extravagant, therefore rests on firmer ground. It is certainly appropriate that England's oldest licensed house should be named after England's patron saint.

Then there are some inns which do not have a very long history as inns, but which have much older buildings, and perhaps inherit a tradition of hospitality

104

even older than the buildings. In early medieval times, for instance, there were many manor houses which were unofficial hostelries for travellers passing through. If you were a gentleman, the lord of the manor would usually think shame not to offer you hospitality, and your retainers would be made equally welcome alongside his retainers, below the salt. Later, a separate establishment for the sub-salt visitors might be established nearby, and a good many inns came into existence this way. The New Inn at Gloucester is one such; and, less famous, the Luttrell Arms at Dunster.

This last was once the town house of the Abbots of Cleeve, and as such must often in its early days have given shelter to wayfarers — at least, if an Abbot's behaviour lived up to his professions. The Luttrell family purchased it in 1499. It was an inn again, officially this time, by 1651 — called the Ship Inn then — and in 1789, the year the French Revolution began, the Somerset countrymen demonstrated their loyalty to their gentry by re-christening it the Luttrell Arms. The Abbot's original house has been knocked round and added to quite a lot, and yet all the bright ideas of the different centuries harmonize astonishingly happily. All, that is to say, except the floors, the levels of which slope unpredictably. The first time I went there I was to meet a distinguished lady, the headmistress of a nearby school. Rising to greet her, I was trapped by an unseen drop in the floor level, and prostrated myself at her feet. A pint tankard on the table contributed to the unfortunate impression. It says much for the Luttrell Arms that even this embarrassment has not prevented me from returning as often as I can.

The George and Pilgrims, at Glastonbury, not far away, is at least architecturally one of the beauties of a town which has many beautiful buildings. The most famous of them, alas, are now ruins, but the George and Pilgrims stands much as it has done for hundreds of years. The date usually given for its foundation in 1475, but again this is a case where it is difficult to be precise about the beginnings.

It was originally, I think, just the Pilgrims, "George" coming in when it was fashionable under the Hanoverians. John of Glaston, who chronicled the early history of the town, tells us that it was built by Abbot Selwood in the fifteenth century for the use of pilgrims and travellers. Glastonbury was not only a famous place of pilgrimage itself, but lay on the route of those travelling to Dartmouth, to take shop to visit that favourite shrine of the medieval English St. James of Compostela. The beach at Compostela was famous for its scallop-shells, and it was customary for those who had been on pilgrimage there (and some who had not) to wear a scallop-shell in their hat: hence Ralegh's poem beginning "bring me my scallop-shell of quiet."

At Glastonbury the Abbey would provide free hospitality for the pilgrims for two nights, but after that period those who stayed — at least if they were of the lower social orders — had to pay for themselves. For these the Abbot built his hotel — the "Novum hospitium", John of Glaston called it, "the New hostel". But "New hostel" implies that there had been an old one. It is very possible that it was on the same site, in which case, remembering Glastonbury's ancient tradition as a centre of pilgrimage, the George and Pilgrims may have a history as lengthy as that of any inn in the land.

It *is* a very handsome building. "At first sight", says Thomas Burke, "it seems almost too good to be true. It is...something out of a troubadour's song or out of the Luttrell Psalter...It has the frozen flush of immortality rather than the pallor of antiquity." Thomas Burke also says that it had the best cheesecakes he had ever tasted. That was a good many years ago, and I do not know whether it is still true. Every time I go there I mean to ask, and I always forget.

The Cott Inn at Dartington, Devon, has subtle ploy of publicity. It claims only to be the second oldest inn in England. Thus, while disputes rage as to which is the oldest, the more moderate assertion of the Cott goes unchallenged. The Cott can at least adduce firm documentary evidence of an early origin. Early in the fifteenth century, Dartington Church was pillaged, and the churchwardens' accounts give some details of its restoration. The Rector contributed 3/4d., which was spent on cider for the workmen at the Cott Inn. As in those days 3/4d. would buy something like sixty gallons of cider, this must have been one of the more memorable parties in the history of the inn. The Cott itself claims, in its publicity, a foundation date of 1320, but this, although perfectly feasible, cannot I think be directly proved.

There seems no doubt, however, that the Cott has been continuously an inn from the fourteenth century until today, although naturally it has had its ups and down in that period, varying from being a rather rough country cider house to the kind of model country inn which delights American tourists. The arrival of the modern version of Dartington Hall nearby, has naturally had a considerable effect upon the inn's fortune. Nevertheless it has retained sufficient of its original and genuine character to appeal to the local countryman as well as the tourist, or the visiting parent. I am inclined to think it was built as an inn in the first place: if it was not, it is certainly a remarkably happy chance that a stream flows through it, just a little underground, exactly where the beer barrels are. This is why, in hot weather, you can always rely on it for a nice cool pint.

One of the oldest inns in the country is *not* the King Arthur's Castle at Tintagel. It is an astonishing piece of architectural effrontery: a twentieth century replica of an Arthurian castle. Thomas Burke records the remark of an American who entered it: "Well, well, well! Say, did Mark Twain ever do anything as naughty as this to King Arthur?" Naughty, perhaps yes. But it is undoubtedly impressive. It reminds me of another building in a very different style, Keble College, Oxford; the finest flowering of the very worst Victorian seeds. Yet you abandon logic, and give in to Keble, just as you give in to King Arthur's Castle. It is chiefly the sheer bulk that does it. Fancy having the unblushing nerve, not only to build such places, but to build them so big! Criticism is daunted.

There is also a real castle at Tintagel, or at least the ruins of one. No-one knows who built it, though excavations have suggested it is on the site of a British camp, and a monastery of the old British church. So here, too, the nearby hotel can claim to be carrying on an ancient tradition of hospitality.

Tintagel is not, or course, the only place which claims to be King Arthur's seat. Its claims have been enhanced by that superb rocky coastline which is certainly the kind of place where one would expect Iseult to wait for her false knight, and where Merlin might have seen the child cast up from the sea upon the ninth great wave the night when Uther Pendragon died. The modern castle so far from marring this illusion — as one would expect — seems to emphasize it. So although when you go there you are not visiting a "genuine old inn", go there you still should. It is the nearest thing to an Arthurian stronghold you will find above the soil, and a lot of careful research went into its making. And if it isn't "genuine" — well, was Arthur? We have discussed that elsewhere, and all we need say here is that we are yet to be convinced.

Once in a broadcast I mentioned that Charles Kingsley wrote most of *Westward Ho!* while he was staying at the Royal Hotel, Bideford; and this led to an interesting correspondence with listeners about the literary associations of other inns in the south and west. These things are, of course, difficult to disprove and prove, and often one suspects that there is an intolerable amount of legend to a pennyworth of fact. But here are some of the less challengeable associations.

Evelyn Waugh has told us that he enjoyed writing at the Manor House, an hotel near Moretonhampstead, indeed finished *Put Out More Flags* there, during the war. A mile or two is the Three Crowns, at Chagford. The porch has a stone seat, upon which Sidney Godolphin lay, and died, after he had been wounded in the civil war. He was a poet of some achievement and more promise. We still sing some of his lines as a carol. Clarendon wrote that Godolphin left "the misfortune of his death upon a place which would never otherwise have had a mention in the world", which is a bit hard on Chagford.

The Alfoxton Park Hotel, Holford, in Somerset, is the house where Wordsworth lived when he and Coleridge were planning the publication of the *Lyrical Ballads*.

Then there is the White Hart, at Whitchurch, in Hampshire. There, John

Henry Newman found he had ten hours to wait for the Plymouth coach, and used the time to begin the work which became known as the *Lyra Apostolica*. I do not know if his distinguished memory is preserved at the White Hart today. At the Jolly Farmer, at Farnham, William Cobbett was born, but though the name is appropriate, it wasn't an inn at that time. And Bill Andrews, the Somerset cricketer, was born at the White House, Swindon. Bill will stand comparison with William Cobbett as a convivial character, but was not up to Cobbett's weight as a journalist. He used to write a weekly sporting column in a Bristol paper, and a friend of his, a local schoolmaster, would reproduce it on the blackboard, with an instruction to his pupils, "Now turn that into English."

The Bear at Devizes, which was the best hotel in the world when my wife and I stopped there for dinner on our wedding day, and near where the unfortunate lady was supposedly struck dead for stealing, was once visited by Fanny Burney and Mrs. Thrale. They were surprised to find that the house was full of books and paintings, and that the landlord's two pretty daughters played the piano. But most of all were they impressed by the ten-year-old son of the house. He seems, Fanny Burney wrote, "to be not merely the wonder of their family, but of the times, for his astonishing skill in drawing." *Sir* Joshua Reynolds had already pronounced him "the most promising genius he had ever met with." The child's name was Thomas Lawrence.

The loveliest inn in Gloucester is beyond question the New Inn. Its fifteenth century creeper covered courtyard, where Shakespeare is supposed to have played, is as fine as anything of its kind in the country. Yet in Gloucester you should also make time for a visit to the Bell, not so much for its architectural merits — it has been much restored — as because of its associations with some distinguished men. On December 16th, 1714, George Whitefield was born there. It was a somewhat unlikely birthplace for a man who was to be, after John Wesley, the greatest evangelist of the eighteenth century. His father, who owned the inn, died when George was only two years old. His mother kept the inn going, not too successfully and in due course married again. Whitefield was educated at the Cathedral School, and then the Free Grammar School, and was clearly a boy of promise, but at fifteen, when the business was still struggling, he — in his own words — "put on the blue apron". He began "washing the mops, cleaning the rooms, and becoming common drawer to his mother's customers" — to be blunt, he was the pot boy. Since he had a sense of humour and a taste for company, he seems rather to have enjoyed it. He won quite a reputation with the customers for his mimicry of various local characters, including a Congregational minister called Cole. On one occasion Whitefield and some of his cronies from the Bell burst in upon one of Mr. Cole's services with loud cries of "Old Cole". At least that is the account given, but I suspect that the comment was a touch more original than that, perhaps a couplet from the familiar ballad "Twankydillo":

Which makes my bright hammer to rise and to fall,
Here's to Old Cole and to Young Cole and to Old Cole of all.

Some years later, this same Mr. Cole became one of Whitefield's travelling preachers.

Some generations later, the owners of the Bell were John and Sybella Phillpotts. They had some remarkable children. One became a barrister, one a general, one a West Indian planter, and the youngest, Henry, became one of the most famous of nineteenth century bishops, a rich and controversial character.

In Wiltshire, there is the Pheasant, at Winterslow, on the London road out of Salisbury. It is on the site of an old inn known as the Winterslow Hut. The Hut, now pulled down, must have been a fine coach-house, and was for some years the home of William Hazlitt. "So have I loitered my life away, reading books, looking at pictures, going to plays, hearing, thinking, writing on what pleased me best. I have wanted only one thing to make me happy, but wanting that have wanted everything." So wrote Hazlitt in one of his gloomier moods, in the collection of essays called *Winterslow*. The first Mrs. Hazlitt had inherited some property there, and it was the Hazlitt home before it became an inn. The years they spent there were not, as the quotation suggests, very happy ones. The present Pheasant is a pleasant place, and makes the most of its literary associations, though one suspects that Hazlitt himself was rather relieved to see the back of it.

But the inn also recalls, with its colour prints, a decidedly unliterary distinction. On the night of October 20th, 1816, the *Quicksilver Mail*, the pride of the western road, drew up at the Winterslow Hut to change horses. During the change, a lioness suddenly sprang upon one of the leaders. It became a favourite subject for prints. The lioness had escaped from a travelling caravan of Wombwell's Menagerie, which had camped nearby (Wombwell was one of the pioneers of the travelling circus). The situation was saved by the arrival of one of the menagerie keepers, and also of a large mastiff, who decided to join in the fun. We do not know what happened to the mastiff, but the lioness was recaptured and the horse, though injured, recovered so well that it was able to go on doing coach work for some years longer.

Samuel Pepys stayed at the Anchor at Liphook; so did John Wilkes, who by a stretch could be called a writer; and a variety of English sovereigns, who could not. Of course, Pepys stayed at a lot of inns and left us recollections of them. He liked the George at Salisbury. The George has a history going back hundreds of years — as many as eight hundred, one writer has conjectured — and certainly its history can be traced from the year 1320, when it was owned by a gentleman known as William Teynterer the Elder. He left it to his son, William Teynterer the Younger, who left it to his wife, who had the splendid name of Alesia, who left it to her second husband. Here the family tradition ended, for this second husband directed in his will that the inn should be sold, and it unromantically came into the possession of the corporation.

However, they looked after their property, and in the city archives it is recorded that a bay window was added, at a cost of 20/-. In a lease of 1473 twelve principal chambers of the inn are listed, as well as a tavern, a wine cellar, a buttery, a kitchen, a parlour and a variety of other rooms. It was one of the great inns of its day. In 1624 a by-law forbidding players to perform at any inn in Salisbury except the George was promulgated (I suspect some officials' pockets were lined in order to put that one over). In 1645 Oliver Cromwell slept there, and he was a man who had high standards of husbandry and liked to sleep and eat well ("I have been in all the counties of England", Cromwell once said, "and I think the husbandry of Devonshire is the best"). Twenty years later Pepys came along and reported:

> Good beds, and the master of the house a sober, understanding man, and I had good discourse with him about this country's matters, as wool and corn and other things. And he also merry, and made us mighty merry at supper, about manning the new ship at Bristol with none but men whose wives do master them. Up, finding our beds good, but lousy, which made us merry. We set out, the reckoning and servants coming to 9/6d.

The George at Salisbury was, sadly, closed in 1961, despite strong local opposition. The Bat and Ball at Hambledon, in Hampshire, still stands, and a pleasant little inn it is, at the corner of Broadhalfpenny Down. "Broadhalfpenny" usually indicates a place licensed by Royal Charter for a market or fair — the words were stamped on the letters patent — and so there would certainly have been some kind of travellers' hostel in this place for a very long time. Yet the fame of the Bat and Ball, and its name, arises from a comparatively brief period in the eighteenth century, when it was the headquarters of the Hambledon Cricket Club.

The Hambledon men were among the pioneers of cricket, and it was upon Broadhalfpennny Down that they played many of their greatest matches against Kent, Surrey, or All England. The secretary of the club, or "general", as they called him, was Richard Nyren, who was also landlord of the Bat and Ball — then, apparently, simply known as "The Hutt". It was the pavilion and clubhouse as well as the inn. Nyren's son John, the historian of Hambledon, has told us of the "high feasting" at the inn at the end of the day's play.

> How those fine brawn-faced fellows of farmers would drink to our success. And then, what stuff they had to drink! Punch!...not your modern cat-lap milk punch — punch bedeviled; but good unsophisticated John Bull stuff — stark! — that

would stand on end — punch that would make a cat speak! Sixpence a bottle! We had not sixty millions of interest to pay in those days. The ale too! not the modern horror under the same name...barleycorn, such as would put the souls of three butchers into one weaver. Ale that would flare like turpentine — genuine Boniface! This immortal viand (for it was more than liquor) was vended at 2d per pint...The quantities the fellow would eat! Two or three of them would strike dismay into a round of beef.

John's son Henry in turn left us a picture of the old days at the inn. "My grandmother, Elizabeth Nyre", he says. "was a splendid old woman, the blood in her cheeks looking pleasingly... [She] was much admired as hostess, whilst her husband and waiters carved the dinner on club days. The dinners were plentiful and old Richard at the head of it by kindness and good manners made all things go pleasantly."

The great days came to an end in 1782 when the club moved its ground to Windmill Down, and a few years later the centre of cricket was transferred to Lord's in London. The Bat and Ball came into the possession of a Hambledon brewer.

Since the city of Bristol was for some time my home, there are a couple of inns there which I should mention. The Grand Spa, Clifton, was built with the money of George Newnes, the magazine man. He was interested in cliff railways, and was given permission in 1893 to build the hydraulic railway from Hotwells Road (not far from the steamer quay) to Sion Hill. But he was only allowed to do it if he built a pump room, to revive the glories of the Clifton Spa. The Pump Room was a failure, but turned out to be the origin of the hotel. The Royal, another Bristol hotel, was the first in the country to have a steam lift, which was ceremonially opened by, for some inscrutable reason, the Chinese ambassador. Staff there have recounted details of the occasion, but no one has explained just why the Chinese ambassador was chosen.

Then there is the Rummer in All Saints Lane. There was an inn on the site called Greene Lattis in 1241, so it is one of the old ones. Its rebuilding in the eighteenth century was done by no less a person than John Wood, when he was preparing a scheme for building the Bristol Corn Exchange. Four monarchs have stayed at the Rummer, as well as Oliver Cromwell.

We have spoken elsewhere about the old harvest customs of the west, and their fitful survival. "Harvest Thanksgivings", says Violet Alford in her book on folklore, are nowadays "entirely Church Festivals, and so-called Harvest Homes, which are flower and vegetable shows, have taken the place of the Harvest Home, which was the supper."

We don't know that this is such a terrible thing. After all, in the Middle Ages nobody doubted that Harvest was a Christian Festival, though it is true that religion and everyday life were then much more mixed up together than they are now. But in any case there is one development of recent years which makes it untrue that Harvest Thanksgivings are entirely Church Festivals, in the sense that they are always conducted in a church. This is the pub harvest festival. I think it would be difficult to trace any descent from the medieval harvest home; but perhaps the result is much the same — something which is partly a religious service, and partly just a binge to celebrate finishing a job of hard work.

These pub services have become increasingly popular lately, especially in Cornwall. They are usually held late in the year, even for harvest, perhaps partly, as one disapproving friend said, "because it's only after summer time ends that the publicans can get their full profit." But can we dismiss them just as an ingenious brewers' racket? I have attended several, and conducted one or two, and this is the kind of thing that happens.

At, say, eight o'clock, the bar stops serving. This suggests that the landlord is not concerned only with profit. On the other hand, the service is not expected to take more than twenty minutes or so, and if you get near the half-hour some thirsty looks are directed towards the pumps. I have known congregations in church with similar impatience towards the end of the service, though they can only give you the traditional cough as a time signal. The service is taken by an ordained minister or by a recognized local preacher. At the end of the bar the harvest fruits have been piled high. They have been brought as offerings by the regular customers, those who stand in much the same relation to their local — although it would not occur to them — as the regular churchgoer does to his church. At the end of the service (the bars open again) the goods are auctioned. They often fetch extravagant prices, and all the proceeds go to a named charity. It is not uncommon for sums nearing £100 to be raised in this way in an hour or so. There will be a good deal of drinking in the bar, and in Cornwall anyway, a good deal of singing, probably finishing up with "Bringing in the Sheaves". But at no service of this kind that I have attended have I found the harvest hymns casually mixed up with the more familiar type of pub song, whether bawdy or just secular. Nor have I ever seen anyone drunk, except once when somebody came in late who hadn't been to the service at all. The sense of occasion persists through till closing time.

These services raise all kinds of arguments, with which we will not become involved. But they do at least offer what the church is always saying that it wants — a meeting-point with a society which largely avoids it, apart from christenings, weddings and funerals. And they also contain an echo, if a faint one, of what the English harvest thanksgiving once was. This is a legitimate function of an English inn.

LITERATURE

Shakespeare Comes West

Normally, we in the south and west of England believe, and justly, that the lot has fallen unto us in a fair ground. We would rather live here than anywhere. But we are not alone in envying our friends in the midlands, for all what we sometimes feel to be cramped accents and smelly cities! They possess Shakespeare, and we do not.

We say "possess", but of course nobody really possesses Shakespeare, "He was not of an age, but for all time", wrote Ben Jonson in his commendatory verse to the first folio. Nor was he of a place, any place, Stratford-on-Avon or anywhere else.

Nevertheless, the Midlands do well to rejoice in him, and it is legitimate that we, too, should relish the associations of the greatest poet who has ever lived with our own part of the country.

We are not going to prove that Shakespeare was a Devonian, say, though he has been proved, supposedly, to be nearly everything else. But that he visited and knew the West, there can be no doubt.

There is a tradition that the young Shakespeare lived for a while, perhaps as a tutor, in Gloucestershire. He mentions Berkeley Castle in two of the plays, and it does sound as if he had some personal knowledge of the South Cotswolds, and what he calls

Those high, wild hills, and rough, uneven ways

Or take this —

There stands the castle by yond tuft of trees.

That sounds uncommonly like a memory of something really seen.

In the second part of *Henry IV*, Falstaff is in the Cotswolds, and Shakespeare has obviously brought him there specially, since it is a long way out of his direct route to his destination in Yorkshire. Perhaps it was a youthful memory of the original of Shallow that made him choose this setting. Shallow tells his servant Davy to sow red wheat, which was a Gloucestershire peculiarity. Shakespeare also mentions a couple of Cotswold worthies: William Visor of Woncot and Clement Perkes o' the hill. There were real families of Vizard at Woodman-cote — which is still usually pronounced Woncot — and Parkes at Stinch-combe Hill. Lord Berkeley owned a troop of players, who at least twice in Shakespeare's boyhood visited Stratford. Perhaps it was there that Shakespeare met them, and decided to cast in his lot with them. But a player's income, especially that of a young one, fluctuated — that puts it mildly, it often disappeared altogether — and so Shakespeare may have been glad to eke out the winter months as tutor to Lord Berkeley's family. This, at least, is the theory put forward by Ivor Brown, who is one of the shrewdest of Shakespearean critics, and one of the most readable.

"Barkloughly castle call they this at hand?" asks Richard II. Since there is no doubt that Berkeley Castle was meant, we are left wondering whether "Barkloughly" is in old pronunciation, or an old spelling. Caroline Spurgeon, in her book *Shakespeare's Imagery*, suggests that the "Temple-haunting martlets" were the martins of Berkeley Castle.

There is another theory about Shakespeare's Gloucestershire association. Hesketh Pearson, noting the ease and familiarity with which he handles legal terminology, thinks that he may have trained as an attorney, probably at Dursley, which was the nearest country town to Berkeley Castle.

And there is yet another of how he spent what are sometimes called "the lost years", that is to say 1577 to 1582, and 1586 to 1592: a theory which also involves the West Country. William Bliss, in *The Real Shakespeare*, puts forward the suggestion that as a boy Shakespeare ran away, and ran away to sea. Where else, he asks, should an English boy run away to? He goes to the nearest port, Milford Haven, and takes a coastal ship to Plymouth, where he finds that Drake is crewing up for a voyage to the Indies — a voyage that was ultimately to take him round the world. What more natural than that the adventurous boy should join Drake, leave from Plymouth with him on December 13th, 1577, and return with him, after that triumphant circumnavigation, in September, 1580?

There is no direct evidence for this thesis, but William Bliss is surely right in saying that Shakespeare often writes as though he had a first-hand knowledge of the sea; much more so than he has a knowledge of the law, with respect to Hesketh Pearson. How else did he learn what the shipboy suffers "upon the high and giddy mast"? — with the winds

Who take the ruffian billows by the top,
Curling their monstrous heads, and harrying them
With deafening clamour in the slippery shrouds.

Shakespeare had a genius, we know, for entering into and savouring other men's experience: but they sound like lines written by a man who had really been to sea.

There is another interesting point to the same effect: from *Pericles*:

115

First sailor: Slack the bolins there! Thou wilt not, wilt thou? Blow, and split thyself.
Second sailor: But *sea-room*, and the brine and cloudy billow kiss the moon, I care not.

And in *The Tempest*, the bo'sun also asks for room, sea-room. Bliss's comment is a valid one. "These", he says, "were no freshwater sailors or longshoremen. They were proper deepsea sailors who hated a lee-shore worse than the devil. They were long-voyage men. Landsmen and coast-huggers feel that to keep in sight of land is comforting. Where would Shakespeare have learned the true gospel that bids the sailor cry out for room enough unless he had been for a long voyage himself?"

This is fair enough: and there are other references in the play which suggest Shakespeare had made a long trip to sea. In *As You Like It*, Jacques refers to the fool in the forest "as dry as the remainder biscuit at the end of a ship's voyage", which, as Ivor Brown comments, is certainly an odd piece of knowledge for Jacques to have come by in the Forest of Arden. "Blow winds, and crack your cheeks" as poor King Lear says, has the ring of a seaman rather than a landsman.

Bliss also suggests that several years after 1580 Shakespeare went on another voyage, in the *Tiger* — which was a favourite ship's name for him — to the Mediterranean, and was wrecked on the sea coast of Illyria. The evidence for this is flimsy, to say the least, but Shakespeare was certainly preoccupied with shipwrecks. There are at least five in the plays (test for Shakespeareans: can you name the five?). Listen to the Clown in *The Winter's Tale*: "I would you did see how it chafes, how it rages, how it takes up the shore! O, the most piteous cry of the poor souls! Sometimes to see 'em and not to see 'em; now the ship boring the moon with her mainmast" — what a phrase! he must have seen that — "and anon swallowed with yest and froth, as you'd thrust a cork in a hogshead. But to make an end of the ship — to see how the sea flap-dragoned it — but first how the poor souls roared, and the sea mocked them..."

That Shakespeare went to sea seems a reasonable guess. But whether he sailed with Drake, or to the coast of Illyria, must be conjectural. After all, you could have scarifying experiences enough in those days in a simple cross-channel trip with a company of players.

There were many occasions when Shakespeare toured the west with his various companies, especially in the years, not infrequent, when plague closed the London theatres. Marlborough was a favourite place for the players; so was Bath. They came to Bristol sometimes and in September, 1597, the Chamberlain's men — Shakespeare's company at that time — received thirty shillings for a performance in Bristol Guildhall. On at least one occasion they came as far west as Barnstaple. Of course there were no theatres, in the true sense, in the provincial towns. Inn yards were the most frequently used substitute: and what a noble setting such a place as, for instance, the New Inn, Gloucester, must have made. In 1603, *As you Like It* was performed at Wilton, the Herbert home near Salisbury, with Shakespeare among those present. William Herbert, Earl of Pembroke, is one of the candidates for being that "Mr. W.H." to whom the sonnets were dedicated — but we will not start arguing about that one! Nor about the authorship of the plays, which has been attributed by some people to Sir Walter Ralegh, a less wildly improbable conjecture than most.

One convincing suggestion is, however, that a good deal of Ralegh went into the character of Pompey in *Antony and Cleopatra*. Ralegh won a notable success on an expedition to the Azores while Essex, his nominal chief, was absent. Ralegh was highly praised, and Essex was not pleased. Thus, says Pompey, it is

Better to leave undone than, by one deed,
Acquire too high a fame when him we serve's away.

On this reading, Essex is Anthony, and Sir Robert Cecil is Octavius. These parallells must not be pushed too far, but this one may well have been in Shakespeare's mind.

There is one more possible association of the West with the plays on which we may touch. It is generally agreed — and almost nothing about Shakespeare is ever more than "generally agreed" — that much of the material for *The Tempest* came from the accounts of a shipwreck in the Bermudas in 1609, when a party of Virginian colonists were blown off course and stranded, though happily they survived. Shakespeare had many personal contacts with leading members of the Virginia Company, which was the principal body concerned with settlement in the New World. It is quite probably that his acquaintances included the Grenville family, which had been involved with colonial development from the beginning. The Grenvilles intermarried with Bevilles, and took over the Beville house at Killigarth, near Polperro.

Sir William Beville of Killigarth had a servant. Carew, in his *Survey of Cornwall*, describes him as "an uncouth servant, whose monstrous conditions partly resembled that Polyphemus described by Homer." *Sir* William had found his servant under a hedge. He was lean and freckled, and at his master's bidding, would eat great quantities of nettles, thistles, raw and living birds and fishes, burning coals and candles: "yet could no man at any time discover of him doing that which nature of necessity requireth." He would take a hot coal from the fire with his bare hand, never changed his clothes if he could help it, lay head-down in straw, spoke little and then strangely, using the word "size"

117

in all sorts of connections — "I'll size him", for "I'll strike him", or "a good size" for "a good man" — so that he became known as John Size.

Now does this description of Carew's remind you of any character in *The Tempest*... one who was "a freckled whelp, hag-born"? one who "did gabble like a thing most brutish"? One who was another man's slave, as John Size was to William Beville? One with "a very ancient and fishlike smell"? Can it be that Caliban was a Cornishman?

Shaksperian criticism is a wine that flies swiftly to the head; but there is no obvious original of Caliban in the Bermuda Pamphlets or, so far as our reading goes, anywhere else. One may choose to think that John Size went up to London with his master, and was shown off, in that callous Elizabethan way, with Shakespeare among the audience. Or perhaps an anecdote or two, thrown into the conversation, helped to fill our Caliban's picture. Or perhaps — and this is fancy, as much Shakespearean criticism probably is, and these our actors

> Are melted into thin air
> And, like some insubstantial pageant faded
> Leave not a rack behind.

Tom Shoel of Montacute

A few miles out of Yeovil, going westward, stands the pleasant little village of Montacute. It is famous for one of the finest Elizabethan manors in England. The village itself is an unpretentious affair, consisting of a large open square, flanked by houses of Golden Ham Hill stone, known as "The Borough". Westward, overlooking the village, is a circular fir-clad knoll, St. Michael's Hill.

> Sweet Michael's loveliest of the hills around,
> With beauty clad, with constant verdure crowned.
> Beneath they shade with name from thee derived,
> Sweet Montacute, through numerous years has thrived;
>
> Baid out with beauty, open, spacious air;
> Blest with a fruitful soil and healthy air;
> Water'd abundant with the purest rills;
> And screen'd from tempest by the surrounding hills.

Those lines were written by a local man, Thomas Shoel. He was probably sitting on top of St. Michael's Hill when he wrote them, for that was his favourite place for composing verses — and not only verses, but music.

Now in the eighteenth century, when Thomas Shoel lived, there was nothing very surprising in people writing music and poetry. They were very fashionable things to do. The interesting thing about Thomas Shoel was that he was a peasant, and one whose life contained a great deal of trouble and hardship (compare Hannah More's milk woman, at about the same time). He was born in 1759 and his parents died when he was still a boy. He tried to become a weaver, but his health broke down and he had to do as best he could as a farm labourer, a member of the poorest section of the community. The wage of a Somerset labourer in 1780 was usually seven or eight shillings a week, perhaps supplemented by an allowance of sour cider. Shoel lived with his family in a small tumbledown cottage just off the Borough. He eked out his wage by doing odd jobs as village carrier, and also by selling his tunes and verses. But in spite of this, his lot remained a hard one.

> Poverty — Thou pale companion of my state forlorn,
> My constant inmate every night and morn,
> Come, prompt my numbers, and inspire my verse
> While I attempt thy sorrows to rehearse.
> Begin with him who with such constant toil
> Ploughs up the field and cultivates the soil;
> Behold while morn's sweet herald mounts the sky,
> How o'er the lea the peasant drives his team,
> To toil and sweat beneath the sultry beam.
> Then homeward see him labour on his way,
> And close the toil of long and tedious day.

Those last two lines will strike a familiar chord if you remember Gray's *Elegy*. Indeed, as a writer Thomas Shoel has sometimes been criticized for barely disguised plagiarism. This is probably unfair. He had a retentive memory, read as widely as he could, and may often have been unconscious of striking echoes from the work of other people. In any case in the eighteenth century this was not an uncommon practice. The hymns of Charles Wesley, for instance, are full of reminiscences of others, and sometimes even whole lines ("Lost in wonder, love and praise" follows Addison). But to go on with Shoel's description of a peasant's life:

> His poor coarse meal then soon behold him take,
> Potatoes salted or a barley cake;

Cold water serves his painful thirst to slake,
Or Indian leaves a half-stain'd bev'rage make;
His lisping prattlers hang on either knee,
Well pleas'd again their father's face to see.
His dear Lov'd partner eyes him with delight,
So well belov'd so pleasing in his sight —
And both perhaps let fall the trickling tear,
While they behold in rags their children dear;
Thus through succeeding weeks is past the day
Which poor eight shillings haply does repay.

These extracts from his writing show you that while Shoel was far from being a literary genius, the standard of his writing was not contemptible. "Peasant poets", working-class poets, have usually been something of a joke. Take Edward Capern, the postman-poet of Tavistock, who was misguidedly hailed as the Devonshire Burns. Here are his lines to the white violet:

Pale Beauty went out 'neath a wintry sky
From a nook where the gorse and the holly grew by,
And silently traversed the snow-covered earth
In search of a sign of floriferous birth.

No: although Thomas Shoel had his share of bad lines and banal thoughts, he had a sound poetic technique, and made good use of his close observation of the country scene. Perhaps the very simplicity and straightforwardness of their chosen theme has caused country poets sometimes to slip into the commonplace or the crude. Here is an example of Shoel's nature poetry at its best, lines which Llewelyn Powys has said should ensure for him a modest, but honourable, place in English literature. "On hearing a small bird sing in the winter":

Pretty little sprightly thing,
That so charmingly canst sing:
Tho' the rough wind keenly blow,
Bringing rain, or hail, or snow.

Lovely songster, sing again,
Whistle loud thy thrilling strain;
Winter soon will pass away,
With his short and gloomy day.

Earnest of the genial year,
Soon the snowdrops shall appear;
Soon the primrose too shall show
To the eye its lovely hue.

Then the furrows shall display
Beauty clad in green array;
Pointing to the eye of hope
Autumn's rich abundant crop.

While along the orchard-rows
Wide the varied blossom blows;
Humming bees and insects round,
Buzzing with delightful sound.

Then the feather'd minstrelsy
Loud shall pour their melody:
While the forest, dell and grove,
Echo to the song of love.

Shoel published several short books of verse, although the editions were so small that he made very little money out of them. He did, however, have his patrons. The poet George Crabbe would often give him a guinea. And sometimes he would set out from Montacute and walk all the way to Bremhill in Wiltshire, getting on for fifty miles, where William Bowles was Vicar. Bowles, himself a poet, a somewhat eccentric character who was known for the special gaiters he wore to protect himself against the bites of mad dogs, was always ready to give Shoel something in return for a copy of his latest poem or tune. On one occasion he started a subscription and raised nearly fifty pounds. In the approved manner of eighteenth century poets, Shoel ought to immortalize his benefactor in verse, but as almost invariably happened with this kind of tribute, the results were undistinguished:

And did my weary feet to Bremhill come,
To find my friend, my patron, not at home?
Have I such long such toilsome tracks walked o'er
My disappointment only to deplore?
How sweet on Bremhill's lovely hill to stand,
And such a beauteous prospect to command,
But ah! how poor my colours, ah! how faint
How poor the pencil such a scene to paint.

Scenes such as these a Bowles's skill require,
A poet's numbers and a poet's lyre.

As a matter of fact, Shoel's verses were much better than the efforts of his patron.

Despite these sundry assistances, Shoel was never free from poverty. Quite apart from the low standard of living suffered by all agricultural labourers, his health often prevented him from earning even a normal wage. During his lifetime he probably earned more money, and indeed more fame, from his music than from his verse. He published three books of sacred music, as well as a great many psalm tunes, hymn tunes, and anthems. The remarkable thing about him as a composer is that he had never had any musical education, and had to teach himself the rules of harmony. And yet, his music is structurally sound. Many of his tunes became exceedingly popular in the West Country, and are still remembered. Mr. Frederick Rogers, a churchwarden of Montacute (who lived to be more than 100) made a collection of them, and in 1966, for the West of England Home Service, collaborated with the Julian Consort of Bath in a broadcast selection. The broadcast, which was produced by the present Bishop of Winchester, and in which June Barrie and Douglas Leach were readers, produced a response which showed that he was far from forgotten.

Tom Shoel has some lines on music in church, recalling those days when the village orchestra led the proceedings from the gallery.

Hark to the viol's deeply solemn note,
With varied descant's modulating sound
That from the gallery doth so sweetly float,
And through the fretted arches loud rebounds.

How doth the soft soprano intervene,
Whose liquid trillings charm the ravished ear,
Till loud the chorus bursts around the scene,
And hallelujah's solemn close we hear.

Shoel began composing his hymn tunes at just about the right time. Up to 1740 or thereabouts, almost all hymns had been composed in two or three standard metres. Then there came Charles Wesley, with his vast output of hymns in every imaginable metre. At once there arose a need for new tunes. Yet they still had to be simple tunes which the congregation could pick up easily. To solve the problem of writing a simple tune to a metre which might be very far from simple, Shoel used the device of repetition, rounding out the lines. He was something of a pioneer in this, and it is easy to see why his tunes became popular with congregations who liked "a good sing".

His facility in composition was remarkable. Once at Montacute feast day the band arrived without their music. Shoel was asked to write a tune for them to play, as they headed the procession round the neighbouring farms for the cider tasting. He sat down on a barrel of beer in the yard of the Phelips Arms, and wrote out his tune, with a separate score for each of the instruments. Its title was "Rejoice, O daughters of Jerusalem", and it was played on every feast day for many years afterwards. He was paid sixpence for it.

And there is a story how Samuel Geard, a member of the Montacute choir, was in bed sick one Christmas when the carol singers began to strike up in the Borough. He left his bed, opened the window and insisted on joining in. When his friends urged him not to take foolish risks, he replied "I can't bide in bed when you be out singing wold Tom Shayell!"

Shoel's first wife died young, and so did the children she bore him save for one boy who was later drowned at sea. In 1797, when he was 38, Shoel married again, and had three daughters. One died young, one took her own life, and only the youngest, Julia, avoided the disasters which seemed to pile on the family. She was still alive in 1886, when the father of Llewelyn Powys became Vicar of Montacute. Shoel himself had died in 1823.

However one looks at it and whatever may be one's critical judgment upon his work, it was a notable thing that a man from such a background, and with so many difficulties and hardships in his own life, should make such a contribution to the literature and music of his time. His verse is little read, less so indeed than it might well be. The style of his music is no longer fashionable. But he does not deserve to be forgotten. So much sadness made him often solemn, yet probably he is best in his more cheerful moods: as, for instance, in these lines heralding the return of spring.

Welcome spring's returning day,
Welcome sun, thy clearing ray,
Welcome to the fruitful showers,
Welcome blossoms, birds, and flowers.

Welcome April's springing scene,
Welcome May's delightful green;
Welcome cowslip's yellow hue,
Welcome to the violets' blue.

Welcome to the shepherd's lay,
Welcome to the lambkins' play;

Welcome richly cultur'd soil,
Welcome future plenty's smile.

Welcome to the orchard's bloom,
Welcome bees, your charming hum,
Welcome insects, buzzing round,
Welcome, purling rills, your sound.

Welcome, hours of soft repose,
Welcome, sleep, respite from woes,
Welcome rest to bless the night
Welcome to the morning's light.

The Decline of the Church Bands

Writing of Thomas Shoel prompts us to add a note about the church orchestras, whose decline was almost complete while his daughter Julia was still living in Montacute. The orchestra — or "band" as it was commonly known in the village — was usually placed in the west gallery, and for the anthem and the psalms (Tate and Brady's metrical version, usually) the congregation would rise, turn round and face them, though they did not often join in the singing, and sometimes were frowned upon if they did. The clerk would read out the psalms verse by verse, and the words of the anthem as well, even with all the repetitions. One such occasion provoked an historic retort from the band leader at Hawkridge. "Who", asked the clerk, "who is the King of Glory? Who? Who? Who is the King? Who is the King of Glory?" "Pass up the rosin, Jim", came the voice from the gallery, "and us'll show 'n 'oo's the King o' Glory!"

A hundred years ago and more the father and mother of a row was going on in the village of Stokenham, in Devon. The father and mother concerned were Mr. & Mrs. John Randall, and they and their family were responsible for the music in Stokenham church. The band was entirely composed of Randalls: Father John played the bass viol, which in Devon was usually in fact a 'cello, son Peter the violin, son Richard the flute, and son William Henry the cornet. The rest of the family sang in the choir. But progress, and the harmonium, had arrived, and gloom descended upon the smithy (John Randall was the village blacksmith). Feelings on this subject were bitter and deep in many West Country villages. There were riots in London at this time about High Church practices: but in the west, where the Oxford Movement had still had little effect, organs versus orchestras was the ecclesiastical issue of the day.

Bands were often family affairs — the Rowe family at Denbury, the Carters at Harpford, who numbered, it was said, …sixteen, and all musicers." The more unconventional instruments had mostly disappeared by this time, though Ashburton had its serpent for many years and Thurlestone its hautboys. At Thurlestone the fat farmer who played the bass viol was always carefully sited at the strongest point of the rather rickety gallery. Sometimes the band and choir were shrouded by curtains until the great moment when they were called into action: bright red curtains at Heanton Punchardon, where the clerk would mark time by stamping with his wooden leg. Girls and women in the choir were a comparative innovation: trebles, tenors, basses and counter-tenors were the traditional arrangement. Newton Poppleford had a famous counter-tenor, a shoemaker called Bastin who, it was said, "could go higher than any girl." Star performers would visit other churches: Sam Peardon of Stratton was a bass who specialized in bottom C, Braunton had a clarinettist who was very popular. I suppose the nearest thing we have to it all today is bellringing.

Of course, though people were sad, the bands went. Hardy describes the fall of the Mellstock band in *Under the Greenwood Tree*. At Stratton they tried adding the harmonium to the orchestra, but the attempt failed, perhaps because it was a home-made harmonium. The Randalls of Stokenham indeed lasted longer than many, and the first edition of *Hymns Ancient and Modern* delivered the death-blow to most survivors. But not quite all: at Countisbury the wardens were charged for repairs to the bass viol as late as 1886.

Stephen Duck

This is the sad story of Stephen Duck, who was born at Charlton St. Peter in Wiltshire, in 1705. He was a poor boy, who married in his 'teens and supported his wife and child on a labourer's wage of 4/6d. a week.

He became a poet, painstakingly educating himself for the task, reading through *Paradise Lost* with the aid of a dictionary, counting out the metres on his fingers. His verses had remarkable success in society, from the royal court downwards. Queen Caroline gave him a pension and made him a Yeoman of the Guard in 1733. *Poems on Several Occasions*, which included his best-known poem, "The Thresher's Labour" was published in 1736. It was rather like Dr.

Johnson and the women preachers — it was sufficiently remarkable that an agricultural labourer should write verse at all, let alone whether he wrote it well. As a matter of fact he did not write very well, though some of his early works, with their pictures of rural life, are pleasing enough. He adopted the poetic conventions of his time, the heroic couplets, the classical allusions, and this had a constricting effect upon any natural flow of expression. The Wiltshire countryside did not fit easily into the world of Pope and Gray — Gray, incidentally, is said to have had Stephen Duck in mind when he wrote of "mute inglorious Miltons." Maurice Hussey has an apt phrase when he writes of Duck's "slender lyric qualities."

Such as they were, they soon faded away when he became a society pet. He was loaded with honours, and given several of those sinecures which were features of eighteenth-century society. Someone had the splendidly witty idea of making him Keeper of Duck Island, in St. James Park, a post which carried a good salary and no significant duties. He was even suggested as a poet laureate — not that, as our laureates went in the eighteenth century, he would have lowered the average much. His verses continued to sell, but as with Swinburne when Watts-Dunton took over his establishment and made him change his socks regularly, the poetry declined. In 1746 he took Holy Orders and in 1752 became Rector of Byfleet. In 1756, at Reading, he threw himself in a stream and drowned.

Stephen Duck did, however, leave two memorials behind him, not counting his poetry, which the little we have read does not tempt us to explore further. The first is the "Duck-Feast", still held each year at his birthplace, Charlton St. Peter, when meat is eaten — not, of course, duck — and ale is downed in gollops in his memory. The other thing is what is surely the dream of every litterateur — he set a trend; he founded a school. He made the rural poet fashionable. They came in droves in the next century, cobbler-poets, bricklayer-poets. The roll of their names included that of Burns, who is believed by many people to have written poetry. Most of the others have been forgotten. "Poetry", wrote a correspondent of Horace Walpole's, "is as universally contagious as smallpox." Perhaps some of the inglorious Miltons would have done better to remain mute. But it was at least a nobler aspiration than filling in pools coupons. So two cheers for poor Stephen Duck.

The Marvellous Boy

We have earlier mentioned Thomas Chatterton and his influence on the Romantic revival. But although this recognition came to him soon after his death, he was still some way from being "the marvellous boy", and his death was noticed a great deal less than was his bicentenary in 1970. In his lifetime, even in Bristol, his home town, he was no more than a provincial lad who went to London to try to make a living by writing, failed, and killed himself with a dose of arsenic in the traditional attic, before he was eighteen.

This neglect was partly his own fault. He had produced, you may remember, a series of poems supposed to have been written by a fifteenth century monk called Rowley, which took in some critics and had obvious merits even when the forgeries had been proved. The Chatterton family had been for two hundred years sextons of the church of St. Mary Redcliffe, which Elizabeth I had declared to be the fairest parish church in England. The muniment room of the church, full of old and uncatalogued documents, became the boy's haunt. He claimed that the poems by Rowley, and others, had been found there. It is understandable that he should try to sell his work in this ingenious way. But it must be added that he had a taste for forgery. At the age of 12 he had offered what he claimed to be a fifteenth-century poem to a master at Colston's School, Bristol, which he attended. He even drew up a bogus pedigree for a worthy Bristol pewterer called Burgum, proving his descent from a knight, De Bergham, who came over with the Conqueror. Mr. Burgum was delighted and gave him five shillings. Not very generous, perhaps: Chatterton was not lucky in finding generous patrons.

He was liable to severe depression, though it is said that after he had composed, at the age of ten, his ode to the last judgment, he became slightly more cheerful. His epitaph for himself, which is on his memorial near St. Mary Redcliffe, says "Reader! Judge not. If thou are a Christian, believe that he shall be judged by a Superior Power. To that Power only is he answerable." It sounds like a parody on epitaphs, and it probably was. Remembering Keats's dedication, an apter epitaph might be, "Peace, ho! The moon sleeps with Endymion, and would not be awak'd."

His influence, and what might be called his myth, have been traced in a book by Linda Kelly. There are sections on Herbert Croft, who wrote a best-selling novel about Chatterton; William Henry Ireland, who was inspired by Chatterton to forge Shakespeare, and even had a bogus Shakespearean play put on at Drury Lane — once; the Romantics, Southey and Coleridge and Keats; Alfred de Vigny and his play "Chatterton", and the vogue for suicide it established, among young poets, so that the roofs of Paris rang with the pistol shots. We are told how Leoncavallo turned him into an opera, the true history of Chatterton becoming more and more vestigial; how Francis Thompson saw him in a vision: and Meyerstein, his twentieth century biographer, restored him to reality, while himself becoming captivated by that elusive Chattertonian magic.

The remaining question about Chatterton is the manner of his death. Linda Kelly accepts the usual view that it was suicide, although she quotes some lines from the poet Mason, written shortly after the event —

> The Youth is dead, *felo da se* or not,
> By pox or poison matters not a jot

— which shows that even then alternative explanations were considered. Richard Holmes, in *The Cornhill Magazine*, has more recently argued powerfully against the suicide theory. "There was no despair in the attic", he concludes; and certainly it would be pleasing to think so.

The Young Coleridge

At the end of the eighteenth century, Bristol was still the second city in England, as it had been for centuries. The new towns of the industrial revolution, in the midlands and the north, were swiftly overtaking it in wealth and population, but Bristol still had plenty of which to be proud. All the best prizefighters came from Bristol. To be called a "yellowman" — for yellow was the Bristol colour — was the highest compliment of the prize ring. If a ship was Bristol-built it automatically remained in Lloyd's first-class register for ten years, a rating as high as Liverpool's, behind only London among the ports of Great Britain. The slave trade, in which Bristol had a large stake, was not yet abolished, though Wilberforce had been making angry speeches. "All I ask of the people of Bristol", he said, "is that they would become as civilised now as Irishmen were four hundred years ago." So Bristol was prosperous, with a fine sporting reputation. It was also acquiring some cultural aspirations. The poet Chatterton had not liked Bristol much, and Bristol had not much liked him. But a quarter of a century after his birth, there was talk of his strange genius, literary people were discussing him, and Bristol was beginning to be proud of him. In 1794, Lancelot Sharpe published an edition of Chatterton's Rowley Poems, which included a "Monody on the Death of Chatteron", by Samuel

Taylor Coleridge. It was the year Coleridge first came to Bristol.

Coleridge was more a poet of the West Country than he was a poet of the Lakes, and the first and most enduring Bristol influence on his life was Chatterton. Indeed, it could be argued that Chatterton was, if not the founder, the first fine fling of the romantic revival in literature. Keats was to dedicate *Endymion* to his memory.

Without attempting to demonstrate any such high-flying thesis, perhaps we might remind you a little of Chatterton's life, because it was so extraordinary, so novelettish, it sometimes seems unreal. He was a provincial poet who went to London to make his fortune, failed, and committed suicide in an attic, with a dose of arsenic, before he was eighteen years old. He had produced this series of poems supposed to be written by a fifteenth century monk called Rowley. Many critics had accepted them at their face value, and they were certainly remarkable. Now they were recognised as the boy's own work. Chatterton had become the type of the provincial romantic, who had died because he went to London. It is understandable that critics, and readers, should sometimes make asses of themselves. It is all part of the fun. The poems, however, *even when you know* they are forgeries, do not lose their appeal.

> Here upon my true-love's grave
> Shall the barren flowers be laid;
> Not one holy saint to save
> All the coldness of a maid:
> > My love is dead,
> > Gone to his death-bed
> All under the willow tree

Its simplicity is its strength, but in order to maintain his fiction that Rowley wrote it, Chatterton had to trick it out as best he could in fifteenth-century words. Thus the line "Dance no more at holiday", is written "Daunce ne moe atte hollie daie", and so on. D.B. Wyndham Lewis said that Chatterton's language reminded him of those signs which say "YE OLDE ELIZABE-THANNE TEA SHOPPE". But never mind about that. Chatteron was recognised, too late for it to be of any use to him, as a romantic poet, although provincial. The thought may have occurred to other writers, that Chatterton had died because he went to London. Dr. Johnson, in his thunderous classical way, had declared that the man who was tired of London was tired of life. But Johnson was dead, Old Dad dead, and a new *Revenger's Tragedy* was at hand. Of the next generation of poets, none drew their inspiration from London, except perhaps Keats. Byron and Shelley were natural foreigners. Wordsworth was from Cockermouth, Southey was the son of a Bristol draper, Coleridge came from Ottery St. Mary. Trying as we may not to be tempted into definitions of the classical and romantic, we may just observe that it is possible to look at the romantic revival in literature as a reassertion of the provinces against the bossy capital. (We will add just one more comment, which cricketers will understand: classicals play forward, romantics play back).

Ottery St. Mary is a town in Devon. In 1760 John Coleridge became Vicar there, and Head Master of the King's School, a fourteenth century foundation which still thrives. Among his pupils were Hurrell Froude, the Tractarian, and his own youngest son, Samuel Taylor. John Coleridge had many of the qualities which were associated with his son. We take this account of him from G.E.J.Holmes's history of the King's School, Ottery.

Although he had left home at 15, become as usher, and married young, he saved enough money to go to Sidney Sussex College, Cambridge, in his 'thirties. By the time he came to Ottery with his second wife , he was regarded as a man of considerable learning — "an exceedingly studious man, pious, of primitive manners and of the most simple habits; passing events were little heeded by him, and therefore he was usually characterized as the 'absent man'. One of his grandsons who became Vicar of Buckerell wrote that he was "as simple as a child, and as learned as Solomon." He sometimes astonished his congregation in Church with long quotations from the Bible in Hebrew which they "believed to be the very words of the Holy Ghost." He was the author of two Latin grammars in which he proposed to simplify the study of the language for beginners by re-christening the ablative case the quale-quare-quidditive case! In one of them was an advertisement which said "The author teaches the Latin and Greek languages, with any branch of Mathematicks if desired. He Boards and Teaches at Sixteen guineas per year. A Writing Master attends for those who chuse it, at Sixteeen shillings per Year, and a Dancing Master once a week, at Two Guineas Per Year." This shows an interesting extension of the curriculum. If parents of prospective pupils wished to obtain the full details of the books and methods he used, they then had to buy another of his works, *Dissertation on the Seventeenth and Eighteenth Chapters of Judges*

Coleridge was clearly much influenced by his father and his neighbour-hood. He was to write an affectionate sonnet to the river Otter. Once he had run away from home, after some childish misdemeanour, fallen asleep on the banks of the Otter, and had been found early in the morning damp and miserable. He was not punished.

I remember, and never shall forget, my Father's face as he looked upon me while I lay in the servant's arms — so calm, and the tears stealing down his face; for I was the child of his old age.

130

LITERATURE

The wedding-guest in *The Ancient Mariner*, you remember, "listens like a three year child", and Samuel Taylor, while no doubt full of words himself even when three years old, must have spent some time listening to his father. Indeed, some more lines from that poem surely contain an echo of early Sundays when they trooped along to Bishop Grandisson's huge parish church at Ottery.

> O sweeter than the marriage-feast,
> 'Tis sweeter far for me,
> To walk together to the kirk
> With a goodly company.
> To walk together to the kirk,
> And all together pray
> While each to his great Father bends,
> Old men, and babes, and loving friends
> And youths and maidens gay!

Coleridge's religion, which he often took very seriously, always naturally turned to the goodness of a loving Father. This meant more to him than the specifically Christian theory of redemption. He once sought to be a minister, but a Unitarian minister. He preached "with a view", in the old Dissenting phrase, at Shrewsbury, and among his congregation was a young man, twenty years old, William Hazlitt; who always remembered it.

> When I got there, the organ was playing the 100th Psalm, and, when it was done, Mr. Coleridge rose and gave out his text, "And he went up into the mountains to pray, *Himself, alone.*" As he gave out this text, his voice "rose like a steam of rich distilled perfumes", and when he came to the last two words, which he pronounced loud, deep and distinct, it seemed to me, who was then young, as if the sounds had echoed from the bottom of the human heart, and as if that prayer might have floated in solemn silence through the universe.
>
> The preacher then launched into his subject like an eagle dallying with the wind...

Coleridge's father died when his youngest son was nine, and through a well-meaning friend, the child was sent to school at Christ's Hospital, where he was very unhappy. No doubt this experience did not make him think any the better of London. Among his fellow-pupils was Charles Lamb, who suffered less because his home was close at hand, but later set down these words on behalf of a "poor friendless boy", thinking of Coleridge.

> My parents and those who should care for me were far away. Those few acquaintances of theirs which they could reckon upon as being kind to me in the great city, after a little forced notice, which they had the grace to take of me on my

131

first arrival in town, soon grew tired of my holiday visits. They seemed to them to recur too often, though I thought them few enough; and, one after another, they all failed me, and I felt myself alone among six hundred playmates. How, in my dreams, would my native town (far in the west) come back, with its church, and trees, and faces! How I would wake weeping, and in the anguish of my heart exclaim upon sweet Calne, in Wiltshire!

Not that Coleridge had come from Calne, though he lived there later, before Lamb wrote that essay. Coleridge confirms Lamb's account in some lines from his poem, "Frost at Midnight".

> How oft, at school, with most believing mind,
> Presageful, have I gazed upon the bars,
> To watch that fluttering *stranger*! and as oft
> With unclosed lids, already I had dreamt
> Of my sweet birth-place, and the old church-tower,
> Whose bells, the poor man's only music, rang
> From morn to evening, all the hot Fair-day,
> So sweetly, that they stirred and haunted me
> With a wild pleasure, falling on mine ear
> Most like articulate sounds of things to come!
> So gazed I, till the soothing things, I dreamt,
> Lulled me to sleep, and sleep prolonged my dreams!
> And so I brooded all the following morn,
> Awed by the stern preceptor's face, mine eye
> Fixed with mock study on my swimming book:
> Save if the door half opened, and I snatched
> A hasty glance, and still my heart leaped up,
> For still I hoped to see the *stranger's* face,
> Townsman, or aunt, or sister more beloved,
> My playmate when we both were clothed alike!

Any boy who had been miserable and forlorn at a big boarding school will recognize how telling are those lines.

From Christ's Hospital Coleridge progressed to Cambridge, where he was happier but unsettled. He left dramatically, enlisting as a trooper in the dragoons, under the improbable name of Silas Tomkyn Comberbacke — that was how it was entered. No doubt he called himself Cumberbatch, a name with a suitable bucolic ring, and indeed there are today plenty of Cumberbatches in the west. But he did nothing much in the dragoons except fall off his horse; and after a few weeks his family secured his discharge, and he went back to Cambridge. Upon his return to Cambridge he was reprimanded, but no more. Already his natural charm, ability, above all his eloquence caused him to be highly regarded, though he suffered, as he was to suffer all his life, from what he called "aberrations from prudence". A girl called Mary Evans seems to have been the principal cause of this particular aberration.

He paid a visit to Oxford, where he met Robert Southey. Very quickly they decided what they were going to do with their lives. They evolved the scheme which came to be known at Pantisocracy, not exactly an original idea even then: an ideal society was to be formed by a group of friends on the banks of the Susquehannah. It was thus described by Thomas Poole, who lived at Nether Stowey, in Somerset, where Coleridge later lived. The two pioneers hoped to enlist Poole.

> Twelve gentlemen of good education and liberal principles are to embark with twelve ladies in April next, fixing themselves in some delightful part of the new back settlements of America. The labour of each man, for two or three hours a day, will suffice to support the colony. The produce is to be common property, there is to be a good library, and the ample leisure is to be devoted to study, discussion and the education of the children on a settled system. The women are to be employed in taking care of the infant children and in other suitable occupations, not neglecting the cultivation of their minds. Among matters not yet determined is whether the marriage contract shall be dissolved, if agreeable to one or both parties. Everyone is to enjoy his own religious and political opinions, provided they do not encroach on the rules previously made. Every gentleman providing £125 will be sufficient to carry the scheme into execution.

Whatever Tom Poole may have thought — and he was to be a lifelong and faithful friend of Coleridge and Southey — his cousin Charlotte wrote in her diary:

> Tom Poole has a friend with him of the name of Coleridge: a young man of brilliant understanding, great eloquence, desperate fortune, democratick principles, and entirely led away by the feelings of the moment.

There is not much more to say about Pantisocracy. It never became even a remote reality. It was very daring at the time, with the French Revolution upsetting all the eighteenth-century notions of a proper society, and England in a wary, authoritarian mood. Southey lived on to become Poet Laureate, and a grumbling old Tory. Coleridge never quite shed historical liberal affections, though he disavowed Unitarianism in excessive language, and made a poor impression on Emerson. But Coleridge was an old man then, old before his time, all that abounding vitality sapped by many years of opium.

Yet Pantisocracy was another illustration of Coleridge's romantic provincialism, of his desire to move away from the centre of things, not towards it; and it was because of this scheme that he came west again, with Southey, and arrived at Bristol in 1794, under the shadow of Chatterton.

He soon made friends among the intellectual Bristol circle. He was particularly impressed by Humphry Davy, of whom he said that he "had never met so extraordinary a *young* man." This was a real compliment, for Coleridge specialized in being an extraordinary young man himself. He found company and entertainment in the strong and by no means foolish evangelical party. Robert Hall was widely held to be the noblest preacher in the land. In the gallery of Broadmead Baptist you would find the craggy figure of John Foster, a distinguished and unreadable essayist, also a preacher who had emptied seven churches: curly wig, dingy white cravat, rusty black jacket, large and ancient umbrella covered in green gingham, speaking to nobody: surely the original of the Dr. Foster who went to Gloucester in a shower of rain!

But Coleridge, Southey and before long Wordsworth soon occupied the centre of the literary scene, with Joseph Cottle paying them zealous court, Coleridge's marriage to Southey's sister-in-law drew them closer together. In retrospect it is fairly clear that Coleridge married Sarah for a variety of reasons: affection for Southey, because it would be a convenience for the Pantisocratic settlement, reaction from Mary Evans — but no doubt more tender emotions stirred him at the time. The Tintern expedition, which we have noticed under Cottle, had begun because Southey had rebuked Coleridge for failing to turn up at an advertised public lecture. Cottle observed that the episode did not seem a good omen for the intended new brotherhood of mankind, but before long all was harmony again.

As we have seen, when the *Lyrical Ballads* appeared in 1798, Coleridge had done most of the talking about it, and Wordsworth most of the writing. But Coleridge's principal contribution was no less than *The Rime of the Ancient Mariner.* In recent years critics have made determined though only partly successful efforts to draw our attention to the merits of Coleridge's less familiar work — *Frost at Midnight* had certainly been underestimated — but it remains that his poetic reputation is still founded on three poems: *Kubla Khan*, a fragment; *Christabel*, never finished; and the *Ancient Mariner*.

Kubla Khan, written in a Somerset farmhouse, the astonishing fragment interrupted by a visit of a person from Porlock, would probably have remained a fragment in any case, because of Coleridge's lack of what he called to Cottle "finger industry". It was written under the influence of opium, a severe and prolonged "aberration from prudence" which the Bristol waterfront encouraged. Substantial proportions of *Christabel* were finished, but despite many attempts Coleridge never achieved a definitive version. *The Ancient Mariner*, however, was complete when it appeared in the Ballads. If you read it today — which is a good idea, especially if you have not read it since school — one of the things which will strike you about it is that (as the child said of *Hamlet*) it is all quotations. So much has it become a classic.

> Why look'st thou so?
> With my crossbow
> I shot the albatross.

In a radio series some years ago, called "Shanty Time", the question cropped up as to why, in maritime lore, to kill an albatross was to invite disaster?

The most popular suggestion was that albatrosses were believed to be inhabited by the souls of dead sailors. Another was that albatrosses were angels in disguise, and that though they appeared to be following the ship, in fact their influence was guiding it, and that you could not hope to get round the Horn without one. Yet another was that in those desperate latitudes, where every man's life hung by a thread, it ill behoved him to kill any other living creature — and albatrosses were just about the only creature around to kill.

But there is a story of Captain Shelvocke, in the year 1719, rounding the Horn in the frigate *Speedwell*, bent on a raiding expedition against Spanish possessions in the Pacific. He had with him Simon Hatley, a sailor experienced in those waters, who had indeed been with Woodes Rogers some years earlier on the famous circumnavigation, had been taken prisoner by the Spaniards, released only after some years, and was nevertheless going once again to the well "We all observed", wrote Shelvocke when they were off the Horn,

> we had not had the sight of one fish of any kind, since we were come to this southward of the Straits of Le Maire, not one Sea-Bird, except a disconsolate black Albatross, who accompanied us for several Days, hovering about us as though he had lost himself; till Hatley, observing in one of his melancholy fits, that this Bird was always hovering near us, imagined from his Colour, that it might be some ill Omen. That which, I suppose, induced him the more to encourage his Superstition, was the continued series of tempestuous Winds, which had oppressed us ever since we got into this Sea. But be that as it would be, after some fruitless Attempts, at length shot the Albatross, noy doubting, perhaps, that we should have a fair wind after it.

At least, they got round the Horn all right; but the voyage was disastrous. Speedwell was wrecked on Juan Fernandez. Shelvocke constructed a bark out of the wreckage, captured a Spanish merchantman, and sold it in China, where he deserted his men and came back to England. Few of the others ever saw home again. Hatley was captured a second time by the Spaniards, and almost certainly came to a sticky end.

According to MacLiesh and Kruger, in their book *Fabulous Voyage*, Shelvocke's account was read many years later by William Wordsworth, who suggested to his friend and fellow-poet Coleridge that it might provide material for a poem.

Shelvocke was a Bristol privateer, and it would have been difficult for Coleridge *not* to hear about him. But it is hardly relevant. *The Ancient Mariner* is a sailor's tale, and must have drawn on many sailors' tales. He was hearing them all the time in Bristol, and for that matter in his childhood in Devon.

Of *The Ancient Mariner's* revolutionary impact on English poetry, much has been written, perhaps too much, so that we begin to think of it as a piece of history and not a poem. One point about it should be made: it shows how strong the influence of Chatterton had been. For one of the features of *The Ancient Mariner* is its deliberate archaisms, and it was Chatterton who had made archaisms respectable. Indeed, as Professor John Livingstone Lowes has pointed out, Coleridge uses some of the same ones as Chatterton did (though be drew on many earlier poets as well).

Because it is narrative, the poem does not offer itself readily to quotation, but in 1970, the bicentenary of Coleridge's birth, it was decided to use some brief extracts in a B.B.C. programme, and the producer, Pamela Howe gave the job of reading them to Douglas Leach. Douglas is a man of many voices, but has always retained his natural Devon. He was born very near Ottery St. Mary, and the effect of his Devon accent upon the verses was something of a revelation.

> And now the Storm-blast came, and he
> Was tyrannous and strong:
> He struck with his o'er taking wings,
> And chased us south along.

One of the authors wrote a piece in *The Spectator*, suggesting that Radio Three should get Douglas to read the whole poem, and thanks to Brian Miller, who read the paragraph, this was ultimately done. It produced more than three hundred letters of appreciation, a remarkable number for such a programme. Gielgud had made a fine recording of the poem, but Douglas Leach had added a new dimension to it.

> And a good south wind sprang up behind
> The Albatross did follow,
> And every day, for food or play,
> Came to the mariner's hollo!

In mist or cloud, on mast or shroud,
It perched for verspers nine;
Whiles all the night, through fog-smoke white,
Glimmer'd the white moonshine.

Mrs. Coleridge, who did not join the others on the walking tour of
Germany (she was expecting a baby) wrote to them dolefully *"The Lyrical
Ballads* are not liked at all by any", but in fact it was not greeted, for a
pioneering work, too badly, and after the second edition in 1800 its popularity
grew swiftly (no profit to the authors or Cottle).

Wordsworth was the better poet, the success, both in his own lifetime and
since. Coleridge wrote fewer bad lines, few bad poems, and perhaps once or
twice reached heights which Wordsworth did not quite touch. Southey was
also a success in his own lifetime, less so since. Coleridge was clearly a much
nicer and more interesting man than either of them, and it is fair to say that
great poet though he was, his fascination even today lies for us in his life as
much as his writings.

Well, there we must leave him, on the threshold, still determinedly
provincial, a disciple of Chatterton, consciously romantic, the aberrations
from prudence already indicating the frustrations of his career. He survived
through the generosity of his friends, and political writing, and lecturing.

His lectures were extremely successful when he turned up. He once missed
an appointment in Bristol because he left the London coach at Bath. He had
discovered a lady in the coach to be the sister of a friend of his, and conceived
it to be his duty to escort her home to North Wales. When he did arrive in
Bristol some days later, he was routed out from his lodging with some
difficulty, and kept his audience waiting an hour: but in five minutes they had
forgiven him. Few such irritating people can have been so loved. The devoted
Tom Poole saw him in a haze of adoration, though like his sister he too had
not yet mastered the spelling of the poet's name:

Hail to thee, Coldridge! youth of various powers!
I love to hear thy soul pour forth the line,
To hear it sing of love and liberty
As if fresh-breathing from the soul divine.

As if on earth it never yet had dwelt,
As if from heaven it now had wing'd its way;
And brought us tidings how, in argent fields,
In love and liberty blest spirits stray.

I love to view the abstracted gaze which speaks
Thy soul to heavenward towering — then I say,
He's gone — for us to cull celestial sweets
Amid the flowerets of the milky way.

J.D.Campbell, who wrote a splendid life of Coleridge, compares this passage with a description by Lamb, twenty years later. Poole, as he says, saw Coleridge entering the battle, radiant as the Michael of Perugino. Lamb saw him retiring from it, but his imagination was still stirred when Coleridge recited the vision of *Kubla Khan*,

....which said vision he repeats so enchantingly that it irradiates and brings heaven and Elysian bowers into my parlour when he sings or says it. His face when he repeats his verses, hath its ancient glory; an archangel a little damaged.

Sydney Smith

Sydney Smith was one of the famous wits of the first half of the nineteenth century. He was a parson, an essayist, something of a politician. Although his origins were middle class, he was a great success in the world of the Whig aristocracy, a world that, as Alan Bell writes in his biography, "soon took him up but never took him over." He was an agreeable man with no enemies, or very few.

The difficulty in trying to write about wits is that what has made people laugh at the time, cannot often be conveyed by the printed word. This is not just a matter of changing backgrounds over the years: timing and inflection has so much to do with it. We read of countless people acclaiming his little jokes, but when they go on to give examples, only occasionally are we stirred to more than a mild smile. For instance: when Sydney was leaving Bristol — he held a living at Combe Florey, and was a Canon of Bristol cathedral — he turned at the top of Knowle Hill, cast his eyes over the city, placed his hand upon his stomach — there was plenty of it — bowed, and declared "Farewell, Bristol, I go, but I take with me the fat of the land." It sounded very funny when once Geoffrey Matthews had the line in a radio play. Also, of course, as time went by, he had the advantage of being known as a comic turn. As W.S.Gilbert said, "An accredited wit has only to say 'Pass the mustard' and they roar their ribs out."

Here is a selection of some of Sydney's remarks, from which you may make your own judgement, and if you are tempted for more, turn to Mr. Bell's biography, or Hesketh Pearson's, a delightful book published in 1934, titled with a phrase of Macaulay's, "The Smith of Smiths".

Of the pavilion at Brighton: "It looks as if St Paul's Cathedral has come down and littered." (Chesterton said of this remark: "It is more than a logical sequence: it is an imaginative vista").

On the village of Netheravon, his first charge, in the middle of Salisbury Plain: "A pretty feature in a plain face."

On Scotland: "that garret of the earth — that knuckle-end of England — that land of Calvin, oatcakes, and sulphur." "It requires a surgical operation to get a joke well into a Scotch understanding. Their only idea of wit, or rather that inferior variety of this electric talent which prevails occasionally in the north, and which, under the name of 'wut', is so infinitely distressing to people of good taste, is laughing immoderately at stated intervals." But he also said, "No nation has so large a stock of benevolence of heart." (He had worked as a tutor in Scotland, and with Jeffrey and Brougham had founded the *Edinburgh Review*.)

A stout Anglican, he disliked the enthusiasm of the Protestant Dissenter and the mummery of the Catholics. But, an equally stout liberal, he fought fiercely for their civic and religious freedom. "I solemnly believe blue and red baboons to be more popular than Catholics or Presbyterians. When a country squire hears of an ape, his first feeling is to give it nuts and apples; when he hears of the Dissenter, his immediate impulse is to commit it to the county gaol, to shave its head, to alter its customary food, and to have it privately whipped." And "no eel in the well-sanded fist of a cook-maid, upon the eve of being skinned, ever twisted and writhed as an orthodox person does when he is compelled by the gripe of reason to admit anything in favour of a Dissenter."

Henry Hallam was an incessant dogmatic talker. Lord Melbourne once began. "I think I may say, without fear of contradiction..." and Sydney interrupted him with "Are you acquainted, sir, with Mr. Hallam."

On marriage: "It resembles a pair of shears, so joined that they cannot be separated, often moving in opposite directions, yet always punishing anyone who comes between them."

On the future: "I am not fond of expecting catastrophes, but there are cracks in the world."

On England: "What two ideas are more inseparable than Beer and Britannia?"

On human nature: "You find people ready enough to be the Samaritan — without the oil and the twopence."

Perhaps Mr. Bell, and even Mr. Pearson, do not quite capture the elusive laughter of Sydney. What they have done, and it is not unimportant, is to make clear the significance of the other aspects of his life, and explained how he used his good humour, his gift of phrase, and his social standing, to advance the causes he had at heart, such as Catholic emancipation, the abolition of slavery, and parliamentary reform. It was during the passions, even the riots — especially in Bristol — that in 1831, at Taunton, he made his most famous speech. It was rapidly read all over the country, and is said to have had a big effect in calming things down. Here is his most famous passage. The Bill had passed the Commons, but the House of Lords had thrown it out.

The attempts of the Lords to stop the progress of reform reminds me very forcibly of the great storm of Sidmouth, and of the conduct of the excellent Mrs. Partington on that occasion. In the winter of 1824, there set in a great flood upon that town — the tide rose to an incredible height — the waves rushed in upon the houses, and every thing was threatened with destruction. In the midst of this sublime and terrible storm, Dame Partington, who lived upon the beach, was seen at the door of her house with mop and pattens, trundling her mop, squeezing out the sea-water, and vigorously pushing away the Atlantic Ocean. The Atlantic was roused. Mrs. Partington's spirit was up; but I need not tell you that the contest was unequal. The Atlantic Ocean beat Mrs. Partington. She was excellent with a slop of a puddle, but she should not have meddled with a tempest. Gentlemen, be at your ease, — be quiet and steady. You will beat Mrs. Partington.

Alfred Austin

In writing about bad poets, we perhaps did not pay sufficient attention to Alfred Austin: he was hardly a good/bad poet, but he was the Laureate. And he was certainly one of the most memorable men — "memorable" would be the just word — ever to hold the office. It is a mistake to imagine that this office has always been dignified by our noblest poets. Nahum Tate, Laurence Eusden, Colley Cibber are not exactly names which ring proudly down the long galleries of our literary heritage. But the nineteenth century had at least provided us with Southey, Wordsworth (after he had stopped writing good poetry) and Tennyson; and Alfred Austin did come rather as a shock. There was a gap of some years after Tennyson's death before the appointment was made, and when Lord Salisbury, who had made it, was asked why he had done so, he said he thought nobody else had applied for the job.

Austin had tried his hand at politics. In 1865 there was an election held at Taunton for two members of parliament to represent the eastern division of Somerset, and he was one of the Conservative candidates. He had taken over from a former M.P. for the division, Arthur Mills, who stated in *The Times* "that by bribery he might have obtained re-election, but not without it." *The Somerset County Gazette* commented, "Truly Taunton has no reason to regret that it has for ever dispensed with the services of such a representative." Austin was supposed to have a little money and to be inclined to spend it. He expressed as few political opinions as possible, which is traditionally a mark of a shrewd candidate, but he came at the bottom of the poll. Nevertheless, this brought him within the rather vague cognizance of Salisbury.

There is a gorgeous account of a conversation with Austin in *As We Were*, by E.F. Benson. The poet, reclining on a couch, explained to a purportedly admiring group of youngsters that he could never write a line without It — his inspiration. Sometimes there were dark moments, when It left him awhile. He recalled how It vanished once at a critical moment of his great work, "The Human Tragedy". He had just written the lines

> As for the twain they vanished in the rattle
> Of jolting tumbrils and the joy of battle —

when It went. So he put his pen away and waited. Finally It returned and the mighty work was resumed. If you have not come across it, you have delights ahead. This is the passage describing how the rejected lover receives a letter from the beloved:

> He tore it open with a trembling hand,
> And with a greedy eye its message read,
> Written, it seemed, in haste and quickly scanned:
> "I write to tell you my last news, instead
> Of leaving it to gossip's busy hand.
> I am engaged and shortly shall be wed.
> Congratulate me, won't you? All here send
> Their best regards. I fear that I must end."

But there are jewels all through Austin. Take this couplet from his poem on the Jameson Raid, which *The Times* published, as it customarily did Laureate offerings —

> They went across the veldt
> As hard as they could pelt.

And the lines on the illness of the Prince of Wales,

Across the wires the electric message came,
He is no better, he is much the same.

The ascription of these lines to Austin is uncertain, but as Benson remarks, the internal evidence strongly suggests that It is operating.

He published twenty volumes of verse, which the *Oxford Companion to English Literature* dismisses as "of little merit". His prose writing is not too bad, and his autobiography, published in 1811, gives some useful background information as to the literary and political life of his time. Perhaps we should be grateful to the electors of Taunton for turning him down, lest he had been tempted "to party give up what was meant for mankind." One doubts if It would have flourished in the House of Commons.

Dr. Bowdler's Legacy

In this book we have several times has occasion to use the word "bowdlerize". Look it up in the dictionary, and you will find: "To expurgate a book, etc., by omitting or altering words and passages considered indelicate", and then, more grimly, "to castrate". Dr. Bowdler, who gave us this word, became famous in the early nineteenth century because of his *Family Shakespeare*, the version which probably your great-grandmother read when she was a girl. He was even mentioned in Gilbert and Sullivan. In *Princess Ida*, Psyche is telling the girl graduates of the wonders of classical literature; Ovid, Aristophanes, Juvenal, but ends

if you will be well advised
You will get them bowdlerized.

And up come the girl graduates,

Ah! we will get them bowdlerized!

Dr. Bowdler's Legacy, "a history of expurgated books in England and America", by Noel Perrin, an American teacher of English literature, has one or two faults. He writes in an American style so relentlessly breezy that his meaning is sometimes obfuscated (or is it perhaps just that the time has come when American books should be translated?) He makes some casual and irritating mistakes in English history. His system of footnotes is new, complicated, and useless. These are small matters. It is a capital book. If you are at all interested in the oddities English literature — which means if you are at all interested in English literature — you will enjoy it.

Mr. Perrin deals not only with Dr. Bowdler and his family (his sister Harriet did much of the actual work), and the various works of expurgation (not just Shakespeare) they carried out from their citadel of delicacy in Bath; he also deals with Bowdler's predecessors and successors. He makes them appear comic. But he is fair. Bowdler's revision of Shakespeare was less contemptible than Dryden's, who sought to improve him by making him *more* bawdy. Bowdler's motives were not mercenary. They were, and this is a conclusion Mr. Perrin bravely reaches after a struggle, honourable. He was concerned with protecting women and children from the rough realities of life. "Women and children first" was not an ignoble principle, though nowadays the women consider it a slur, not to speak of the children.

The delight of the book is the many examples that it gives of bowdlerization in action. Just two examples. Iago says of Othello

> I hate the Moor
> And it is thought abroad that 'twixt my sheets
> He has done my office.

This is holily revised to

> I hate the Moor,
> And it is thought abroad that with my wife
> He has done me wrong.

As Mr. Perrin points out, Frankie and Johnnie. The other example is from the *Liberal Translation of the New Testament*, by Edward Harwood, the purpose of which was to refine "the bald and barbarous language of the old vulgar version". This has Jesus saying, "Thomas, because thou hast seen me, thou hast believed . Blessed are those that have not seen, and yet have believed." Harwood's version went: "You are convinced, Thomas, of the identity of my person, merely because of the testimony of your senses — be assured that those who discover a better disposition, who though they have not ocular demonstration, are yet persuaded." Even the *New English Bible* can't beat that.

Henry Sewell Stokes

Worthies of Cornwall! long the Roll
That bears your proud historic names.

These are the opening lines of a poem written by Henry Sewell Stokes, who
was born in the nineteenth century. That odd word "worthy" used as a noun,
so popular with our Victorian forebears for describing a man who had done
the state some service, has today a slightly pompous and ridiculous ring to it.
But most of our West Country worthies were interesting enough people, who
in a latter day would probably have become stimulating contributions to local
radio (think what an asset to broadcasting Sabine Baring-Gould would have
been). And Henry Sewell Stokes was undoubtedly a lively and capable man,
whose life work qualifies him to be a Cornish worthy himself.

That life's work was done in Cornwall, though his father was a Tavistock
man, and he himself was born in Gibraltar. He came back to the west in his
early twenties, and set up as a solicitor in Truro. There he became the founder
and editor of the *Cornish Guardian*, a newspaper which, through its merging
with the *West Briton*, still survives. He was mayor of Truro; later, town clerk;
later, the clerk of the peace for the county, which caused him to move to
Bodmin, where he died in 1865.

Besides his journalism, he was a poet: in fact he was known, in his time, as
"Cornwall's laureate". His poems are mostly concerned with local subjects,
and they are not to be despised, although he did not have the power to sustain
a major work. "The Vale of Lanherne", which his contemporaries regarded
as his finest poem, is a struggle. When one of us had read it through he could
not help wondering how long it would be before anyone would do it again. But
some of his shorter poems have charm:

Should beauty fade?
   I'll love the rose when pale,
And shield its frailty from the winter gale.

Or this, on a winter wedding:

Love will not wait the vernal hour,
   To love all months are May;
Old Christmas leaves his holly bower
   To give the bride away;
No lilies twine sweet Marian's hair,
   But then her cheeks the roses wear.

144

And there are such graphic phrases as this, in a rollicking poem called "The Times of the Cavaliers", in which Stokes describes the giant Anthony Payne, Bevil Grenville's huge and faithful servant —

Payne, whose spear look'd like an elm
Torn from the countryside.

Stokes was a friend of Landor, Lytton, Longfellow, Matthew Arnold, Kingsley — a brilliant literary circle — and also of the mighty Tennyson, who visited him more than once in Cornwall. Tennyson could be a difficult guest, as was discovered by the lady lion-hunter whom he told "Your stays creak"; before chasing her all over the garden to make the correction, "I beg your pardon. It was my braces." I do not know the provenance of this story, but for some reason it is associated in my mind with Stokes. He was unlikely to be perturbed by the upset, because everyone who writes of him speaks of his equanimity and calm throughout a long and busy life. A stout friend in Cornwall; a poet with his own little niche in the gallery; a worthy worthy.

Conan Doyle in Plymouth

Conan Doyle had brief, but hectic associations with Plymouth. He came to the city in 1882, shortly after he had qualified as a doctor, at the request of a friend and former fellow-student, Dr. George Budd. Budd, the son of a Bristol doctor, had failed in the medical profession in his father's town, and started again in Plymouth with highly unorthodox methods. Conan Doyle spent several months in uneasy but diverting partnership with him. Although it ended in disaster, it was a period which provided the future author with material he was to put to good use. There are many traces of Budd's powerful, brilliant and perverted personality. He is the original of Dr. Cullingham in *The Stark Munro Letters*. Professor Challenger certainly owes something to him, and even, though we say it with hesitation, Sherlock Holmes.

Budd met Doyle at North Road station with a carriage and pair, and a coachman who asked to which of his houses he would like to be driven. He had three, none of them properly furnished. The big house on the Hoe had thirty empty bedrooms. He explained to Doyle that there was no point in buying a bedroom suite for forty pounds, and then having to throw it out of the window to make room for one costing a hundred. The rooms that *were* furnished were luxurious, and all the rest in due course were going to be the same. This optimism seemed to be justified by the state of the practice. No.1 Durnford

Street, Budd's consulting rooms, was packed every morning (Durnford Street now in a "down-town" area, was then extremely fashionable, as one might guess from its faded elegance even today). Every room was full of patients, to say nothing of the coach-house and stable. There were three main ingredients in Budd's success. He gave consultations free — patients only paid for the medicine, or if they wanted to jump the queue. He bullied his patients savagely, yelling at them to shut up, never listening to a word they said, cursing and hitting them. On Doyle's first day he saw Budd throw out a fat, middle-aged man with the words, "You eat too much, drink too much, and sleep too much! Knock down a policeman, and come again when they let you out." From which you may gather that the second element in Budd's success was a rudimentary but shrewd psychology. The third was a boldness in the use of drugs which would find less disfavour today than then, and effected some remarkable cures which gossip elevated almost to the status of miracles. But he did not know enough about the drugs, and in the end one or two critical remarks at coroners' inquests set his meteoric career into swift decline.

But that was after Doyle's time. In the summer of 1882 all was prosperity and even Budd's enormous practice could not exhaust his energies. He decided that they should run their own weekly paper, to be called *The Scorpion*, to sting Mayor and Council and everybody else, especially other members of the medical profession. Budd hated them, and his disregard of etiquette was such that it was not surprising the hate was mutual. At the end of the day, he would walk through the medical quarter, loudly jingling the day's takings in a canvas bag. Budd was to write the news and comment in the paper, Doyle the fiction and poetry. Doyle protested, not then having had any success as a writer, but Budd insisted — another example of his discernment. Budd was also an inventor: he had made a steel jacket for soldiers, and a magnetic device which would ensure permanent naval supremacy to the power which possessed it. He managed to increase the power of a magnet in such a way that it would deflect a steel bullet, fired at point-blank range, on to itself and not the target. He experimented successfully on his wife, Doyle declining to join in. Apply this principle to battleships, and clearly they are invulnerable! But long arguments with the Admiralty failed to convince them. The negotiations came to an end when they asked Budd what he would fix his magnet to, and he replied, any solid impenetrable object, such as the head of an Admiralty official.

All these excitements finished, so far as Conan Doyle was concerned, because Budd, for all his entertaining qualities, was unfortunately a good deal of a blackguard. He seems to have been jealous of Doyle, because Doyle equably refused to be jealous of *him*. He opened Doyle's letters, and found some unfavourable references to himself written by Doyle's mother. The partnership broke up, in unpleasant circumstances which troubled Doyle but never made him waver from his own straightforward and tolerant path. The great Dr. Budd stayed in Plymouth, while the unsuccessful Dr. Doyle went to Southsea, a largely non-existent practice, penury, and then — before very long — to Professor Challenger and Sherlock Holmes.

L. A. G. Strong
(written upon his death, 1958)

We cannot really claim L.A.G.Strong as a Westcountryman, but he lived a lot of his life in Devon, and made it the scene of two of his most famous novels, *Dewar's Ride* and *The Swift Shadow*. *Dewar's Ride* made a great impression on me as a boy, and would have made an even greater one had I then known the shadowy vastness of Dartmoor, and awe-inspiring heights of Dewar's Leap. Some of the critics have been suggesting that *Dewar's Ride* was marred by excessive brutality. It was a great deal less brutal than the average boy's magazine — what we used to call the "tuppenny blood" — and a great deal better written. As for the idea that his so-called brutality was an over-compensation for the physical weakness which afflicted Mr. Strong after a boyhood illness, that is nonsense. *Dewar's Ride*, like most of his novels, is a thundering good story, well and vividly told, It can be ranked with *The Hound of the Baskervilles* as an adventure story of the moor: and there were some brutal passages in that, but nobody ever suggested that Conan Doyle was over-compensating for physical weakness, because he was one of the fittest men who ever hit a six over long-on.

We ought also to remember Strong's book on boxing, *Shake Heads and Come Out Fighting*. Boxing, as practised in the modern professional set-up, is not appealing, even though the days of the old prize ring were worse, but it makes stirring reading; one of the best books on the subject, in the Hazlitt tradition.

As a poet, I doubt if Strong has had justice done to him. For instance,

This is the house where Jesse White
Run staring in one misty night,
And said he seed the Holy Ghost
Out to Lowery finger-post.

In that verse we have metrical precision, accurate observation, and genuinely evocative atmosphere. It makes you want to read the rest of the poem, which a first verse should.

But, of his poetry that we have read, this is the favourite –"The Knowledgeable Child":

I always see — I don't know why,
If any person's going to die.
That's why nobody talks to me.
There was a man who came to tea,
And when I saw that he would die
I went to him and said, "Goodbye,
I shall not see you any more."
He died that evening. Then next door
They had a little girl: she died
Nearly as quick, and Mummy cried
And cried, and ever since that day
She's made me promise not to say.
But folks are still afraid of me,
And where they've children, nobody
Will let me next or nigh to them
For fear I'll say goodbye to them.

Let us not spoil a good case by over-stating it, but that has tragedy in farce, and beauty in both: in the same strain as the great tragi-comedians of the twentieth century, Waugh and Beerbohm and Chesterton and Belloc.

A Letter from Eden Phillpotts

As it happens, we had access to a letter written by the Devon author more than eighty years ago, which seems to us to deserve wider circulation. It is written on the notepaper of *Black and White*, 34 Bouverie Street, the magazine on which Phillpotts was then working. It is a higgledy-piggledy letter, wandering through a mass of single and double sheets, so that one never knows where to find the next bit. It was written to Silvester Horne, one of the great Free Church leaders of the early part of this century, and it is through the courtesy of Silvester Horne's equally (though differently famous son, Kenneth, that we can quote it. It does give an insight into the mind of this admirable Devon writer during the earlier, formative years of his life.

Horne, writing to thank Phillpotts for a novel he had written, had evidently made some reference to the "theatre" of a book. "I always try", says Phillpotts, agreeing, "to get a thorough grasp of the environment of my puppets, for then only do they grow alive to me. I like to see the colour of the mud on their boots and smell their country smell. A novel only gives at best a few passages out of a few lives: but if the writer is in earnest, and not merely playing at making men and women, he lives with his folks by day and night, and follows them through a hundred events, interviews, crises for which there is no room in the book."

Then Eden Phillpotts talks to Silvester Horne about religion. In his novel he had been hitting out at the lunatic fringe of nonconformity, but he says, "Nonconformity itself I have far greater sympathy with than that musty and monstrous machine we call the Established Church...Christianity lies buried deep today under such hideous accumulations of dogma that nothing less than the appearance of a genius only second to Christ himself will bring us back to the notable faith of the Founder."

"As an agnostic....I am disposed to think that Faith and Reason cannot run in double harness, unless tandem fashion; for each man must decide which he shall choose for leader. But so a man has a guide, and lives obedient to nature, and to the dictates of his conscience...that man commands our respect and sympathy."

He then turns to his own life history. "I was brought up in a little circle of wealthy Ritualists, made a member of various Romish guilds, adorned by medals, taught to "serve" at strange Popish services in a rich priest's private oratory, and "educated" for the church. Poor myself, I depended upon this man, and when I reached an age for going to college, he designed to place me there. Then I found I could not believe, and told him so. The scene was painful; he turned his back upon me and I had to seek a career elsewhere, for my dreams of college were of course at an end."

"I design", Eden Phillpotts adds, "to hear you next Sunday, for sometimes Reason points along a cold road and one envies men the sheet anchor of faith which has been denied to me."

Apart from the main theme of his letter, there is this comment on the two south-western counties: "The Devon man has more humour in his nature than the Cornish, and goes easier in matters of religion." And there is this remark: "Childhood is the time of luxuriant imagination, for reason and experience chill and wither it in adult life." But for Eden Phillpotts, happily, they never did.

The Tangyes from Illogan to Minack

A book which seems to have been oddly neglected — indeed, we do not often hear it mentioned — is *The Rise of a Great Industry*, by *Sir* Richard Tangye, published in 1905. Certainly there is nothing in the title to attract any special interest, but our attention was drawn to it by the crest of Cornwall on the cover.

That was a characteristic touch of Richard Tangye's because until the day of his death (only a few weeks after his book was published) he rejoiced in his Cornish origins. He was born at Illogan, on the road between Camborne and Redruth, in 1833, in a poor but good home, and he died at the head of a great engineering factory in Birmingham called "The Cornwall Works". The book is mainly the story of how he, and his brothers, built up that business from nothing, but the most interesting parts for Westcountrymen are the early chapters, with their vivid description of a Cornish childhood in the first half of the nineteenth century.

Richard's grandfather was a St. Columb man, put to the land when a boy. His master would call his boys together at night and say, "Who will go to bed without supper for a new penny?" (Boulton and Watt's "cartwheel" pennies had recently been introduced). The boys would take the pennies and make their supper from raw turnips. But they would be hungry in the morning, and would be greeted with the suggestion, "Who will give a penny for an extra large breakfast?" This character deserves to have found his way into Dickens.

However, grandfather Tangye survived it all, saved enough to buy a few acres of poor land, worked as a night driver on a mine pump as well as farming the land, raised a family and lived to be ninety-four. His grandson remembered him well, so he did his great-grandmother, who was born in 1750 and had taken tea with John Wesley.

Richard Tangye's father was born in Redruth, and went down the mine. Later he exchanged the mine for a smallholding. He also exchanged the Wesleyans for the Society of Friends. Richard was brought up a Quaker and remained one (John Bright was his hero, and became his friend).

In the 1830s, he recalls, Cornish children still lit bonfires and danced around them on Midsummer Eve, singing

Midsummer Eve is passing away, passing away,
  Hip, hip, hooray!

There were fairly fierce "battles" between the boys of neighbouring parishes, again with appropriate words,

150

Redruth boys, Redruth boys, up in the tree
Looking as wisht as wisht could be,
'Logan boys, 'Logan boys, up in the oak,
Knocking down Redruth boys at every stroke.

(The *Shorter Oxford* gives wisht as "dreary, uncanny, sickly": it is still used in Cornwall, usually with the meaning "exhausted"). It had not been so long since men, and not boys, engaged in these fights, and they could easily become savage. Breage men and Wendron men used to met in regular strife beneath "the great tree at Cury." Rugby football no doubt helped to sublimate such animosities.

It was dangerous, in Cornwall then, to try to count the stars, or to whistle after dark. So it was believed, but superstition began to fade with the coming of the railway, which ran through the Tangye holding — though the railway was at first regarded with deep suspicion, as making more fire and smoke to torment poor sinners in hell.

The mines worked a shift system, three spells of eight hours, and in consequence of this most miners could manage to cultivate a little land. But their tenure of the land was held under the iniquitous "three-lives" system. The lease had to be signed by three people, and when they were all dead — which could, by misadventure, happen quite soon — the holding lapsed. Richard Tangye has some justifiably bitter comments to make about the working of this system.

He was even more infuriated by the church rate. At that time everybody in a parish, irrespective of their religious allegiance, had to pay tithe. The Tangyes refused, and in consequence, year after year, the Anglican vicar distrained upon their goods. Once he seized the cow on which the family depended for their breakfast bread and milk. Once he seized a side of bacon — curing bacon was an art in which Mrs. Tangye excelled — and afterwards sent a message to say he had never tasted better bacon in his life. The church rates were abolished in due course, but the bitterness was not. At that time in Cornwall there were parishes where not one in ten was an Anglican, but all had to pay the rate. It is not surprising that ideas of Christian reunion are sometimes greeted coolly by Cornish Nonconformists today. Memories are long in the south-west.

Sir Richard Tangye — he was knighted in 1896 — was a self-made man, in a sense in which — for better or worse — it is hardly possible to be in the welfare state of today. One of the key writers of the period was Samuel Smiles, the author of *Self-Help and Thrift* and similar volumes describing how men of humble origins made their way in the world by the faithful exercise of the Victorian virtues. "A place for everything, and everything in its place" was one of the maxims of Samuel Smiles. Richard Tangye might have been made to measure as a Smiles hero, and it is not surprising that *Self-Help* was one of his favourite books. He went from the local school to Sidcot, a Quaker foundation, where for a time he acted as a student teacher, for his keep and a salary of a pound a year. But his bent was for engineering. His heroes were Watt and Stephenson, and ultimately he and his brothers set up a small engineering shop in Birmingham. By rigid personal economy and a frightening industry they built it up to be the Cornwall Works at Smethwick. Their trade was worldwide, and Tangye travelled the world himself to promote it. They invented a patent hydraulic jack which had much success, and was used, among other things, to launch Brunel's *Great Eastern* and to set up Cleopatra's Needle on the embankment. One of the jacks is buried in the foundations of the Needle. They were good employers and conceded the nine hours' day to their workman unasked. A happy staff was good for business. They were completely dedicated to the principles of John Bright, abhorring state control but completely confident that righteous dealing was also profitable dealing. In fact Tangye's autobiography is a deliberate justification of one of the typical Victorian attitudes.

"Had Ruskin known this place thirty years ago", he says, "and were he to revisit it now, doubtless his anger would be kindled, and he would anathematize those who had invaded the pleasant meadows and turned the cherry orchard and flower gardens into a place where nothing is heard but the hissing of steam, the clanging of iron, and the perpetual thud of the steam hammer. And yet, thirty years ago, the land on which the works stand gave employment to less than a dozen people, who lived in houses damp and undrained, whereas now nearly two thousand men and boys earn a comfortable livelihood under conditions much more conducive to health and happiness." There stands the case for the defence. As for the prosecution, you remember Ruskin's comment: "There was a rocky valley between Buxton and Bakewell, divine as the vale of Tempe. You enterprised a railway, you blasted its rocks away, and now, every fool in Buxton can be at Bakewell in half an hour, and every fool at Bakewell in Buxton." But Victorian authority had no doubt on which side virtue lay.

There are times, as Richard Tangye tells his story, when he seems priggish as well as broad-minded; times when he seems hard as well as compassionate. One thing he always remained, through and through: a Cornishman. He would be pleased that there are still Tangyes in Cornwall today, notably Derek and his wife Jeannie in the cottage at Minack, near Lamorna Cove. They both gave up successful London careers to settle in what was at first a tumbledown cottage on a nearly derelict smallholding. Derek has told the story of their adventures in a series of books, of which the most famous is probably *A Gull on the Roof.* These are passages of autobiography, describing the ups and downs they had before Minack became an efficient flower farm. Probably the most interesting as we look back on the years is *The Way to Minack*, which is autobiographical in a stricter sense. He deals with his life from schooldays up till the time when he and Jeannie took the decision to go to Cornwall. In doing so, he enables us to weigh the attractions, and the virtues, of his two lives, and understand much more than before about the great renunciation.

There is some confusion about the Tangye books, even among some of those who have read them. They have charm, of course: all those almost-human animals which they adopted, and the famous and humble alike dropping in at Minack for a bite of home-baked bread. But that is not really what the books are about. They are important social documents. The Tangyes have found their philosophy, however unfashionable, and live it. After reading *The Way to Minack*, it is no longer a puzzle why Derek Tangye abandoned a career in journalism which often touched brilliance. The puzzle is why he stuck it so long as he did, because temperamentally he was clearly unfitted for it. He spent four years of his life doing something that he had stumbled into almost by accident, doing it well, but not in his heart wanting to do it at all.

His chief unfitness was that he was an exceptionally kind man, and could not suppress it. He can be cruelly frank about himself in his books, but he is almost always kind about everyone else, and some of them must have taken a lot to be kind to. There are two exceptions, both interesting. One is Dawson of *The Times*, who has "Hard eyes behind a bland smile", and who advised the young man: "You may wish to become a journalist but I warn you never *never* work for Lord Beaverbrook or Lord Rothermere. Such men would destroy you." The advice was not appreciated, or taken. He worked for both. And they very nearly did destroy him, and would have done if he had not got out in time: but Derek Tangye does not make this point himself. His talent was such that he was given the William Hickey column in the *Express* after Tom Driberg; but his character was such that he resigned after three days. He was insufficiently waspish.

The other person mildly criticized is Jean Nicoll the tennis-player, who had the same maiden name as Jean Tangye and got married from the same hotel in the same week, a situation ripe for the shambles. And this is significant because the one sure way to ruffle Derek Tangye is to slight or upset his wife. And rightly; for though Jeannie has been the mortar of Minack, the first wrench must have been for her more difficult, since she was not only highly successful in her job at the Savoy but clearly very happy in it. She writes a chapter in *The Way to Minack* but does not tell us much about her inner thoughts. Perhaps that is her strength. (She has become a successful writer herself).

One more thing about the Tangye books. It is easy not to notice how well they are written. Derek has a fluent command of English, but he does not waste words, and rarely commits a solecism, possibly owing to the influence of the master A.P.Herbert. Whether the Tangye philosophy is valid can be argued, but it is expressed with much distinction. Of this, certainly, old *Sir* Richard would have been proud.

T.S.Eliot and East Coker

"As pretty a place as there is", wrote Edward Hutton of East Coker more than half a century ago. That is still true. It is very much what is called a "chocolate box" village, thatch and cob, Perpendicular church, seventeenth century almshouses, fifteenth century manor house, lilac trees, wistaria and roses in season, oak beams and log fires: a kind of synthesis of all that Somerset villages are supposed to be. It is a surprising place to have inspired some of the most disturbing and challenging verse in the English tongue.

T.S.Eliot was born in St. Louis, Missouri, in 1888. He went to Harvard and Oxford, settled in England in 1915, and in 1927 became a British subject and a member of the Anglican Church. His *Four Quartets*, among them "East Coker", where he lived for some years, were published in 1936 and the following years. East Coker had been the village whence his ancestors went to New England in the seventeenth century. He was buried there on January 4th, 1965, by which time he had won the Nobel Prize for Literature and received the Order of Merit.

> In the beginning is my end. Now the light falls
> Across the open field, leaving the deep lane
> Shuttered with branches, dark in the afternoon,
> Where you lean against a bank while a van passes,
> And the deep lane insists on the direction
> Into the village, in the electric heat
> Hypnotized.

But of course East Coker is more than a picture of a village. It is a meditation on time and eternity, and man's place in nature and history. The *Four Quartets* reached a wide public and communicated the fundamentals of Christian faith and experience.

The many tributes at Eliot's death stressed his traditionalism, his loyalism, even his monarchism. J.B.Priestley has called him a poet of the Establishment:

he wrote, "a major poet in a bad time should make powerful enemies." Eliot did in fact make enemies, though they were not always Mr. Priestley's enemies: but he did not make very many, because he was a humble man.

> The only wisdom we can hope to acquire
> Is the wisdom of humility.

This is not the voice of the Establishment; it is a revolutionary voice, just as the New Testament is a revolutionary book. Only the poor are rich; your only possessions are those you have given away; the mark of the King is that he ministers to others. It was this clear restatement of challenging truth, restated with all the vividness which a consummate poetic technique could command, which made Eliot, to many young men of that generation, so disturbing, so exciting a writer. When we turned from him to Spender, or Ezra Pound, or even Auden, we were reminded that genius does what it must, while talent does what it can.

So perhaps, on reflection, it is not so surprising that East Coker should have been one of the sources of Eliot's inspiration. Look down on it from the churchyard on a sunny winter's afternoon, and it seems a very humble place, contented to be sure, but contentment is not a sin. It is sometimes mistaken for self-satisfaction, just as humility is sometimes mistaken for smugness. This is the mistake we have sometimes made about T.S.Eliot; but our descendants will not.

An Unsentimental Cornishman

It has been said that there is a love-hate relationship between Cornwall and A.L.Rowse: with all the love on Dr. Rowse's side, and all the hate on Cornwall's. There is this amount of truth in it: that Dr. Rowse loves Cornwall too well to do other than paint her warts and all, and that Cornishmen are particularly susceptible about their warts. Hence the rumpus, many years ago, about the first volume of his autobiography, *A Cornish Childhood*, which was given a very stiff review by J.W. Hunkin, the Bishop of Truro, in *The Oxford Magazine*. But feelings have mellowed, and it is hard to imagine any literate Cornishman not enjoying his collection of Cornish stories published in 1967. The opening story, "How Dick Stephens Fought the Bear", has become a classic. The stories depend less on plot than on evocation of atmosphere and character, and can therefore be read again and again. The parallel with Q is obvious and to some extent valid: but perhaps there is a closer similarity with

Henry Williamson's stories about Devon. There is the same careful observation, the same tautness and economy of style. It is not a style which one would expect to yield warmth and affection, yet these things are there. I suppose one could say that this is an example (as is Williamson) of a man writing with real sentiment, and yet not, as we usually employ the word, sentimentally.

Something of the quality also comes out in Rowse's Cornish poems, a volume of which was published at about the same time. Dr. Rowse once said that it was his greatest wish in life to add something to the rich store of English poetry. It must be said, however, that his achievements in this field so far fall short of his work in so many others. The best things in *Poems of Cornwall and America* are the Cornish poems, by far. This is the immediate reaction, but do we think this because we know Cornwall and do not know America? Even if this is so, it suggests a failure of communication by the poet. He makes deft use of Cornish place-names, but sometimes he reminds us of Betjeman in one of his less inspired moods, almost seems to be parodying him:

In the late afternoon of my life I lie and doze
In the residents' lounge of the hotel at Lytham St. Anne's

— we almost expect it to be followed by Betjeman's self-deprecating comment, "Not very good, is it?"

Dr. Rowse has soaked himself in the English poets: a reminiscence of Milton, a line of Hardy, will illumine his verse. A former pupil remembers being told firmly that the best two poets "to begin with, and carry on with so long as you like" were Milton and Wordsworth. The perceptive eye, the wide but precisely used vocabulary which we find in the stories, we find again here. But it is not enough. He might be a better poet if he subjected himself more severely to the disciplines of rhyme and metre, as his fellow-Cornishman Causley does. The "Child's Verses for Winter" with which he ends suggest it. What would happen if he were to set himself to write a long, metrical poem, possibly rhymed, on a big subject? Something like "The Armada", of which Macaulay left us only a fragment. It would be very interesting to see him try, and — as the Cornish say — one wouldn't be "frightened" if it came off.

LAW

The Unsolved Mystery of Rode
Kind, Good, Lamson
The Misfortunes of Edith Pegler
Tea with Major Armstrong
The Lewannick Soil
The Boy from Bath

The Unsolved Murder of Rode

On the night of the twenty-ninth of June, in the year 1860, at the village of Rode, on the borders of Wiltshire and Somerset, Francis Seville Kent was murdered. He was a little boy, not quite four years old. During the night he was taken from his cot, his throat was cut — though probably he had been suffocated first — and his body was hidden in a disused earth closet in the garden. It was a thoroughly nasty, brutal murder, and yet it has always exercised a powerful fascination, simply because nobody is quite sure who did it.

The murder had a classic detective-story setting. Rode Hill House, where it took place, was carefully locked, and there was no sign of any forced entry. The murderer must therefore have been one of the eleven inmates — that number includes the servants. The obvious suspect was the nursemaid, Elizabeth Gough, who slept in the same room as the child. She had, she said, awakened early in the morning, and seen that Francis was not in his cot, but she had not been concerned because she imagined he had been picked up by his mother. This apparently was a not uncommon occurrence. It was only when she visited the mother's room, after getting up at the normal time, and found Francis still missing, that the alarm was raised.

A blanket had been taken from the cot, and used to wrap the body in. The bedding had been carefully made up again, so that it could not be seen that the blanket was missing until the bed was stripped. This oddity, while not perhaps very significant, is characteristic of the case: there seems no logical explanation of it on any theory.

A woman's night-shift, much stained with blood, was found in the flue of the scullery stove. This might well have been an important clue, though it was argued later that there was a natural explanation for the stains. But this could never be established, nor even whom the garment belonged to, since, incredibly, it was allowed to be destroyed while the policemen on duty were having their supper in the kitchen — locked in.

The local police were in fact clearly overawed by having to deal with the gentry. For though Mr. Samuel Kent, the child's father, was a factory inspector — not a particularly exalted position — he was, in the social context of Rode, well above the salt, approximating almost to lord-of-the-manor status. There was strong public feeling, too, that at the inquest the coroner was chiefly concerned to avoid giving offence, and did not do enough to bring out all the evidence. Mr. Kent himself was not called. Eventually Chief Inspector Whicher came down from London to take over the investigation. His was one of the great names in the early history of the C.I.D., indeed he is supposed to have been the original of Sergeant Cuff, in the pioneer detective novel, *The Moonstone*, by Wilkie Collins. But in *The Moonstone* Sergeant Cuff, for all his talents, is wrong in the end, and though Whicher seems to have made up his mind fairly quickly about the Rode case, and never to have wavered from his beliefs, *he* may have been no wiser.

After the inconclusive inquest, Elizabeth Gough was brought before the magistrates and examined. But there was no evidence against her, save the delay in reporting that the child was missing, and they let her go. Whicher then arrested the child's sixteen-year-old stepsister, Constance Kent. This caused a further public outcry. One contemporary report declared, "The grounds on which this accusation was made were so frivolous, and the evidence by which it was attempted to be supported so childish, that the proceedings can only be described as absurd and cruel." Constance had lost a night-dress. She explained that it had been lost in the laundry, and things had certainly been lost in the laundry before. A housemaid said that she had been sent away by Constance on a pointless errand while the laundry was being got ready, presumably so that Constance could hide the night-dress. This did not amount to very much, and it is difficult to avoid the conclusion that Whicher was hoping that Constance might break down in examination and give herself away. She was a cool, calm young person and did nothing of the kind. She was therefore discharged, but since she had not been formally on trial, she was not formally acquitted. This proved to be crucially important, since under English law a person once acquitted of a crime can never, whatever the circumstances, be charged with it again.

Why was Whicher so sure, without being able to produce sufficient evidence, that Constance Kent was the murderer? Someone in the household had done it, and one can only assume that, from his study of the characters it contained, he thought her the one capable of such a thing. She certainly was a young woman of courage and aplomb. (Her bearing in her various troubles reminds one a little of another enigmatic woman who was suspected of murder, Madeleine Smith). A few years earlier, Constance had run away from home with one of her brothers, cutting off her hair — a Victorian sacrilege — and dressing as a boy. It was not a successful escape attempt, but a spirited one. Looking at her picture, the cheekbones high and chilling, the lips firm and slightly sardonic, it is possible to imagine that she had the will-power to commit a murder; much more difficult to imagine that she had the inclination.

But who else could have done it? The vague, lordly Mr. Kent? The flustered, pathetic Elizabeth Gough? No-one else could have done it, Whicher decided.

All the same, after the magistrates had released Constance, Elizabeth was brought back to them, with no different result. There was no new evidence.

She, too, was discharged; and there the matter rested — apart from endless speculation — for five years.

The speculation centred mostly on the suggestion that Elizabeth Gough and the father had committed the crime together. They were suspected of carrying on what was called "an intrigue": and the theory was that the child had woken in the night, and peered over the edge of his cot, and seen something which he would with innocent interest mention to Mummy in the morning. There was no evidence for this theory: there is really hardly any evidence for anything in this irritating case. Still, the theory covered the known facts.

The extraordinary feature in the case is, of course, how anyone could have taken Francis from his bed, cut his throat, left the house and thrown him down the privy, without causing any disturbance — remembering that Elizabeth Gough was sleeping in the same room, that the house was locked, and that it was very quiet in the countryside at night-time — much quieter than we can easily imagine in a mechanical age. This points, in our view — though no-one can do more than hazard a guess so much later — to Elizabeth having at least some knowledge of the crime.

Constance Kent left her family, and went to a convent in Brittany. After three years she moved to another at Brighton. This was under the charge of the Rev. A.D.Wagner, whose personality is one of the key features in the rest of the story. He was a well-known man, a leader of the extreme High Church party in the Church of England, and constantly at the centre of controversy because of his theological views and practices. He does not seem, quite apart from his beliefs, to have been an attractive person. Baring-Gould, who was a high churchman himself, calls Wagner "a peculiar man with a peculiar voice, grossly fat, and the voice did not comport with the body." Wagner's own father, also a clergyman but of much "lower" opinions is said once to have preached on the text: "Lord, have mercy on my son: for he is lunatic and sore vexed."

A few days after Easter, in 1865 — two years after Constance Kent had gone to Brighton, five years after the murder — Wagner travelled to London and gave the Home Office a written confession that Constance had killed her little stepbrother.

The authorities — partly, one feels, out of a distrust of Wagner — made repeated attempts to dissuade Constance, but she quietly persisted that the confession was true. She was brought to court at Trowbridge, sent to the assizes at Salisbury, pleaded guilty, and was sentenced to death.

Since she pleaded guilty, no evidence was called. It is safe to say that if she had, even at the last minute, pleaded not guilty, she would not have been convicted. There was no more evidence against her than there had been five years earlier, save her own confession. Now this confession, which was set out at length in a letter to the press by her solicitor, is manifestly incorrect in many vital details. That does not in itself prove that Constance was innocent. What it does demonstrate is that she could not have committed the murder in the way she says she did. And why, if anyone confesses to a murder, and is ready to suffer the consequences, should they make such a transparently inaccurate and incomplete confession?

You will find the details set out in *The Case of Constance Kent* by John Rhode, and *Saint — with Red Hands?* by Yseult Bridges. A third distinguished criminologist, F.Tennyson Jesse, has an essay in her book, *Murder and its Motives*. After close study, all those three reach different conclusions — all arguing from the same body of evidence.

The Home Secretary was conscious that it was an unsatisfactory situation, but all he could do, and did, was to commute the sentence to one of life imprisonment. Constance Kent, therefore, spent twenty years in prison, a normal "life sentence" in those days. When she came out, she went to Canada and worked there, apparently happily and well, as a nurse. She spent part of her imprisonment at Portland, where some rather beautiful mosaics in the prison chapel still testify to her industry and ability.

Even after all this time, Constance Kent is the sort of person you take sides about. We will therefore tell you what we think happened. We do not think she committed the murder. We think she knew who did. We think that her father, sleeping with Elizabeth Gough, *was* surprised in the middle of the night by an interested three-year-old nose poking over the side of the cot in the same room. The two of them together, panicking, killed the child and disposed, for the time being, of the body. This hypothesis leaves less questions unanswered than any other — certainly less than Constance's supposed confession.

Then why the confession? Father Wagner, and a Mother Superior who seems to have been an even more formidable person in the Brighton establishment, had debarred Constance from communion, and possibly even refused her confirmation, until she told them what she knew of the murder. Of course she knew more than she had publicly admitted. But could she, even under the seal of the confessional, — of which Father Wagner made much play, as if trying to force an issue on this vexed legal point — could she inculpate her father, whom she loved? Would it not be simpler to take the blame herself, and thus keep everyone more or less happy? Father Wagner revered martyrs, and it was in a spirit of martyrdom — of one who lays down his life for his friend — that Constance made her rigmarole of a confession. She certainly achieved one object — she distracted attention from her wretched father, who had been forced to leave his home, seeking anonymity but always pursued by suspicion. Miss Tennyson Jesse says that if Constance had confessed falsely she would have been unable to participate, as she subsequently did, in the sacramental rites of the church. This is a misunderstanding of the way in which Constance's mind — and those of many other would-be Christians — worked. Hers was not, except outwardly, a sacramental religion. It was a sacrificial one.

Well, that is what we think happened. But we don't know. Nobody knows. Nobody ever will.

Kind, Good, Lamson

Almost everyone who knew Dr. Lamson said what a kind, pleasant man he was. Indeed, among murderers he seems to have been equalled in these respects only by another doctor, Palmer of Rugeley — and as Robert Graves has shown us, it is extremely doubtful whether Palmer was a murderer at all. The odds are against Lamson having been equally unlucky. There are, nevertheless, some curious points about the story.

He was a Bournemouth doctor, who was tried in the year 1882 for the murder of his brother-in-law, Percy Malcolm John. Lamson was 29 at the time, a very personable young man with some lively experience behind him. He had served Serbia and Roumania as a volunteer surgeon in their wars against the Turks — a cause which appealed deeply to many Britons at the time — and for his services had received several decorations, including an order of knighthood. One of the Roumanian leaders said of him, at the time of the trial, "Kind, good Lamson is the last man in the world whom I could conceive capable of a base and cruel action."

He was not, unfortunately, well suited to general practice. For a time he had been at Rotherfield, in Sussex, and when he was trying to sell the practice he had to employ people to keep ringing his bell, in order to create for a prospective purchaser an illusory prosperity. After his conviction for murder, hands were held up in horror at this abominable duplicity. He did no better at Bournemouth. He got into financial difficulties, and had to sell him home. Twice he visited America. It is not clear what he did there, but it brought him no relief, and before the end of 1881 he was back in Bournemouth. It was presumably too hot to hold him, and he went to stay in a hotel in London, living in a miserable world of creditors, pawnings and dud cheques.

His financial situation is important, because it provided the motive for the murder. His wife — who was, and remained through everything, devoted to him — was one of five children. One girl had died before her parents. The other four were left sums of money — a few thousand pounds apiece, to be theirs on coming of age or on marrying. If they died before either of these things happened, the money would be divided equally among the survivors.

Lamson married in 1878, and received his wife's share of the patrimony — it became automatically his, since this was before the days of the Married Women's Property Act. In 1879 one of her brothers died. It was later suggested that Lamson was responsible for the death, but that was a retrospective suggestion, and there was no evidence for it. However, as a result, he received a useful legacy. There were now three children remaining: Mrs. Lamson, a married sister in the Isle of Wight, and Percy, who was 18 years old. Percy's legacy was £3,000, and therefore, if he died before marrying or coming of age, Dr. Lamson would receive £1,500. It was a large sum in those

Percy was still at school: Blenheim House School, Wimbledon. He suffered from curvature of the spine, and could not walk. However, he managed pretty well with wheelchairs and helpful schoolfellows, and was otherwise in reasonably good health. He seems to have been a likable, cheerful young man, on good terms with his doctor brother-in-law.
on good terms with his doctor brother-in-law.

On 1st December, 1881, Lamson wrote to Percy from his London hotel saying he hoped to see him the next day, before leaving for the continent. The next day he did indeed travel to Wimbledon, but did not call on Percy. He told a friend, however, that he had found Percy's illness worse, and that he had postponed his trip to the continent, as the headmaster had told him the boat that night was a bad one. It was later assumed that Lamson had intended to commit the murder that day, but his nerve failed him. The needless elaborations are a little odd, though said to be characteristic of a certain type of psychopath.

The next day, December 3rd, Lamson *did* call to see Percy, about seven in the evening. They met in the company of the headmaster, Mr. Bedbrook. Lamson had brought some empty capsules, in which powders could easily be given to the boys, as a small gift to Mr. Bedbrook "While in America", he said, "I did not forget you." To show how easily they could be swallowed, he filled one with sugar and gave it to Percy, saying "You are a champion pill-taker." Percy obliged. Lamson also produced from his bag some sweets and a Dundee cake, already cut. He gave a piece to Percy, and a piece to Mr. Bedbrook, and had a piece himself. Mr. Bedbrook provided a glass of sherry — in fact, it was because Lamson had asked for a little sugar with his sherry, as he said to counteract the alcohol, that the sugar-basin was on the table.

These festivities concluded, Dr. Lamson left in a hurry — an unnecessary hurry, as he had plenty of time before the next train. He told Mr. Bedbrook on departing that he "did not think Percy would last much longer." It was now about seven-twenty. Ten minutes later, Percy was taken ill. He said, "I feel just the same as I did after my brother-in-law gave me a pill at Shanklin."

163

This referred to an occasion when they had both been on a visit to Mrs. Lamson's sister, and Dr. Lamson had prescribed some medicine for Percy.

Before long, sickness and convulsions set in, but although the later accounts stress the horror of his suffering — the matron giving a particularly harrowing account — there cannot have been much alarm at first, for he did not see a doctor until nine o'clock. When the doctors did come, they could do nothing for him except give morphia to ease his pain. He died at eleven o'clock. Poisoning was suspected before his death — some kind of a vegetable poison, it was thought. (It turned out to be aconitine, the monkshood poison).

At once, Dr. Lamson was sought. He had in fact gone on to Paris, as planned. But when the news reached him that he was required, he promptly and voluntarily returned, and presented himself at Scotland Yard. Was this, asked the defence with some force, the behaviour of a guilty man? Why had he not fled to a country — easier to find then than now — with whom Britain had no extradition treaty? It was true that he had very little money, but he was young, strong, adventurous and his neck was in danger. One can only suppose that his return was a bold piece of bluff — unless, indeed, it was connected with his mental instability, to which we shall return.

By the time Lamson's trial had opened in the following March, the evidence against him had piled up formidably. He was prosecuted by the Solicitor-General and defended by Montagu Williams. Mr. Justice Hawkins presided, and that was not a sight to bring any prisoner encouragement.

Motive and opportunity for the murder he had in abundance. Means, too, for in November he had purchased aconitine from a London chemist. He had given his own name — another oddity, for he could easily have given that of another doctor. As it was, as soon as the name Lamson was mentioned in the press, the chemist's assistant reported the sale to the police.

There was also found, in his pocket-book, a detailed description of the symptoms of aconitine poisoning. Among Percy's belongings were found some pills and powders which Lamson had given him. They were supposed to be quinine pills, but some of them contained aconitine in amounts which would have been fatal.

Montagu Williams was a counsel who relied on aggression and emotion — rather like a Marshall Hall with the genius left out. He concentrated upon trying to shake the medical evidence — an easier task in those days, but he had no great success. He called no witnesses — the prisoner himself could not give evidence as the law then stood. Possibly Williams took this course in order to have the right of speaking last to the jury, but this was somewhat harshly denied him, the Solicitor-General exercising his superior privilege as a law officer of the crown. In spite of this, Williams pulled out all the stops in a speech lasting two days. He made particular play of the loyalty of Mrs.

Lamson, who every evening as the court rose would go to the dock and touch her husband's hand. A friend of Williams said to him of the speech, "I have never in my life been so terribly moved." It did not move Hawkins, nor the jury, who were out only half an hour before finding Lamson guilty.

Lamson himself felt it was a mistake calling no witnesses on his behalf, but he seems to have been thinking of witnesses to his good character, who could not have availed him much. There were, however, two other matters which might have been raised. The first concerns the administration of the poison. The prosecution's theory was that it was contained in the sugar-filled capsule. But Lamson had been under Bedbrook's eyes all the time he was filling the capsule, and Bedbrook had provided the sugar. The defence never questioned him on this. It seems altogether more likely that the poison was contained in the Dundee cake, which you will remember was already cut when Lamson produced it, and which he distributed. Indeed, a raisin-skin impregnated with aconitine was found in the stomach at the post-mortem. Then what was the capsule for? A red herring? Then why did the defence not seek to draw it across the trail? If the prosecution had been forced to recast their theory in the middle of the trial it could scarcely have brought anything but benefit to the prisoner. Or was the capsule just another of Lamson's oddities?

He has been called a "particularly cunning and subtle murderer", but in fact, as this narrative has made clear, he was nothing but a hopeless blunderer, his conduct logical only in terms of a subconscious death-wish. This brings us to another matter which the defence must have considered: his mental condition. According to his own account, he had been subject to mental disturbances from his early years, and these had been exacerbated by an excess of drugs, particularly morphia. After sentence he is said to have made a confession in a letter to a friend, but actually he does not quite do so. The key sentence is: "In my right and normal state of mind the compassing and committing of such a crime as that for which I must now die would have been utterly and absolutely impossible, and altogether foreign to my whole nature and instincts." He also says that the news of Percy's death "roused me as from a species of cloud." His great popularity with all sorts of people, and his wife's unshaken affection, lend force to this. There would seem to have been the makings of a defence of insanity under the McNaghten rules — did he know what he was doing, and did he know that what he was doing was wrong? A forlorn hope, perhaps, especially with Hawkins on the bench, but surely less so than the line Williams took. But at that time the defence could not run a plea of "Not guilty" and a plea of "Guilty but insane" simultaneously — nor indeed can they now, though the concept of diminished responsibility has given them more room to manoeuvre. They had to choose one or the other. Lamson pleaded not guilty, and short of returning the brief, that was how

Montagu Williams had to defend it. He could not say "We plead not guilty but if we were guilty we were insane"; and if the plea was "not guilty" there could be no investigation of the mental state of the accused by the trial court.

He retained public sympathy. Women left flowers for him at the prison. A meeting was held at Exeter Hall which urged his reprieve. Charles Reade, the author, was one who was convinced Lamson was insane. His execution was twice postponed because news came that a large number of affidavits on his behalf was being sent from America. But the Home Secretary, after studying them, decided that the law must take its course.

The Misfortunes of Edith Pegler

In the year 1908, at number 368, Gloucester Road, Bristol, there lived with her mother a young lady called Edith Mabel Pegler. She needed a job, and on July 1st she advertised her availability as a housekeeper, stipulating that it must be in a house where a servant was also kept. A dealer in second-hand furniture, who lived just up the road at number 389, answered her advertisement. He regretted that he could not afford a servant, but she liked the look of him and accepted the post. Indeed, she was so attracted by her George — that was his name — that after only a week she accepted his proposal of marriage as well. He was vague about his financial position — an aunt, he said, allowed him money, and he went about the country "dealing", but in those days it was not unusual for women to know very little about their husband's business affairs. They were married by special licence at St. Peter's Registry Office on July 30th.

They began a wandering married life, moving from one set of furnished apartments to another, as George pursued his business around the country. At the end of October, 1909, the business caused him to leave Edith in Southampton, but after a few weeks she was able to rejoin him at Southend. These absences were to become frequent, and Edith often did not know where her husband was. She must often have been hard up, because he rarely sent her money. However, she would return to him uncomplainingly. At Southend he had good news for her. He had made a successful deal in a seascape by Turner, and he bought a house with the proceeds. But he still could not settle down, and in 1910 they were back in Bristol, living in Ashley Down Road.

George was soon hard up again. Wherever he went, he made a half-hearted attempt to keep a furniture and antique business going, but it never showed a profit. Soon he was forced to raise money on the Southend house. But in August and September, he undertook another business trip, "to London and round the country", as he said. Once more he was successful, paid off his debts, and took Edith off to Southend again. Four months there, then to Walthamstow, then in 1912 back to Bristol, at a house on the Bath Road.

George's next absence was more prolonged. He was away for five months, and during that time he sent his wife only £2. His letters gave no address other than the building society with which he dealt. In the end Edith was forced to sell the antique business for what it would fetch — five pounds or so — and returned to live with her mother.

Then her husband wrote to her and asked her to join him in Margate. This time the reunion was less smooth. She naturally asked him what he had been doing, and was unwise enough to disclose that she had been making enquiries for him — and had not been so far from finding him, since her information had suggested he might be in Ramsgate. George was furious at this, and told her never to do such a thing again. However, he relented so far as to tell her that he had just got back from Canada, where, among other things, he had been lucky enough to buy an ancient Chinese image on the cheap, and sell it for £100.

For more than a year now they were together, coming west again and living at Weston-super-Mare. George invested his money, several thousands in all, in an annuity, and in buying some houses. But he was a bad judge of property, and sold them again after a few months at a loss of more than £600. Because of this, he explained, it was necessary for him to take to the road again. He was away about three months this time, but once more his gift for business stood him in good stead. He reported a successful deal in antique jewellery in Spain.

It was 1914, and still George and Edith continued their restless wanderings: Bournemouth, Torquay, Cheltenham, Bournemouth again, Weston again, Bristol again. George was away in September, but only for a week or two. His financial gains from the trip were not very great, but he brought his wife some lady's clothing which he had "picked up in a London sale."

They had been married more than six years now. Was it a happy marriage? In spite of George's eccentricities, the fact that Edith always went back to him suggests that she cannot have been too miserable. He was certainly mean, but there is no suggestion that he was physically cruel. Divorce was very difficult for poor people, but Edith could always have gone back to her mother. He was certainly strict about keeping her out of his business life. In November, 1914, or thereabouts, Edith made some comment about his annuity, and he told her, in rather strange terms, that if she interfered with his business, she would never have another happy day, as the world was wide, and he would forfeit it all. He was, however solicitous for her welfare, and about the same time as this conversation, when she announced her intention of having a bath, he said, "I advise you to be careful of those things, as it is known that women often lose their lives through weak hearts and fainting in a bath." This was certainly not a risk he ran himself, for she could only recall him taking a bath once, at Weston-super-Mare.

In December, 1914, though his financial state was now reasonably good, George decided he would "have a run round before Christmas with a young fellow I've met in Clifton." But Christmas came and no George. Edith heard nothing of him till February, when Detective-Inspector Cole and Sergeant Page called to see her.

For, as most of you will have known or guessed by this time, Edith Pegler had married — or thought she had married — George Joseph Smith, who was now under arrest, and in due course to be charged, tried and executed for the murder of three other of his supposed wives.

There is probably no more famous murder case in this century than that of "the brides in the bath", and we will not go through the whole story again. But it is interesting to compare in outline the events as they happened with the course of Smith's life as it appeared to his faithful and undoubtedly unsuspecting Edith.

He had been "married" three times before he met her. His first wife left him when he was sent to prison for receiving stolen goods. His second and third wives he deserted. He married his fifth wife while he was at Southampton with Edith, going to London for the honeymoon. Again he left her as soon as he had obtained her money and possessions. This money bought the house at Southend. His second absence from home was to marry Beatrice Mundy at Weymouth — number six. It took him three weeks to get her ready money out of her. He then decamped, writing her a false and vicious letter in which he accused her of infecting him with venereal disease.

But he had not done with Miss Mundy. Eighteen months later, apparently quite by chance, he met her on the front at Weston-super-Mare. Unbelievably, she agreed to go away with him again at once. This was the five months' absence when Edith went home to mother. He now tried to obtain control of the main body of Miss Mundy's estate, which had been previously denied him since it was in trust. He realised that he could only get at this money if she made a will in his favour, and then died. She made the will. He bought a £2 bath, beating the ironmonger down by half a crown, drowned Beatrice Mundy in it, and returned the bath, unpaid for, as he had no further use for it. He had already taken her to see a doctor, and talked much of her suffering from fits — he used this device in all three cases — and the coroner's jury brought in a verdict of accidental death, with no hesitation. Back he went to Edith, with

168

news of the Canadian trip and the Chinese image.

An odd incident now took place. George and Edith were now living at Weston, and both became friendly with a young governess named Burdett. George proposed to insure Miss Burdett's life for £500, and Edith actually went with her to the insurance company's doctor. But George, after paying the first premium, changed his mind and cancelled the policy, which was no doubt extremely fortunate for Miss Burdett. Edith disapproved of the idea — or so she later said — but still does not appear to have been at all suspicious. All the same, George may have decided it would be more prudent to stand by his repeatedly declared principle, and keep his home and business affairs apart.

On the next trip away, George Joseph Smith married Alice Burnham — number seven — at Portsmouth, and murdered her in just the same way at Blackpool a week later. The Burnham family were not at all happy about things, but again the coroner's jury found nothing suspicious about the death. Smith had clearly been revolving the possibilities of insurance and had insured Alice's life for £500, which the company duly paid. She also had had about £140 of her own. These sums were the profits of the Spanish trip and the antique jewellery, so Edith was led to believe.

Wife No.8 was a domestic servant called Alice Reavil, whom Smith met at Bournemouth, and, after the usual brief interval, married at Woolwich. He did not, or could not, insure her, so he was content to desert her with what money and property she had — not much more than £100 worth. His manner of departure was typical of how he managed these things. They went for a walk in a Battersea park, he left her to go to the lavatory and did not return. Alice's belongings had already been taken away, as she had thought for Clapham station, *en route* for a new house; her trousseau was the "lady's clothing bought at a London sale" which George brought home for Edith.

Wife No.9, and last, was the "young fellow from Clifton", with whom George thought he would take a run around. Margaret Lofty was a most respectable woman, and yet she left her family and ran off with Smith with very little persuasion, having insured her life first. She married him at Bath, and — after the usual visit to a doctor — was murdered by him the next day at Highgate. it was on this occasion, and so far as is known only on this, that after the murder he played for a spell on the organ — or more accurately harmonium — in the parlour. Once again the coroner's jury had no thought of murder. But the death was reported in the press. Alice Burnham's father saw the report. Mr. Joseph Crossley, the landlord of the house where Alice died, saw it. They wrote to the police. Although Smith used a variety of names for his marriages, the similarity of the Blackpool and Highgate deaths caused the police to start an investigation. It soon proved that there was plenty to investigate.

The character of George Joseph Smith has caused endless speculation. He was uneducated, not to say uncouth, and yet he exerted this remarkable influence over women — and women of very different backgrounds. Both Alice Burnham and Margaret Lofty were what that age would have called "ladies". There is no parallel with, for instance, Christie, whose victims were, apart from Mrs Evans, from the dregs of society. Edith is an almost equally perplexing, and infinitely more pathetic figure. Five wives deserted, three murdered, and yet to her he always returned, and if he was mean — as he was with everybody — at least he never harmed her. To her alone he wrote from the death cell. This affection, for what it was worth, she more than reciprocated. She gave evidence at his trial, but not vindictively. She did not, as some of the other survivors did, try to make money out of her misfortunes. Let us hope that the rest of her life was more tranquil and rewarding.

Tea with Major Armstrong

Herbert Rowse Armstrong was born at Newton Abbot, in Devon, in the year 1869. Thanks to the devotion of the two maiden aunts who brought him up, he was able to go to Cambridge. He read law, was admitted a solicitor, and practised in his home town and then in Liverpool. In 1906 he moved to Hay-on-Wye, on the borders of England and Wales, as managing clerk to a Mr. Cheese. He became a partner and took over the whole of the business when Mr. Cheese died.

There was only one other solicitor in the town, Mr. Griffiths, and he too was ageing and unwell, and forced to take a partner. So Oswald Martin came to Hay, and was soon practically running Mr. Griffiths' business. Two new solicitors, both with their names to make, and naturally a good deal of rivalry between them. Mr. Martin had been invalided in the first world war. Mr. Armstrong had served, too, but he had always been stationed in Britain, and managed to keep his business going.

Mr. Armstrong — Major Armstrong, as he like to call himself — was more popular than Mr. Martin, but either he was not a good solicitor, or he mishandled his own affairs, for in the years after the war he was in considerable financial difficulty. Perhaps part of his popularity sprang from sympathy. He had been married since 1907, and there were three children, but he was almost a caricature of the henpecked husband. He was a little man — he only weighed seven stone — and his wife was a termagant. She was, everyone said — especially after her death — such a *good* woman, so dutiful, so talented; but

Armstrong may be forgiven for taking a different view. No alcohol in the house; smoking confined to one room; but far worse than this was the way she humiliated him in public. "Come home, Herbert, it's your bath night." And once at a tennis party, in the middle of a set: "Six o'clock, Herbert. How can you expect punctuality in the servants if the master is late for his meals?" However, her conduct may partly be explained in terms of a nervous disorder, for in 1920 she entered a private asylum in Gloucester and spent six months there. She seemed better when she came home, but relapsed, and died a few weeks later, in February 1921. In those few weeks she had made a new will, leaving everything to her husband. Previously her children had been her chief heirs. About two thousand pounds was involved.

Neither the doctor, Dr. Ian Hinks, nor anyone else had any suspicion that the death was not natural. It was understandable that Armstrong should not seem too upset, and he settled down to lead a considerably livelier social life than he had previously been permitted.

Then several things happened which, in retrospect, seemed rather odd. After one of the dinner-parties which Armstrong liked to give, the local inspector of taxes was taken very ill with stomach trouble on the way home. It was later held to be significant that also at the party had been the clerk to the justices at Talgarth, an old man. Armstrong was already clerk to the justices at Hay, and it was known that he was hoping for the Talgarth position.

Then Mr. and Mrs. Martin — Oswald Martin had recently married — received through the post, with no explanatory letter, a box of chocolates. They were not chocolate-eaters, and put the box aside until some guests came: one of the guests who ate them was taken ill. An estate agent who had a business difficulty with Armstrong was taken ill after having a meal at his house, and died, after an operation for appendicitis. None of these incidents came to court, and it is quite possible that hindsight reads false meaning into coincidences.

Mr. and Mrs. Martin declined the invitations which Armstrong proffered so freely. However, he persisted and on one occasion Martin did take tea with him. During the meal, Armstrong handed Martin a buttered scone, saying "Excuse my fingers." Martin was taken ill as soon as he got home. Dr. Hinks was called, and became a little perplexed at the severity of the bilious attack. He had an analysis made, and found that Mr Martin had swallowed arsenic.

This was the moment of truth. Dr. Hinks began to think of the death of Mrs. Armstrong, and realised to his horror that many of her symptoms, which had been set down to nervous disorders, could very well be the result of arsenical poisoning. He consulted with the doctors at the Gloucester asylum, who also recognised the possibility, and the facts were placed before the Home Office.

There followed a period in which the comic and tragic made a macabre mingling. The Home Office naturally wanted to make the most careful investigations before taking any overt action, and Hinks and Martin were adjured to give no hint of their suspicions. In the meantime Armstrong kept asking Martin out to tea. A constant stream of invitations flowed across the street. Martin began to run out of excuses. When he persistently refused to stop at Armstrong's house on the way home, Armstrong started having tea in his office, and inviting Martin to slip across for a cup. In desperation, Martin started having tea in *his* office as well, to provide himself with a reason for refusal. The situation was complicated because inevitably the two men were involved in a good deal of mutual business, and so Armstrong was never short of an excuse to suggest a friendly chat with refreshments. Martin naturally found it a great strain — suppose more violent methods were to be attempted? — and he and his wife took turns to keep watch at nights. But Armstrong took no action save maintaining the barrage of invitations.

It is not quite clear why Armstrong should have sought to murder Martin — assuming that he did, for this again was a question never formally decided in court. Was he simply trying to put him out of business? — but the business would still have gone on, for old Mr. Griffiths' son was now qualified and back from the war. Did he fear Martin suspected him? Or had he reached the stage of self-confidence where he believed killing was so easy that it was the simplest course of action to take with anyone who displeased or inconvenienced him?

Arsenic has always been a popular poison. It is easily obtainable. Its effects are not at all easily distinguishable from a normal gastric illness. On the other hand, it is uncertain in its results — quite large quantities have failed to kill — and it can be readily identified at a post-mortem examination.

Thus when the Director of Public Prosecutions acted, and Armstrong was arrested for the attempted murder of Oswald Martin, Mrs. Armstrong's body was immediately exhumed. As soon as the coffin was opened, Dr. Hinks and Bernard Spilsbury felt they knew the truth. Arsenic preserves the body, and Mrs Armstrong's, ten months after she had died, was astonishingly well preserved. The Home Office pathologist later reported that he had never before discovered so much arsenic in a body.

The trial of Armstrong for the murder of his wife began in April, 1922, before Mr. Justice Darling, who was a good judge but is chiefly remembered today for the tediousness and frequency of his witticisms. Fortunately he restrained himself on this occasion. In retrospect, it seems that the whole question was decided by the opening exchanges. Was the evidence concerning the attempted poisoning of Martin admissible? After much argument, Darling held that is was, a decision that was sustained by the Court of Appeal. Thus the buttered scone, the arsenic in Martin's stomach, the grisly farce of the tea invitations, could all be brought out in court, and was bound to have

172

a powerful effect on a jury which might distrust — as they were to do in the case of Mrs. Hearn — the expert medical evidence concerning the dead woman.

Even so, *Sir* Henry Curtis Bennett, who was defending, put up a good fight. His strongest point was that Mrs. Armstrong had been of unsound mind and suicidal tendencies. Had she not been in a mental hospital, and had it crossed the minds of any of the doctors that her complaints had anything but a nervous origin? Less convincingly, he urged an absence of any sufficient motive. Little, henpecked men had been known to round on their wives before, and the money would be useful. There was, of course, no direct evidence that Armstrong administered arsenic to his wife, but equally there was no denying that he had ample opportunity.

The theory of suicide would become immensely more probable if it could be shown that Mrs. Armstrong had died of a single dose of arsenic, taken shortly before her death, and had not already been suffering from arsenical poisoning when she went into hospital. The earlier symptoms would be evidence of unsound mind, as the doctors thought them to be at the time, and suicide is inherently more likely as the result of one sudden impulse than a protracted series of doses. The medical evidence, however, claimed to show that arsenic had been in the body for well over six months before death. Curtis Bennett challenged this with the evidence of a Dr. Toogood, who declared it was possible for part of the arsenic to have become encysted, remained attached to the wall of the stomach, and distributed around the body *after* death. This theory, though perhaps no more fanciful than Birkett's theory of arsenic in the soil in the Hearn case, made no impression. The doctor cited a dubious precedent on which unfortunately the judge was better informed than he. As one writer has said, with a wit worthy of Darling himself, "Dr. Toogood's evidence was not good enough."

Opportunity, yes; motive, a qualified yes; and it was common ground that Armstrong had the means to commit the murder. He used arsenic in the classic tradition, as a weed killer; but his method of killing weeds was a peculiar one. He made up the arsenic into little packets — one of them was found on him when he was arrested — and, with a syringe, he injected the contents of these packets into the dandelion roots: one packet, one dandelion. He had, he said, made up twenty packets this way. The prosecution's suggestion, of course, was that they were a handy size for the tea-table. But one must add that Armstrong was just the kind of fussy, meticulous man to set about his weed-killing in so unnecessarily elaborate a way.

There was a stir in court when Curtis Bennett announced that Armstrong had, after his arrest, told his solicitor to look for a further, large packet of arsenic in a drawer to his bureau. The bureau had already been searched by the police, but sure enough the solicitor found the packet, caught up at the back of the drawer. Curtis Bennett claimed that this, with the dandelion packets, accounted for all the arsenic which Armstrong was known to have purchased — but this did not really help very much, for how many of the dandelion packets had gone to the dandelions? (Incidentally, though this was not allowed in evidence, some of the mysterious chocolates which the Martins had received were found to contain arsenic, introduced into them by a hole in the bottom, and the hole matched Armstrong's syringe).

There was a general feeling that Armstrong would be acquitted, in spite of a hostile summing up. One's impression, looking back, is that the suicide theory might well have been accepted had it not been for Mr. Martin's tea party. But the jury seem to have had no doubts. It was reported in a newspaper that the foreman asked everyone to write his verdict on a slip of paper. Eleven wrote "guilty" and one wrote "not proven". Pressed for an explanation, the twelfth said, "Well, you know what not proven means. I really believe the man is guilty." The foreman then supposedly said, "We've heard enough of the case and we needn't discuss it any more. Let's have a quiet smoke before we go back into court." This story has been quoted as a tribute to the jury system, but however casual their methods, it can hardly be doubted that as the law stood Herbert Armstrong was justly hanged.

The Lewannick Soil

On June 18th, 1931, Mrs. Sarah Hearn (more commonly known as "Annie") stood her trial at Bodmin Assize for the murder of her friend Mrs. Thomas. Some people spoke of it as "an open and shut case". It was not that: but it did seem that only two people could possibly have committed the murder — Mrs. Hearn, and the dead woman's husband, Mr. Thomas.

Mrs. Hearn and the Thomases had been friends and neighbours at Lewannick, a Cornish village. One afternoon in the previous October the Thomases had taken Mrs. Hearn on a motor drive to Bude. There they had tea together in a cafe. They ordered tea and cakes, and Mrs. Hearn brought out some sandwiches, saying she hadn't been sure what they were doing about tea. The sandwiches were arranged in two piles of three. Mrs. Thomas took one first, and then both the others took one. It seems almost certain that the sandwich Mrs. Thomas took contained arsenic.

She was taken ill on the way back, and put to bed as soon as they got home. Dr. Saunders was called in, and diagnosed ptomaine poisoning. Mrs. Hearn generously offered to stay and look after her friend. She did this for the next eleven days, cooking the food and giving the medicine. She had plenty of experience of this sort of thing, for she had nursed her sister Minnie, who had died of a stomach complaint, after a long illness, five months earlier.

But during this time her new patient's condition fluctuated, with no overall improvement. On the eleventh day Mrs. Parsons, Mrs. Thomas's mother, took over the nursing from Mrs. Hearn, but Mrs. Hearn stayed on and still did the cooking. There seemed to be some improvement, and the doctor thought she might safely eat more, suggesting mutton. When mutton was served for lunch, Mrs. Parsons brought back her daughter's helping almost untouched, but later Mr. Thomas took the plate in and persuaded her to eat it. Mrs. Thomas complained of a "sweety taste in her mouth", which was just the phrase she had used after eating the sandwich at Bude. From this time her condition deteriorated swiftly. Dr. Saunders became suspicious and called in a specialist, who diagnosed arsenical poisoning. Mrs. Thomas, delirious by now, went into hospital at Plymouth, and soon died. Her body was found to contain more than a fatal dose of arsenic, and it seemed that only Mr. Thomas or Mrs. Hearn could have put it there.

They had a conversation on the evening of the death. Mr. Thomas's manner towards Mrs. Hearn was unusually cold. He asked for an I.O.U. for a long-standing loan which he had never bothered about before. He then said, according to Mrs Hearn, that people were "saying things. They will put the blame on us, but the blame will fall heavier on you than on me." Later, there were some unpleasant scenes at the funeral, with Mr. Percy Parsons, the dead woman's brother, dropping heavy hints that Mrs. Hearn knew more than she should.

Mrs. Hearn now did her best to attract suspicion by running away, staging an unconvincing fake suicide by leaving a note for Mr. Thomas, and a coat on top of a cliff near Looe. She took a post as a housekeeper in Torquay, where she was traced the following January. In the meantime, the body of her dead sister, Minnie, was exhumed. It was established that there was arsenic in the body; and its presence in the hair led the Home Office pathologist to state that doses had been given during the last seven months of her life. Mrs. Hearn was charged with the double murder. She was tried only for the murder of Mrs. Thomas, but evidence concerning the death of her sister could be introduced. Henry du Parcq was briefed for the crown, Norman Birkett for the defence. The young Anthony Hawke held a watching brief for an unnamed third party.

The course of events as outlined was presented by the prosecution, and Birkett was unable to shake the evidence in any material particular. Quite early in the trial he abandoned any attempt to suggest that either death had an alternative cause to arsenical poisoning. The medical evidence was far too strong. He did, however, have one asset. For neither murder did there seem to be any kind of motive.

It is worth repeating that in a murder trial it is not necessary for the prosecution to establish a motive. But naturally when they can, they do; and equally the defence are entitled to point out an apparent absence of motive; and questions of motive, whatever the law may say, frequently have a powerful influence on the minds of juries.

It is therefore important that there seemed no conceivable reason why Mrs. Hearn should have killed her sister Minnie. Indeed, there was plenty of evidence that they had been on affectionate terms, and that Mrs Hearn had been a devoted nurse, not only for a few months, but for a great part of her sister's life — Minnie had always been sickly.

As far as Mrs. Thomas was concerned the situation was slightly different. When Mrs. Hearn was arrested at Torquay, Sergeant Trebilcock — the Lewannick sergeant — declared that he had heard her say, during her interrogation, in a low voice, these words: "Mr. Thomas used to come over every day with the papers, but of course that was only a blind." Sergeant Trebilcock could not be shaken on this in the witness-box, but not only did Mrs. Hearn deny saying anything of the kind: the two other police officers, who were both nearer to her than Trebilcock, did not hear anything either. During the trial the prosecution and the judge both hinted at the relationship between Mrs. Hearn and Mr. Thomas as a possible source of motive. Was an intrigue going on? It seems inconceivable that it could have been, in a village, without a shred of evidence or even rumour. Did Mrs. Hearn hope that with Mrs. Thomas out of the way she might marry him? There was nothing to suggest she had ever been given the least encouragement to think it possible. She was in her mid-40's, not particularly attractive, though she had some modern tastes — she liked jazz and smoked cigarettes. Mr. Hearn was a shadowy figure — he had left her after a brief marriage, and was believed to be dead. During the trial it was questioned whether he had ever existed. But what all this amounted to was that Birkett was entitled to say that there seemed to be no real reason why Mrs. Hearn should wish to kill Mrs. Thomas. (Mrs. Thomas had no motive either, except in so far as it is held a husband and wife may always have motives for killing each other).

As against the absence of motive, there was abundant evidence that Mrs. Hearn had both means and opportunity for both murders. Nobody else could have administered a series of doses of arsenic to Minnie over a period of months. Mrs. Thomas had taken at least two doses. The second one, presumably in the mutton for lunch, could have been given by either Mrs. Hearn or Mr. Thomas. The first one, presumably in the sandwich at Bude, if it did not rule out Mr. Thomas altogether, pointed very strongly to Mrs.

176

Hearn, who had made the sandwiches. Birkett sought to show that this dose might have been taken with the midday meal, which would have pointed to Mr. Thomas, but the five hours which elapsed between lunch and the onset of illness made this highly improbable. Birkett persuaded Dr. Lynch, the Home Office pathologist, to say it was "just possible there had been an abnormal delay", and made the most of this: but it was little enough. He did not seriously try to bring the crime home to Mr. Thomas — he had not the material for that. But by stressing points of this kind he did his best to draw the jury's mind away from Mrs. Hearn, to suggest other possibilities, however impalpable, which might cause them to hesitate. It is not one of *Sir* Norman Birkett's more famous defences: yet on reading over the evidence one wonders if an advocate has ever used so skilfully every scrap of evidence, however flimsy, which could be turned in his client's favour.

The supreme example of this is the question of the arsenic in the soil of Lewannick churchyard. It contained 125 parts of arsenic to the million, an exceptionally high proportion. Naturally Birkett wanted to suggest that this had somehow worked its way into Minnie's body after death. He cross-examined the medical witnesses in the closest detail about this. Without following all the intricacies of the argument, it is fair to say that he had no success whatever in establishing his point. Only a tiny proportion of the arsenic was soluble, and the amount that might have found its way into the coffin in water could not possibly account for the quantities found in the body.

But if this was so, how did the arsenic get there? Birkett had to have an answer, and the one he found was characteristically audacious — or, as it was also put, "sheer damned cheek". He simply ignored the expert evidence altogether. He had the right of the last word to the jury, since he had called no witnesses save Mrs. Hearn herself. By all accounts she made a good witness, though relying on nothing more than what P.G.Wodehouse called "stout denial". In his closing speech, despite all that had been said, Birkett dwelt repeatedly on this question of arsenic in the soil. He was concerned with the jury, and juries, especially country juries, are often sceptical about experts. Could it, he was inviting them to think, could it possibly be coincidence? — distracting their attention from the question as to whether it could be coincidence that two people to both of whom Mrs. Hearn, and only Mrs. Hearn, had access, should have died successively of arsenical poisoning.

It was a superb closing speech, with the kind of moving peroration which only Birkett could do, and not overdo. But according to one shrewd observer, a journalist reporting the case, one of the most significant moments of the trial had occurred during the previous speech of Mr. du Parcq.

Du Parcq was in full flow when Birkett passed a message to him via his junior, Patrick Devlin. The interruption appeared to distract him, and a few minutes later he collapsed in a faint. He was only able to resume after a break of some hours, and finished his speech seated. This, of course, detracted from its effectiveness, but — according to our observer — the atmosphere of the trial was changed from that point.

Very few of those in court, however, had much doubt about the result when they had heard Mr. Justice Roche's summing-up. While he duly and correctly explained to the jury that his views must not bind them, he can scarcely have left them in any doubt that he thought the prisoner guilty. Yet the jury were out for less than an hour before returning a verdict of "not guilty". According to custom the crown offered no evidence on the second charge, and Mrs. Hearn went free. She was shortly afterwards smoking a cigarette on the courthouse steps. When last heard of, she was holding a position as a housekeeper-cook.

The question has always been, what impelled the jury to acquit, in the face of an undeniably strong body of evidence and so hostile a summing-up?

First, it needs saying, and perhaps has not been said often enough, that the evidence *was* circumstantial and any jury might hesitate to convict in the face of such lack of motive. To say "Who else could have done it? How else could it have happened?" is not quite the same as saying that Mrs. Hearn was a murderer.

Mr. John Chandos, whose life of Norman Birkett contains the best study of the trial, quotes some words of the foreman of the jury, from a source, he says, "too reliable to be disregarded. We thought they were in it together", he said, "but we did not want to see her swing on her own." This may indeed have been the way the jury's collective mind worked, but there was nothing in the evidence to support the idea: moreover, the foreman was speaking in a pub to a crowd, and public feeling was very hostile to Mrs. Hearn. He may have given the reason he felt would be most acceptable to his audience.

The journalist observer of whom we spoke has his own theory. He believes that the jury were shocked and alarmed by the dramatic collapse of Mr. du Parcq. There is, of course, a strong religious streak in the Cornish, and there is biblical precedent for guidance by "signs from heaven". He believed that, though they might have hesitated to put it into words, this incident affected the jury deeply (they came from West Cornwall, since it was felt that feeling ran too high for Mrs. Hearn to be tried by a local jury).

There are also those who think that, in spite of its technical fairness, the force of the judge's summing-up produced a counter-reaction in a people notably disinclined to be bullied.

Finally, it is surely true that Mrs. Hearn would have been found guilty without Birkett's advocacy, and above all his mastery of a jury, on her side. Here we return to the arsenic in the soil. Despite the categorical expert assertions that it was a completely nugatory point, this was just the kind of matter, especially as Birkett handled it, on which a jury — *this* jury might seize. If today you ask anyone in Devon or Cornwall old enough what they remember about it, almost invariably you get an answer to this effect: "Ah, yes. That was the time Norman Birkett found arsenic in Lewannick churchyard, and saved Annie Hearn's life."

Birkett left the court immediately the jury had retired, and caught a train to London. At Exeter his clerk, Bowker, left the train and bought a paper which carried the good news. Birkett was in court next day in London, and at the beginning the judge passed down a note to him which read "With his honours thick upon him...".

The Boy from Bath

Nobody really liked the Homicide Act of 1957. Those who favoured the abolition of the death penalty were disappointed because it did not meet their main point. Those who believed that crime was encouraged by an undue tenderness towards criminals felt that the Act, with its introduction of "diminished responsibility" for murderers, was a step in the wrong direction. "Because thou art neither hot nor cold", the general opinion seems to have been, "I will spew thee out of my mouth."

Nevertheless, had the Act been in operation in 1952, it would have avoided many of the incongruities, even absurdities, which attended the trials of John Thomas Straffen. This is a singularly unpleasant case, even as murders go, but it does throw some light on the always vexed problem of a murderer's mental responsibility.

Straffen was twenty-two when he became a murderer. Let us begin with a look at his earlier history. He was born at Borden Camp, Hampshire, the son of a soldier, the third of six children. After some years of service in India his father retired, and settled in Bath, where it soon became apparent that John was a difficult, indeed a mentally retarded child. He was a truant; he stole things, and after several warnings he was brought to juvenile court and put on probation. The probation officer found him impossible to deal with, and it was decided on medical opinion that the boy must be certified as a mental defective.

There is a statutory definition of mental defectiveness. It is a condition of "arrested or incomplete development of mind existing before the age of eighteen years, whether arising from inherent causes or induced by disease or injury." There are further divisions of mental defectiveness, with which we need to concern ourselves here. The important point is that it is in quite a different category from insanity. An insane person, by legal definition, is one who has possessed sanity, but lost it through the onset of a nervous or physical disease.

When Straffen was aged ten, it was reported that he had a mental age of six. He went for six years to a school for sub-normal children. On the whole, he did well there, though a timid child who kept himself to himself. On one occasion he was suspected of strangling two geese, but this was not reported at the time, and can hardly be accepted as valid evidence since it only came out when he was accused of strangling other creatures than geese: hindsight is always ready to provide such stories on such occasions.

He returned to his family at Bath, and for some time he worked reasonably well in a clothing factory. But before long he was in trouble for a series of petty and usually pointless thefts, as a result of which he was committed to Hortham Colony, Bristol, under the Mental Deficiency Act. It was stated on his certificate that he was not dangerous or violent; and this was unfortunate because he had by this time been accused of strangling chickens and also of threatening to strangle a thirteen year old girl. Neither charge had been proceeded with, neither appeared on his record, and since his behaviour at Hortham was good, it was not surprising that after nearly two years the authorities released him, on licence, to an agricultural hostel near Winchester. Another small theft lost him his licence, but in 1951, though still on licence, he was allowed to go home. He now had a job on a market garden near Bath. He was twenty-one — still certified, but everyone was pleased with his progress.

On July 15th, 1951, a Sunday, Straffen paused in a field, on his way to a cinema, and strangled a five-year-old girl, Brenda Goddard. He was one of many interviewed by the police, simply because of his criminal record, but there was no evidence to suggest that he had any connection with the murder. Just over three weeks later, in another Somerset meadow, he strangled a nine-year-old child called Cicely Batstone. He had been noticed in the girl's company by a policeman's wife, whose description was sufficient to identify him. Thus Straffen was arrested, confessed, and was charged. At Taunton Assizes, he was found unfit to plead, and sent to Broadmoor.

There is no need to go into the harrowing details of these murders; except to say that there is no shadow of doubt that Straffen committed them, and that they were not sexual murders in the sense that no direct sexual attack was made on either child. Of course, there are doctors who hold that strangling can be a sexual perversion. The interest in this case lies in Straffen's mental condition, and the reactions to it of his judges, his guardians, and, ultimately, the law of the land.

After six months in Broadmoor Straffen escaped, and the same afternoon strangled a third child, Linda Bowyer. He was captured by Broadmoor nurses shortly afterwards — they had no idea that another murder had been committed — and fought violently before he could be taken back. By the next morning the body had been discovered, and Straffen had been charged in Broadmoor. He was tried at Winchester, found guilty, and sentenced to death. He was then reprieved, after he had been medically examined by order of the Home Secretary. He was sent to an ordinary prison to serve his life sentence.

Now, if Straffen was sane, there were no grounds for reprieving him. If he was insane, then the proper place for him was Broadmoor. The decision taken not only seemed illogical but affronted both main sections of public opinion — and public opinion was very vocal.

Possibly the Home Secretary was influenced by the feeling that if Straffen had escaped from Broadmoor once, he might do so again. He does seem to have escaped with ridiculous ease, and there was very rightly a strengthening of the security precautions there. At the same time, Broadmoor's escape record had been good — twelve in half a century — and the authorities had to face the classic dilemma of all mental hospitals: that you reduce the chances of a patient's recovery in much the same proportion as you forcibly detain him. Broadmoor is, of course, a hospital: and it was sad that a long record of successful rehabilitations, under the guidance of the then Medical Superintendent, should have been so grievously marred by the Straffen tragedy.

And now, hesitating as laymen must and even doctors will, what can we gather of the state of mind of this man who committed three such appalling crimes? We cannot really hope to get very far from its edges, but here are some clues.

There is his sheer ignorance, which must be expected in a mentally-retarded person. He appeared to think that he could not be convicted of murder unless someone had actually seen him doing it.

There is his total lack of moral sense, as we usually call it; at no point did he ever seem to feel any kind of remorse for what he had done. Psychiatrists looking for guilt complexes must have had to dig very deep to find any. He readily demonstrated how he had murdered Cicely on a policeman, showing no emotion whatever.

The policeman was perhaps taking a risk, for the grudge against society which every mental defective bears, seems in Straffen's mind to have become concentrated into an intense hatred of the police. This was the only motive he ever gave: "I did it to spite the police." It was not, perhaps, a hatred of the police as such; it was simply because they were the symbol of authority, and nearly all his life, or what he could remember of it, he had been subject to authority. Authority kept sending him to places where he did not want to go. Authority could govern his life by issuing a licence, by withdrawing it. His constant series of petty crimes, continued even when he was out on licence, brought him into contact with an endless series of probing, prying policeman: this is how it looked to him. It was no use explaining to such a mind that he brought their interference on himself, or that they were only doing their duty.

I suppose that it is possible Straffen might have lived out his life as no more than a minor nuisance to society, had it not been for two quite separate events which both occurred on July 10th, 1951.

That day, the Medical Officer of Health for Bath saw Straffen, considered his condition slightly improved, but was unable to recommend that he could be discharged from his licence, even though he was now over 21. Straffen, emotionally unaffected by much graver matters, was deeply upset by this, even though it made no difference to his immediate life: he was allowed to go on living at home, on licence, as he had been doing before.

That same day, July 10th, a small girl called Christine Butcher was strangled near Windsor. Straffen was not the murderer. No-one to this day knows who was. But the case received enormous publicity in the newspapers, particularly on the following Sunday, by which time the savage details of the story were fully reported. Straffen usually only read newspapers on a Sunday; and it was on that Sunday, pausing on his usual trip to the cinema, that he strangled Brenda Goddard. The coincidence of an acute personal disappointment, reviving all his hatred of authority, with a vivid suggestion of the possibilities of strangling as a means of annoying the police — who, as every newspaper implied, were in a great state of vexation and bafflement over the Windsor case: this coincidence precipitated the mentally deficient Straffen into murder. Of course, it can be argued that if he had not done it one way, he would, being what he was, have done it another. Nevertheless, such a particularly pregnant coincidence need not have recurred.

Straffen's story must surely have been in the minds of those who framed the 1957 Homicide Act. In his case, the mid-nineteenth century McNaghten rules still held sway. Did he know what he was doing? And that what he was doing was wrong? It is possible to give a qualified assent to both propositions. He knew that he was murdering children. He knew that what he was doing was — we will not say "wrong", for that word was meaningless to him, but at least he knew that it was against the law. On the other hand, as Laetitia Fairfield and Eric Fullbrook have pointed out in their admirable study of the trial, Straffen came very near to meeting the acid test of a murderer's responsibility — "would he have done it with a policeman at his elbow?" He was completely careless about being recognised and described even when in the company of the children he murdered. Only a few minutes before killing

Cicely Batstone he deliberately stood up in the field and showed himself to a passing courting couple. For all the efforts at concealment he made, a policeman might well have been at his elbow. No case, perhaps, had so thoroughly demonstrated the inadequacy of McNaghten as a guide to the responsibility of a criminal. Indeed, under their guidance two diametrically opposing conclusions had been reached. Straffen was insane, and then became sane because he escaped from a home for the insane and committed another murder. Then, after sentence, he was judged insane again, and so not hanged. One is inclined to use the word "insane" to describe, not only Straffen, but the entire muddled legal system which tried to deal with him. And though, as we began by saying, the 1957 Act was an improvement on what went before, our legal judgements of criminal mental responsibility still quaver inconstantly between the savage and the feeble.

SOCIAL AND INDUSTRIAL PICTURES

War in the Countryside
The Last Labourers' Revolt
"For the Term of your Natural Life"
St. Andrew's Day
The Boy Sweepers
Yeovil Gloves
The Lunacy Laws
Shaftesbury in Trouble
Kingswood School
The Poole and Dorsetshire Herald
Bristol and the Black Trade
Aeronautics at Chard
Up in a Balloon
Davy and the Lamp
A Somerset Mining Village
The Fifth of November
A Cold Christmas
The Ballot

War in the Countryside

In 1813 Britain's war against France was approaching its climax: but quite a different war, often just as savage, was occupying the attention of most English villagers. It was the war of the landlords and the poachers.

The war boom in agriculture did not benefit the labourers, most of whom were struggling along at a bare subsistence level or below it. In these circumstances they poached game. Since almost everybody did it, popular opinion was overwhelmingly on the poachers' side. It is very difficult to enforce a law which the majority of the public regards as a bad one, and so the landlords, who commanded parliament, had recourse to a series of increasingly savage penalties.

An Act of 1800 made imprisonment with hard labour the consequence of poaching: two years with whipping for a second offender. Alternatively, the criminal could be sentenced to serve in the army or navy, a fate which, especially as far as the special "condemned" regiments of the army were concerned, was usually thought much worse than imprisonment. Now that the consequences of being caught were so severe, poachers naturally took to carrying guns and hunting in packs. In 1803, therefore, an Act was passed which made any armed poachers liable to hanging. In 1816 even unarmed poachers became liable to seven years' transportation — which meant, in fact, transportation for life, since the state did not pay the return fare. A Wiltshire magistrate who had sentenced many men to transportation for various periods, proudly declared that he did not know more than one who had ever returned.

A haze of romance now surrounds the jolly poachers ("Tis my delight on a shiny night", etc) just as it surrounds the penalty of transportation, which was in fact so brutal a punishment that many men preferred death. A novel now largely forgotten, *For the Term of his Natural Life*, by Marcus Clarke, should be read by anyone who harbours doubts on this point. For his background, Clarke drew on authentic records. He did not need to invent anything to make the picture grimmer.

As for the poachers, we cannot match the description of J.L. and Barbara Hammond: "The woods in which Tom Jones fought his great fight with Thwackum and Bilfil...now echoed on a still and moonless night with the din of a different sort of battle: the noise of gunshots and blows from bludgeons, and broken curses from men who knew that, if they were taken, they would never see the English dawn rise over their homes again." And there is Cobber's story of the young man breaking stones on the roadside, who was asked how he could live upon half a crown a week. "I don't", he said. "I poach.

It is better to be hanged than to be starved to death."

The Last Labourers' Revolt

Whenever we get a bitter autumn in the south and west, with east winds and rain, our minds go back to the year 1830, and the tragedy of what is known, with some picturesque exaggeration, as the Last Labourers' Revolt. There was hardship that year of a degree which often reached starvation, and the countrymen, desperate for bread, stormed round in mobs, breaking up the threshing machines which they blamed for their unemployment, demanding money with menaces from the gentry and farmers and parsons. But it was all far too haphazard, far too unorganized, and, for that matter, often far too mild-tempered to deserve the title of rebellion.

All through October and November there was a grumbling discontent in Kent and Sussex, but in the last week of November it spread westward to Hampshire, Wiltshire and Dorset, and simultaneously became fiercer and more explosive. Wages in Wiltshire were seven shillings a week, sometimes lower, and in Hampshire eight shillings. The demand was for two shillings a day, and sometimes the men wanted a family allowance as well, say one and six a day for each child up to a total of four. There was considerable destruction at Fordingbridge where the mob was led by a gypsy called Cooper, who rode on horseback and took the name of Captain Hunt. Some think he was the original of the notorious Captain Swing, whose threatening letters were sent to landowners all over the south. At Selborne, the mob confronted the vicar, and told him "We must have a touch of your tithes: we think three hundred pounds a year is quite good enough for you." The farmers had agreed to raise the wages if the labourers could make the parsons reduce the tithes. The vicar signed a paper agreeing. After that, the labourers marched to the workhouse at Headley, and destroyed it, taking precaution to see that the old people and the children were not harmed. It seems a strange way of demonstrating against poverty, until we remember that the workhouses had become the symbol of a system which made poor relief necessary, and yet provided it only under the most humiliating circumstances. At Wilton, where the mob was led by an eighteen-year-old boy, four hundred pounds worth of damage was done in a woollen mill. At Quidhampton, another cloth factory was attacked, and this time the ringleader was aged only seventeen. At Pythouse, Tisbury, the house of Mr. John Benett, one of the M.P.s for the county, was attacked. He was a man who years before had threatened to pull down every cottage on his estate if Parliament should make length of residence a legal method of gaining security of tenure. He made a speech to a mob of five hundred or so people, and subtly pointed out to them that they could not trust each other, for any man, by informing against the rest could easily obtain rewards of hundreds of pounds. The labourers rejected this suggestion with contumely, and as one looks back on the scene from this distance, it is not they who come out of it without dignity. They threw stones at Mr. Benett, without apparently hurting him, and broke up some of his machines. A troop of yeomanry was summoned, and after a volley of blank cartridges had proved ineffective, they charged; there were many wounded, and one dead. At the inquest on the dead man, the coroner refused a warrant for burial, saying his action was equivalent to suicide.

All the same, there was a great deal of panic among the ruling classes, and in many places wages were raised, either as a result of trouble or for fear of it. It did look as if the labourers were not protesting in vain. "If", say the Hammonds in their great work on the village labourer, "the rising of 1830 had won back for the labourer his lost livelihood, the day when Headley Workhouse was thrown down would be remembered by the poor as the taking of the Bastille." But the glimpse of victory was an illusion.

Harsh retribution followed. The scattered bands of agricultural labourers were protesting against unbearable living conditions, and sometimes the protests had got out of hand. But there was no thought of an organised revolt, and no hope of withstanding a government ready to use force to restore order. The Whigs had just taken over from the Tories — the first true Whig government for nearly fifty years — a government to live in fame as the authors of the Great Reform Bill. Yet in the suppression of the rioters they showed themselves as remorseless as any Tory could have wished. It was only a few years since Shelley had written:

I met murder in the way,
He had a mask like Castlereagh.

But now the mask of Castlereagh, the methods of this grimmest repression, were assumed by the Whig Home Secretary, Lord Melbourne, the dear old man who was to be so kind to the young Queen Victoria. In the first week of December, he circulated a memorandum to the magistrates of the affected areas: there must be no more concessions. The rigours of the law must be enforced.

No life had been lost in the riots except that of one of the rioters when the yeomanry charged at Tisbury. Now there were many death sentences, a few of which were actually carried out, and more than 450 men — perhaps many more, we cannot be sure — were transported. There were terrible scenes as

188

they were parted from their families. One man asked permission to take his nine month old baby with him, her mother having died in childbirth, and was told by the judge he should have thought of that before. Some pardons were granted later, but no free passages back. It is not surprising that Australian stock should be so vigorous when one remembers this infusion of the best blood in the south and west of England.

Many of them were young. John Jennings, the 18-year-old who led the attack on the wool mill at Wilton, was transported for life. John Ford, who was 17 and one of the Quidhampton rioters, had the same sentence, though it was later committed to imprisonment. Henry Cook, a ploughboy of Micheldever, was 19. He could not read nor write — that was true of very many. He had been earning five shillings a week. He had gone round with the mob, and aimed a blow with a sledgehammer at Bingham Baring, a justice of the peace. Baring's hat was seriously damaged but not its contents. Cook was hanged. When his execution was questioned in parliament, Lord Denman gave a wildly inaccurate account of his circumstances and crime, and according to Cobbett the labourers of Micheldever subscribed their pennies to put a correction in the papers. When Cook's body was brought home, the whole parish went out to meet it, and for long afterwards they said at Micheldever that the snow lever lay on his grave.

"For the Term of Your Natural Life"

Perhaps a word or two more about the punishment of transportation would be in order: its savage reality, as opposed to the romantic empire-building myths with which, retrospectively, we associate it.

You are a Devon country labourer, and you have been caught poaching. You have been sentenced to death, but a generous authority has commuted your sentence to transportation for the term of your natural life. You have been torn away from your wife and children. You will never see them again, and they will probably starve to death without you. Now you are on the convict ship, and if you can get a glimpse from a porthole, you see the ramparts of Plymouth Sound dropping out of your sight for ever. In the prison ship, which is so crowded that you can probably only lie on your side at night, you are surrounded by criminals of a different kind — the footpads and the housebreakers. If you are young — and boys of 10 or 12 were sometimes transported — the long journey will have its special miseries.

When you reach Tasmania, you are assigned to an employer for labour. Your situation then is described by the governor, a stern man, defending himself against suspicions at home that the prisoners were not suffering enough.

> "Deprived of liberty", he says, "exposed to all the caprice of the family to whose service he may happen to be assigned, and subject to the most summary laws, the condition of the convict in no way differs from that of a slave, except that his master cannot apply corporal punishment by his own hands or those of his overseer, and has a property in him for a limited period only...Idleness and insolence of expression, or even of looks, anything betraying the insurgent spirit, subjects him to the chain-gang, or the triangle or to hard labour on the roads."

This was the life which Lord Ellenborough described in the House of Lords in 1810 as a "summer airing by an easy migration to a milder climate." He was not the only one to be worried at this feather-bedding of criminals, and of course transportation had to be made as unpleasant as possible if it were to be an effective deterrent, because the normal life of a country labourer was grim enough already. Ellenborough was speaking on a bill of *Sir* Samuel Romilly, the social reformer — proposing that death or transportation for life should not be imposed for the offence of stealing goods worth five shillings or more. Romilly's bill had passed the Commons, but was thrown out by the Lords. He tried again in 1813, and again the Lords threw it out. The voting was twenty to fifteen, and five Bishops voted with the majority. "The hungry sheep look up, and are not fed."

St. Andrew's Day

We regard St. Andrew's Day (November 30th) as a Scottish occasion, or possibly a Russian one, for at one time he was regarded as the patron saint of Russia as well (the Greeks whom St. Andrew brought to Jesus were presumably the founders of the Greek Orthodox Church). We were surprised to find that at one time the festival was celebrated with enthusiasm in many other places, including parts of the south and west, notably Sussex and Wiltshire.

St. Andrew's Day, like so many other saints' days, was a splendid opportunity for all the young women to find out about their future husbands; there are so many legends of this sort that one becomes inclined to think that young women in the past did nothing but conduct a series of intricate ceremonies which were supposed to give them information on this point. But this is an older tradition than most of the mistletoe-under-the-pillow legends. There is a medieval Latin prayer to St. Andrew on the subject, and these lines, written, at latest, in the seventeenth century:

> To Andrew, all the lovers and the lustie woers come,
> Beleeving, through his ayde, and certain ceremonies done,
> (While as they to him presentes bring, and conjure all the night,
> To have good lucke, and to obtaine their chiefe and set delight).

The "certain ceremonies" and the "conjuring" do not appear to have been exactly innocent rites; in fact, poor St. Andrew seems to have acquired something of a pagan hangover.

More interesting, and less easily explained, is that St. Andrew's was the great day for squirrel and owl-hunting. The object of this operation was *not* to catch squirrels and owls. It was an ingenious device, sheltered by ancient tradition, for a day's poaching without penalties. This was the day, according to one account:

> When the labourers and the lower kind of people, assembling together, from a lawless rabble, and being accoutred with guns, poles, clubs and other such weapons, spend the greatest part of the day in parading through the woods and grounds, with loud shoutings, and under pretence of demolishing the squirrels, some few of which they kill, they destroy numbers of hares, pheasants, partridges, and, in short, whatever comes in their way, breaking down the hedges, and doing much other mischief, and in the evening betaking themselves to the alehouses, finish their career there, as is usual with such gentry.

The growth of enclosed property, and the increased ferocity of the poaching laws, gradually brought this genial occasion to an end. But as late as 1905, it was reported that there were many living people in Sussex who remembered taking part in it. It is perhaps a pity that this festival has now gone so exclusively north of the border. Whether St. Andrew would have approved may be doubted, but probably Bobbie Burns would.

The Boy Sweepers

In spite of Lord Shaftesbury, in spite of Victorian philanthropy, in spite of Kingsley and *The Water Babies*, as the nineteenth century advanced, small boys were still being sent up chimneys to sweep them. A Children's Employment commission, in the 1860's, reported a widespread disregard of the laws against the practice. A houseproud housewife knew that the newfangled brooms were far less efficient than the good old familiar method: and as the demand continued, so did the supply.

Luke Bull of Andover had started as a boy of 6. He was, he told the commissioners, about 45 now, a master sweep, employing a small son of his own. "About 7", he explained, "is a common age for beginning, as a boy at 8 is getting too large to learn the work for which he is most wanted." He claimed to dislike the practice, but some chimneys had so many bends and turns that it was the only way, "and though I never saw a chimney where this could not be got over by putting in one or more traps, these dirty and spoil the place so, that some people will never consent to have them. The law now is not enforced, gentlemen's places cannot be spoiled so."

James Brown, a journeyman sweep of Winchester, had started climbing in Jersey before he was five. "A boy can learn as young as that, it is according as he gives his mind to it. Some chimneys are rough, and of course that skins you on the elbows, knees and back. Saltpetre, what they call brine, is the only way of getting over it." "Did you ever", asked the commissioner, "find any chimney that could not be swept without climbing?" "No", said James Brown.

John Taylor was the only sweep in Chard. After the Act against Climbing Boys, he gave up using them. "But since then the gentlemen have complained terribly of the machine, and said they must have climbers." So John Taylor had started training his 12 year-old son, but had still lost the custom of one gentleman, a county magistrate, who fetched a boy from Axminster instead.

Hezekiah Currie was a master-sweep in Sidmouth. He had never learnt climbing himself, but he had boys to climb for him. There were, he said, many chimneys with flat flues and no traps, which *had* to be climbed. William Salter, one of the boys, aged fifteen, had begun at eight. "Till then", he told the commissioner, "I used to go to school a bit, but cannot read or write." The commissioner reported that he knew the letters and a few words. Asked what the figure one seven meant, he said, "seventy-one".

Kingsley quotes the master-sweep, Mr. Ruff, describing how the children, ideally aged 6 or 7, were trained:

> The flesh must be hardened. This is done by rubbing it, chiefly on the elbows and knees, with the strongest brine, close by a hot fire. You must stand over them with a cane, or coax them by the promise of a halfpenny, if they will stand a few more rubs. At first they will come back from their work with their arms and knees streaming with blood, and the knees looking as if the caps had been pulled off; then they must be rubbed with brine again.

Perhaps the whole history of nineteenth-century industrial conditions, with all its harshness, does not contain a more brutal picture than that. Think of your own six-year-old.

Yeovil Gloves

In the glove industry of Yeovil, in the middle of the last century, work in the factories would begin at eight in the morning and continue until ten at night. In the small workrooms, where much of the manufacture was still done, the hours were often longer. Mr. Cleal ran a small workroom, with four or five girls under him, the youngest 8 years old. He was worried about one of the girls. She would arrive at half-past four or five in the morning, and stay until eight or later at night. "She was always for being at her work", Mr. Cleal told a parliamentary commissioner, and her mother said she could not sleep at night for wanting to be there. Unfortunately we have no corroborative evidence from the child, because she died.

Mr. Cleal's own daughter had begun under a glove mistress before she was nine, working fourteen or fifteen hours a day, less an hour and a half for meals. The mistress was very punctual. "If we were not there at six, she would not let us come in, and so we used to lose a quarter of a day. I left her at fifteen years old; I only got 1s 3d a week then. I could get much more at home working for myself. For a long time after I had learned I was paid only ninepence a week."

Emily Butcher was nineteen, and had been sewing since she was six. But her mother thought things were improving. "I have brought my younger ones up to service, for I think that is much better for their health than glovey; but I shall teach them glovey too, that they may have that to fall back on. I don't think they begin so young now; not many begin before 8 years old; one reason is that schools are so much cheaper. There is this one of mine I have kept at school till she is near nine, and I shall try to keep her there for another year, but I don't know how the work will go."

Mrs. Tompkins of Yeovil had ten children living. A seven-year-old daughter was just beginning work. Sometimes they worked all through the night when things were busy. "They do suffer in health", said Mrs. Tompkins, "and get very little schooling; they only go on Sundays." When she told this to the commissioner, a manufacturer standing by questioned her. He seemed, said the commissioner, very strongly opposed to any interference. Mrs. Tompkins replied, "If the Queen was to tell me that I must send all my children to school, I should just ask her to take one or two of them off my hands altogether, and be glad if she would." But these were not heartless parents:

they saw the choice as one between education and bread.

The girls worked at what they called the engine: a brass vice, of which they held the stem between their knees, sitting on a low stool. It was a cramped position, and the machine was heavy for young children. Mr. Hill, of Messrs. Bide and Hill, thought the continual stooping was the chief source of injury to the health. Two girls told the commissioner the stooping hurt their chests. There were many complaints of failing eyesight, which they attributed to the bright brass of the machine, but was more probably due to the feeble lighting in many cottages and factories. "The engine hurt me very much", said Mary Cleal. "My side used to hurt me, and sometimes I couldn't see...I know one now, a mere doll of a child, whom they set upon a stool at the engine. I am sure it is very bad for her."

Young Miss Cleal regretted her lack of schooling, and wanted to go to night school. But she was too frail to risk the night air. "Besides", she explained, "it is hardly respectable for a girl to be out in Yeovil in the evening."

The Lunacy Laws

Even today most countries are less advanced in our treatment of mental disorders than physical ones. A hundred years ago the position was far worse, even though a number of wise and good men — Lord Shaftesbury, one need hardly say, among them — had been striving for many years to make things better. Several Acts of Parliament were passed and a Lunacy Commission had been established: but its powers were limited, and the Select Committee on Lunatics which reported in 1860 showed how much had still to be done — how it was still possible for supposed lunatics to be incarcerated on the flimsiest evidence, and kept in appalling conditions.

The private asylums were often the worst. There was one at Plympton, of which some years earlier the commissioners had reported: "The cells were as damp and dark as an underground cellar, and were in such a foul and disgusting state that it was scarcely possible to endure the offensive smell. We sent for a candle and lantern to enable us to examine them." But just a few private asylums were among the best, and St. Thomas's, Exeter, possibly the best in the whole country at this time.

An Act of 1845 had made it obligatory for counties and boroughs to provide their own asylums, but it had been largely evaded. Gloucester had a good one; fifteen years later Bristol was only beginning to build. At Bath, the asylum was only a ward attached to the workhouse. Lord Shaftesbury told the Committee, rather quaintly: "I am bound to speak with great respect of everything that takes place at Bath, but the truth must sometimes be told. Bath affords a fair instance of the objections to these lunatic wards where there is not proper supervision and control, and no proper attendants. The person in charge stinted the wretched patients of their food, and it was discovered only by the increasing wanness and pallor, and by the decline in health and strength of the inmates. The whole sixty might have died of inanition."

At Winchcombe it was complained that the visiting doctor came to the workhouse three times a week, but into the lunatic ward only once a fortnight, though one of the patients was falling incoherent and could not eat. Since the doctor would probably have prescribed bleeding, however, this may have been just as well. In the countryside the lunatics usually fared worst: the workhouse would probably have no special ward, so they might simply be chained by the leg to a table, or, as at Okehampton, "boarded out". To be "boarded out" at workhouse rates very frequently meant a cellar and leg-iron, and food when the host happened to feel like it.

If the patients were not in fact mad when they entered the asylums, the chances were that they soon would be. Shaftesbury demanded the abolition of private asylums, run for profit, and the acceptance of care for the insane as a public responsibility. This was far too strong meat for the Committee, who suggested various safeguards, but came to the comfortable conclusion that confinement was rarely unwarrantable and treatment not all that bad. It is difficult, looking back, to see how they could have reached either view on the evidence available to them. Lunatics — the very name suggests it — still inspired much more fear than sympathy.

Shaftesbury in Trouble

We have had frequent occasion in this book to comment approvingly upon Anthony Ashley Cooper, the seventh Earl of Shaftesbury, and his efforts for social reform. Some would say he was the greatest Westcountryman of his time, taking things all round. Certainly in the bright Victorian galaxy his light shone with a rare steadiness and purity. He had many of the attributes of a saint, including that, not unknown among saints, of being difficult at times. He was a political philanthropist who changed the face of society, with a passionate hatred of cruelty and hardship. But *indignor quandoque bonus dormitat Homerus*: Homer nodded.

In the year 1860 Shaftesbury was occupied, among other things, with the hours and conditions of work of the hundreds of thousands of people still outside the scope of the Factory Acts; with boy chimney-sweeps; with the care of lunatics; with organising religious services for working men in London theatres — an experiment which was extremely successful, and for which he was much abused. He was so busy that he could spend only a short time each year on his Dorset estates: and this situation led to disaster.

When he succeeded to the earldom, nine years earlier, Shaftesbury himself with heavy responsibilities and nothing like enough money to meet them. The condition of the estates in his father's lifetime had often been heavily criticized. The factory owners of the north and midlands, who felt that their profits were endangered by his activities, liked nothing better than pointing out that he did not seem very concerned with human suffering on his own doorstep. The Rector of Durweston, Sidney Godolphin Osborne — a striking character — joined in the attack. A series of articles in the *Morning Advertiser* pointed out that agricultural wages and houses in Dorset were the worst in the country. One of the Shaftesbury tenants kept hunters, and paid his labourers six shillings a week. Another, in consequence of a trivial dispute, turned his head carter on to the roads, at five shillings a week. The accumulated evidence was damning.

Shaftesbury did what he could, even selling family pictures and land, to raise money. His house at Wimborne St. Giles was kept closed for most of the year. He began an extensive drainage scheme on the estates, and placed his agent, Mr. Waters, in charge — thus, it proved, making an unnecessarily complicated and awkward arrangement about the financing of the improvements. Waters was incompetent, extravagant, and almost certainly dishonest. All through 1960 the work was going on, the estimated cost being about £15,000. Soon after, the crash came; a long history of litigation added to the costs, and though Waters was ruined, Shaftesbury himself lost many thousands of pounds — and the condition of the estates was little better. In 1867 a Royal Commission reported that boys in Dorset were employed before the age of 6, and more young people employed than in any other county. The cottages were more ruinous and contained worse accommodation than those of any other county except Shropshire. Five villages were singled out as "a disgrace to the owners of the land." One of them was Cranbourne, a Shaftesbury village. The picture is a terrible one, and when all allowances have been made, it does leave a scar on a noble reputation. After all, Shaftesbury himself would not recognize the financial difficulties of the millowners as an excuse for the savage conditions in their factories.

The next report, in the eighties, gives a much happier picture. Shaftesbury had kept the estates much more in his own hands, and there had been many improvements by the time of his death in 1885. But Dorset farm wages were still the worst in England: ten or eleven shillings a week, at the height of Victorian prosperity.

Kingswood School

Village education, and indeed town education, was in a fairly primitive state even for those children who could go, at least until the passage of Forster's Education Act in 1870, which laid the foundations of a national system. But there were of course an increasing number of private schools, of varying merit. The evangelical revival had a considerable effect on the education of children, especially their religious education. One result of the movement was the foundation of Kingswood school, Bristol (now near Bath) which is described by Paul Sangster in his book *Pity my Simplicity*, a work both scholarly and readable. Possibly no educational institution has ever been the target of so much hostile criticism, and Sangster does something to redress the balance.

Let us begin with the criticisms. Kingswood was the embodiment of John Wesley's theories of education. It was to be, he said, a school "which would not disgrace the apostolic age." The curriculum was terrifying in its scope. A child of seven was expected to translate the *Praelectiones Pueriles*. There was no leisure. The day began at four o'clock in the morning and ended at eight in the evening, and every moment of it was occupied, save for meals, with work or devotions. A light was left burning in the dormitory all night, so that the children should never be without supervision. There were no holidays.

These rules were beyond the power of boys to keep, or masters to enforce, and as a result the life of the school was usually one of chaos and corruption, punctuated every few years by hysterical and shortlived religious revivals. Southey was led to say of Wesley that "no man was ever more thoroughly ignorant of the nature of children", and declared of the no-holiday rule that "no rule could better forward the purpose of those who desire to enslave mankind." W.H.Fitchett wrote that the system "was admirably calculated to make [the boys] either lunatics or hypocrites." Even Leslie Church, who is devoted to Wesley and his works, confesses that he "failed to understand the outlook of the child."

Mr. Sangster faithfully records the catalogue of condemnation, but adds a countervailing point or two. He quotes *Sir* Leslie Stephen as saying that Wesley "forgot that human nature existed in boys as well as men." But, he pertinently points out, this was exactly what Wesley refused to accept in men as well, and is one to call him a failure on that account? Undoubtedly Kingswood had its bad times, and the supposed revivals, for which Wesley himself must accept some responsibility, were the most nauseous features of all. Yet when he visited the school in 1786, five years before his death, he says "I found all things just according to my desire: the Rules being well observed, and the whole behaviour of the children showing that they were now managed with the wisdom that cometh from above." No-one who knows Wesley's character will imagine that this was a case of an old man having the wool pulled over his eyes: He had previously been acutely conscious of the school's shortcomings.

There is another interesting aspect of Wesley's educational theory. He believed that whenever possible schools should not be in large towns, but in the peace of the countryside, and the boys of Kingswood have always benefited from this principle. When L.K.Elmhurst was planning the foundation that was to become Dartington Hall, he said to his estate agent, "We're going to have a school, so it *must* be beautiful." It is an unexpected but a striking parallel.

There is also the point, which Mr.Sangster does not make — I suspect from the proper modesty of an Old Boy —that Kingswood today is one of the best schools in the country, and while one must not press an analogy too far, it is not usual for good crops to grow from bad seed.

It is good to have perspective restored on this remarkable educational experiment, so typical of one of the moods of its time, but when all is said, no-one can really *like* the early Kingswood. How *can* one like a school where all play was prohibited, and where the children were expected to sing the nastiest lines Charles Wesley ever wrote:

> We for no worldly pleasures plead,
> No innocent diversions need.
>   And Satan calls his joys:
> His rattles let the tempter keep,
> Or his own children rock to sleep
>   With such amusing toys.

The Poole and Dorsetshire Herald

Driving into Bournemouth from the west, one passes the familiar sight of the offices of the Bournemouth Times and Poole Herald, a low, handsome red-brick building set in attractive gardens. The forerunner of this modern, well-equipped newspaper, the *Poole & Dorsetshire Herald*, was first printed on a press behind a bookseller's shop in Poole on April 9, 1846.

The story of the *Poole Herald* from that day onwards has been one of steady success. But we are less concerned now to recount its history than to pass on some recollections of its early days, for which we are largely indebted to the anonymous author of an interesting article in the Dorset Year Book for 1954.

SOCIAL AND INDUSTRIAL PICTURES

When the *Herald* began, newspapers had to pay a heavy tax, and at fivepence, as money then went, its circulation was mostly restricted to the wealthy. It was not until Gladstone repealed the "taxes on knowledge", as they were sometimes called, that newspapers became a popular indulgence. With a population of only ten thousand or so, it cannot have been easy to run a newspaper in Poole. The *Herald* succeeded by adopting a policy of "something for everybody." Indeed, it still does: and it is remarkable, when one allows for the obvious differences of type and lay-out, how much a local paper of the 1850s had in common with its modern counterpart.

The local courts, for instance, were a mainstay, though reporters' comments were often more outspoken than would be risked today. William Bailey is convicted of "an unmanly outrage on a respectable-looking woman who has the misfortune to be his wife." He set the dog on her when she refused to give him money for drink, then brought back a pawnbroker and sold up the home. The magistrate fined him £5, two months' imprisonment as an alternative, and expressed regret he could do no more. The reporter, who to distinguish between the man and the dog referred to the former as "the human brute", criticised the magistrate and said he could have committed Bailey to trial. It is strange to find a lenient punishment at this period. A sixteen-year-old boy, by contrast, had six weeks' hard labour for throwing stones at railway trains.

The journalistic ambiguity was not then unknown. A young lady took a draught from the wrong bottle in the middle of the night, and instead of Epsom Salts consumed a quantity of sheep-dip, which contained arsenic. The report goes on, "in spite of all the aid which human skill could devise, she lingered until 12 o'clock."

Readers' letters: bad roads, a crowded cemetery — one correspondent claims the sexton had to go around prodding with a spike to find a free spot, and "I am sorry to complain about the dirty state of your town, but a more disagreeable place in wet weather I do not think you will find in the west of England."

Small ads: "a most extraordinary cure of nervous headache of upwards of 40 years' duration", sailings from Poole Harbour, those pathetic Victorian requests for employment from those who described themselves as "respectable", the shabby-genteel companion-governesses — and even the hit parade of the 1850s. In the sales of sheet music "My Mother's Grave" was fighting it out for the top spot with "O, Sacred are a Mother's Tears".

Bristol and the Black Trade

When William Wilberforce first decided to dedicate his life to freeing the slaves, Bristol was one of the principal slaving ports; only Liverpool had a bigger share of the trade. He first came to Bristol, to gather material for his campaign, in 1788. He found — in his own words — that "everybody seemed to execrate [the trade], though no one thought of its abolition." This was hardly surprising, since slavery contributed substantially to Bristol's prosperity. Wilberforce saw the slave ships for himself. They sailed from Bristol to the West African coast, where by duplicity, bribery or force the human cargo was collected; then across to the West Indies, where the slaves were sold; then home again. During the so-called "middle passage", from Africa to the Indies, the cargo was accomodated in the 'tween-decks. This was about five feet high, divided by shelves on each side, with a narrow passage down the centre. The slaves were chained and packed side by side on the shelves. In fine weather they were allowed outside briefly, and made to dance in their chains — to keep them healthy — while their quarters were cleaned. In stormy weather they lay, and often died, in a welter of vomit and dung. Wilberforce measured the allowance of space per slave in two ships lying in Bristol. In one, it was four square feet to a person; in the other, it was two square feet. He saw the quayside shops stocked with manacles, leg-irons, thumbscrews, and all the other necessary apparatus of the slaver.

Slaves, incidentally, did not come to Bristol itself. For some reason this seems a slight disappointment to modern Bristolians, who took certain pride in such local place names as "Black Boy Hill". There even used to be pictures of slaves standing on the scales, at Temple Meads Station. Yet it had been laid down, before the time of Wilberforce, that any slave stepping on English soil became automatically a free man. But the city's hands were badly stained by the business.

Wilberforce won in the end, as we know. The slave trade was abolished in 1805, slavery itself, throughout British possessions, in 1833. But the struggle was prolonged and bitter, during which the merchants of Bristol fought him at every turn. Oddly enough, Bridgwater was one of the earliest towns to petition against the trade. The Bristol merchants attributed this to jealousy. One Bristol man who did his best to save the city's reputation at this evil time was a surgeon called James Arnold, who had served on slavers, and gave damning evidence at the committee of enquiry about the unbelievable cruelties practised by captains upon their male, and more particularly their female victims. In 1789, Wilberforce delivered his most devastating attack upon the city. "All I ask of the people of Bristol", he declared in the Commons, "is that they would become as civilised now as Irishmen were four hundred years ago. Let us put an end to this infamous traffic! let us stop this effusion of human blood!" But it took another sixteen years to do it; sixteen years during which the Bristol merchants, between attending services at St. Stephen's, continued to safeguard the prosperity of the city and themselves by the profits of the infamous traffic. Long after the trade had been abolished, when Wilberforce was seeking to end slavery itself, Bristol kept fighting him. "If all that was published about me were true", Wilberforce said in 1816, in reference to yet another Bristol petition at the House, "nothing but a special providence can have prevented my being hanged thirty years ago."

But when Wilberforce's victory was complete, the economy of Bristol did not collapse. Over the years, indeed, it grew stronger; scarred in nothing but honour.

Aeronautics at Chard

The little town of Chard, in Somerset, has a niche in aeronautical history which has largely been forgotten. It was there, in 1848, that John Stringfellow built the first powered aircraft to sustain itself in the air.

Before any one says "What about the Wright Brothers?" let us explain that is was only a model, unmanned. Furthermore, Stringfellow's work has come under heavy criticism in recent years, and it certainly seems true that his former colleague, Henson, was the man with most of the ideas. Nevertheless, Chard has its place.

Henson was a Chard man, who worked in the lace trade. In 1842, he designed an "aerial steam carriage", which caused quite a stir, though a company formed to promote it failed. For several years he and Stringfellow worked on a model, with a twenty-foot wing span and a steam engine driving two screws. It was launched from a ramp, but the most it could achieve was a slow, descending powered glide. Henson was disappointed, and left for the United States. Stringfellow carried on. He built a ten-foot span model, based on Henson's designs, to be launched from a wire. This is the account which he gives of the Chard experiments, which took place in a long room in a disused lace factory:

"In the first experiment, the tail was set at too high an angle. The steam was again got up and the machine started down the wire, and upon reaching the point of self-detachment, it gradually rose until it reached the farther end of the room, striking a hole in the canvas placed to stop it." Later Stringfellow took his machine to Cremorne Gardens in London, and had one considerable success, which he describes as follows: "arrived at the spot where it should leave the wire, it met with some obstruction, and threatened to come to the ground, but it soon recovered itself, and darted off in as fair a flight as it was possible to make, to a distance of about 40 yards."

It was not, the modern experts say, a really successful aeroplane; they judge from the surviving relics that its capacity for sustaining itself was only marginal. Stringfellow's later attempts to improve or vary it were less successful still. Yet it was, after all, a remarkable achievement, not only for what was done but for what others were inspired to do: a step forward on a long road.

Up in a Balloon

We now take all kinds of aeronautical exploits so much for granted, that it is difficult to comprehend the fever of excitement that possessed the staid town of Cheltenham when in the autumn of 1813 Mr. Sadler and his son William prepared the ascent of their balloon.

There were several delays, but at last the weaknesses in the equipment were eradicated, so far as might be, and the weather — the governing factor — was favourable. At ten in the morning the balloon and its pendent car were brought out from the Assembly Rooms and taken to the yard of the Iron Railway Company, on the Gloucester road. Then the wind became too lively, the poles holding the balloon in position were blown down, and it was half past one before they could begin filling the balloon with gas. This took several hours, and it was not until nearly five o'clock that everything was ready, the ropes were cast off, and the balloon began to go up.

It was pear-shaped, made of white and crimson silk, and it impressed every spectator with its beauty, but few of them thought it was really capable of lifting Mr Sadler's son, who was to make the flight, and who was aged sixteen or seventeen. However, when the signal was given — we quote from a contemporary account — "the youth ascended with the greatest fortitude, waving a flag in the most exulting manner, the multitude cheering him with repeated huzzas."

Mr. Sadler, senior, set off in a carriage to follow the balloon's course as best he could; but he lost it when the wind freshened again.

However, son William was not discomposed. His balloon rose without difficulty to a great height — it is impossible, on the evidence, to say how high — but he encountered a heavy fall of snow. This decided him to open the valve and come down. He had a job to do it. He saw he was coming down on

Wedgwood Forest, which was no kind of landing-ground, and with considerable aplomb for a youngster, pulled the valve back into position, and looked for somewhere else.

He had been up for nearly an hour, the weather getting worse all the time, before he finally descended safely in a field near Chipping Norton. A labourer rushed towards him with a pitchfork, crying out — possibly the account is expurgated — "Lord, sir, where did you come from?" But the appearance of the Vicar saved him from any harm. He was taken to Oxford for the night, and next day returned in triumph to Cheltenham, where he was chaired round the town.

The only unfortunate thing about this gallant effort by the Sadler family was that they gained in reputation rather than cash. They had optimistically opened a paying enclosure to watch the balloon's ascent, but the surrounds were not high enough to conceal even the preliminaries, and the citizens of Cheltenham were content to look on from outside. Nor is there any record that, despite the enthusiasm upon William's return, it occurred to anyone that his exploits could be acknowledged by anything more permanent than applause. But this, as Kipling pointed out, is a common fate of pioneers.

Davy and the Lamp

Our father/grandfather, as we have mentioned, was a parson, but he had begun work in the pit at the age of twelve, and he worked at the coal face for a dozen years. Mining is not without its hazards even today; early in this century they were more forbidding still. But there had been a big improvement in the nineteenth century, and for this one man, and one invention, had been chiefly responsible. Father, who was proud of having been a miner though glad enough to leave the pit, treasured, to the point of reverence, his Davy Lamp.

Sir Humphry Davy, as he became, was born in 1778 in Penzance, where a fine statue in Market Jew Street commemorates him. His father was a woodcarver and gilder with some private means — enough to make him idle, insufficient to make him rich — and Humphry threatened to follow the same feckless ways. It seems to have been the responsibility brought about by his father's death, leaving him the eldest of a family of five with a load of debt, that caused him to pull himself together. Once he got started, his remarkable talents soon became obvious. His work in chemistry and galvanism at the Hotwells Institution at Bristol soon advanced his reputation. Had he never given safety lamps a thought, he would be remembered as one of the leading chemists of the nineteenth century, a distinguished President of the Royal Society, the patron and partly the inspiration of Faraday. Yet it is the lamp which rightly caught the public imagination.

A succession of terrible accidents in the pits, of which the chief cause was highly inflammable coal-damp, led in 1813 to the formation of the Society for Preventing Accidents in Coal Mines. Its first report declared that "it is to scientific men only that we must look for assistance in providing a cheap and effectual remedy", and their thoughts naturally turned to Davy. But Davy had left for the continent, and nothing was achieved for two years. On his return, he was approached by the Society's chairman, Dr. Gray (who was afterwards Bishop of Bristol) and immediately offered to do all he could. His very first letter of acknowledgement contains the seed of the idea from which the safety lamp was to grow. He started visiting the mines at once, and in two months had produced a prototype, and gave his famous lecture to the Royal Society on the problem. A few months later, John Buddle, a leading member of the Prevention society, after testing a safety lamp in one of the most dangerous pits, proudly declared "We have at last subdued the monster." Davy refused to patent his design, as he did not want in any way to limit its happy effects. The Durham colliery proprietors presented him with a service of gold plate; eighty-two miners at Whitehaven, forty-seven of whom could not sign their names, wrote him a touching letter of thanks "for his invaluable discovery of the safe lamps, which are to us life preservers." There were many such humble tributes.

It was not quite so good as it seemed. The early models of the lamp had their faults. Furthermore, the increased safety they provided led, unforgivably, to the taking of increased risks. But when every allowance has been made, it was still a revolutionary achievement. We can understand why, for father, many years later, his lamp was still a talisman.

A Somerset Mining Village

During their industrial troubles the miners have always had at least one argument to create sympathy. Pit closures can destroy communities. Villages, small towns, with a life of their own, built up over many years, would become derelict. There is always something sad about a deserted village, even if "wealth accumulates and men decay", even if it has not itself been a thing of beauty. One of us lived for years in a village which was, not so long ago, entirely dependent on coal. The coal has gone. The pits were "uneconomic". At High Littleton, in the middle of what was once the North Somerset coalfield, the last pit, Kilmersdon, closed in 1973.

Everyone knows about Somerset, or imagines they do. Somerset is where cider apples grow. It is where the green hills go rolling — or is it striding to the sea? It is where Alfred burnt the cakes, a considerable achievement since he had to do it at Athelney, which spends much of its time under water. We're all king's men in Somerset as we were long years ago, cries the song: another piece of nonsense, because one of the epics of the Civil War was Blake's defence of Taunton, for the parliament. Summoned to surrender, on the point of being starved out, he replied that he still had three pairs of boots left, and would eat two of them first. You can see his statue at his home town, Bridgwater. Later he took to the sea. He was probably a better admiral than Nelson: Nelson won his battles against much feebler opposition. Somerset was also, as we have seen, where Jesus landed, at Glastonbury, "with his uncle, Joseph of Arimathaea." Arthur, on the improbable assumption that he ever existed, is buried at Glastonbury. Et cetera. A long and lovely catalogue. But we do not think of Somerset as industrial territory.

Yet coal was worked here, in the northern part of the county, near Bristol and Bath, for centuries: possibly so far back as Roman times. Down and Warrington, in their *History of the Somerset Coalfield*, record 79 pits which have existed since 1750, though not all of them lived very long.

Coal mining has always been a dirty and dangerous business, and the Somerset mines can never have quite harmonized with the rest of the county. But what were the Welsh valleys like before they were mined? "Look what the bastards did to Wales!" Aneurin Bevan is reported to have said when he surveyed the wreck of what had once been a beautiful valley. We did not suffer so badly down here. We had some thoughtful coal-owners, notably the Jarretts of Camerton and the Rees-Moggs (yes, that family) of Clutton. It was because of such ownership that strikes, even in hard times, were rare. But the coal was not so good. The seams were thin. The great port of Bristol, the natural market of first instance, preferred Welsh coal, even though it meant bringing it across the Channel. So it petered out. There are still a few slag-heaps around, and a lot of those knobbly little green hills where the grass has covered the slag. But nearly all the equipment was taken away for scrap, and you could walk for miles about the pleasant countryside without realising you had been walking in coal country.

We come back to High Littleton, which may stand for many neighbouring villages. How has it fared? There have been losses. For one thing, the railways have gone, because most of their trade was in freight. The Somerset Coal Canal is mostly a brambled dry ditch. We are only about a dozen miles from Bath and Bristol, but buses are rare and eccentric. For another thing, there used to be three pubs in the village, when the miners had money to spend, but now there is only one. For a third, the village does tend to separate into two parts: the commuters (teachers, dons, businessmen, social workers) and the locals. You might almost say that the division can be marked by the doors between the parlour and the public bar at The Star. Some like juke-boxes, some don't.

Yet it is probably a happy village. There are no vandals, barring one family who become less of a nuisance as they grow older, and spend more time in gaol. There is some unemployment, but not very much, compared to the country as a whole. An old-established printing firm from the neighbouring small town of Paulton, Purnell's had a fine new factory built, playing fields and all, with some government assistance. They have had occasional bothers at Purnell's, now part of the B.P.C.C., notably at the time when the future of the *Observer* was in doubt, since they were responsible for its colour supplement. But redundancy has not been high. Most of the sons and grandsons of the miners are printers. They are not so high up the League table for wages, but it is a pleasanter job.

High Littleton is not one of the chocolate-box villages. A walk down the main street (which is practically all there is, except for two or three small housing estates branching off) still suggests the mining tradition of stern, grey cottages. The common accent is sharp, with an industrial twang, not the old Somerset burr. The centre of life is the pub. It ought to be the church (an admirable medieval building) but the church, at least until a year or two ago, rather kept itself to itself, or its own small flock. The remaining Methodist chapel, though it has no minister of its own, is a much livelier affair. But it is on The Star that most of the communal action centres. The landlord, a former policeman, has two darts teams running, two at pool, one at shove-ha'penny, and has hopes for a skittle alley soon. There is a soccer side, for which The Star sponsored jerseys. Rugby sides have been entered, with some success, in the Clifton Pub Sevens. There is an excellent representative on the county council, and a post master who, apart from running his business efficiently, is working on a book about the history of the village, though he is so conscientious about it, it may be wondered whether it will ever be finished. What is not yet achieved, though the battle is in progress, is a village hall, badly needed.

There is no need for a village, because what it has believed to be its staff of life is snatched away, to become a desert. Yet in a wistful way the mines are missed. Old Mr. Hathway died a year or so ago, one of the last of the "Greyfields" men (Greyfields was the biggest colliery in the whole field early in this century). His son is the village bookmaker, and one of his grandsons a Methodist local preacher. We can still see the old names on the maps and the signposts: Woody Heighgrove, Frys Bottom, Bilboa, Sweetleaze, Vobster, Ruth's Arse (we have never discovered where Ruth's Arse is, but it is in the records). Oh yes, we are proud of our mining tradition. But we doubt if, should the opportunity be given, there would be a rush to return. For better or worse, that's that. Life goes on.

The Fifth of November

The abortive conspiracy of Guy Fawkes, which we still honour with fire and mirth, occurred in 1605. Its observance seems to have become more widespread after 1688, when, on November 5th, William of Orange landed at Brixham and sounded the long-delayed knell of the Stewarts. For some time after that is was often celebrated as a political festival, a triumph of the Hanoverian Whigs over the Stewart Tories. But nowadays it is exclusively Gunpowder Treason which we remember, remember on the Fifth of November.

Bristol seems to have been about the first city in the country to make a formal occasion of Guy Fawkes' Day. In 1607, only two years after the plot, two great fires were lit by order of the Corporation, one at the High Cross before the cathedral, the other in front of the mayor's house. For many years the celebrations there and elsewhere remained much more a public observance than a private family party, such as we know today, with the squibs and the rockets, which Daddy fails to light properly, and the genteel glasses of sherry disturbed by a jumping cracker in the drawing room.

In the middle of the nineteenth century there was no eager expectation by a hundred thousand children. But there were, here and there, huge parties when the whole town turned out. At Rye a boat was pulled through the town, and burnt on a bonfire on the Salts — a form of remembrance which suggests disapproval of William of Orange rather than Guy Fawkes. At Lewes the Bonfire Boys led a huge procession with flaming torches. Bridgwater was *en fête*. Beacon Hill, above Bath, was alight, as it had been at this time for many years. Burning tar barrels went hurtling through the streets at Ottery St. Mary. Every inn then provided its own barrel, though today the business is more respectably catered for by the Carnival Committee. From the Plume of Feathers in Yonder Street the blazing barrel was carried, high overhead, by a succession of heroes, their hands swathed in sacking, towards Broad Street, till it grew too hot to hold, and finally burst. And this celebration, and some of the others we have mentioned, still goes on in a modified form, and attracts crowds from the neighbourhood. Cullompton had its tar barrels in the nineteenth century; so did Torquay. They would shake up Torquay a bit today.

In North Devon, they sang the familiar lines, "Please to remember", and so on, with this addition:

> When the old pope her doth return,
> In to the bonfire he shall burn.

So the origin of the feast, the overthrow of a catholic conspiracy, was still vaguely remembered. Sometime in the middle of the century the catherine wheel was invented, that pretty little thing which portrays the martyrdom of the popish St. Catherine.

In West Cornwall, a hundred years ago, they let off their fireworks in midsummer, on the eve of St. Peter, the fisherman's saint. The Mayor of Market Jew (the old name for Penzance) sent round the town crier at dusk announcing that fireworks were forbidden. Nobody was expected to take any notice, and nobody did, but the Mayor felt that is absolved him from legal responsibility for accidents. A writer in 1890 says that Guy Fawkes remembrance had quite died out in Cornwall, except for Launceston and a few other of the eastern towns. This assertion was premature.

The wilder Guy Fawkes celebrations undoubtedly owed something to the proximity of Hallowe'en: then the dead walk, hell opens, and hell is a place of fire. Born partly of paganism, partly of religious hatred, there is really very little to be said for the Fifth of November festival at all: except perhaps William of Orange.

A Cold Christmas

A hundred years ago the girls in the Scillies were going to church dressed all in white, for pride is never a-cold, and we should be proud at Christmas-time. In Somerset and Devon they still wassailed the apple trees on Christmas Eve. At Mellstock the village choir was setting out on its rounds, with fiddles and 'cello but, alas! no serpent, an omen of decline for the church bands. We still decorate our houses, but today mostly with coloured paper and tinsel and fairy lights, and then just with evergreens, the holly and the ivy. In Cornwall you bought a little made-up bunch of evergreens for a penny. It was called "a penn'orth of Christmas". In Devon, on Christmas Eve, they burnt the ashen faggot, for Joseph made a fire of ash wood in the stable. The ashen faggot is sometimes still burned, though perhaps more to honour the tradition than the faith. An observer in the Ashburton district wrote in 1870: "It is usual when the fire is well lighted and the wood beginning to crack, to place the youngest child of the household on the faggot; and its nerve or timidity is regarded by the old people as a sign of future pluck or otherwise." We trust no antiquarian zealot will revive this particular charming old custom. In Cornish villages — still Christmas Eve — children are dancing round painted candles burning in boxes of sand (but this practice was reported as dying). On Christmas morning, Porthminster Beach, St. Ives, is full of young men playing bickens, a kind of rounders.

Some things are the same; some, indeed, are new. Father Christmas came down far fewer chimneys then. Turkey gave pride of place to roast beef at Christmas dinner. Mincemeat still sometimes contained meat, especially in Cornwall. To eat twelve mince pies between Christmas and the New Year meant twelve happy months to come. Christmas puddings were made in all but the poorest cottages, though in the country only the manor houses had the brandy to set them alight. Christmas crackers are new, and Christmas cards as we know them, and Christmas stockings.

And the weather: the weather stays much the same, or at least complaints about the weather. The Christmas of 1860 was bitter cold. It snowed all over the country. In Hampshire the fall was the heaviest for many years. The railway lines converging on Bishopstoke were choked with snow from three to five feet deep. Christmas Day was the coldest day recorded in England for fifty years. The Severn was frozen above Worcester, the Avon on its whole course through Gloucestershire. A temperature of one degree Fahrenheit was recorded at Gloucester, and three degrees at Brighton. Cornwall did comparatively well. It was twenty-six degrees at Truro, and at Helston, the highest temperature recorded, just freezing-point. "The admirers of 'real Christmas weather', said a report, "will never wish for such another example." How the girls in the Scillies must have shivered in their white frocks! But pride is never a-cold. That is something that has never changed. It is still the same blessed child in the same manger.

The Ballot

In 1862, a Mr. Berkeley sought the leave of the House of Commons to introduce a Bill "to cause the votes of Parliamentary electors to be taken by way of ballot" — in other words, secretly. This was then a matter of some substance: when voting was public, a tenant, for instance, might well hesitate before voting against the known wishes of his landlord. Yet there was strong feeling against the change. Palmerston, the member for Tiverton and the aged but still lively Prime Minister, expressed himself strongly about the indignity of Britons "sneaking up to a ballot-box." *The Times*, equally contemptuous, declared that "the crazy old question had had its day, and...the panacea of our political evils had lost its credit with every set of men in the House of Commons.... The good sense of educated Englishmen has already rejected secret voting, and we hope that in a few years it will not be necessary to seek the favour of the crowd by falsely professing a conviction of its justice."

Mr. Berkeley's motion for leave to introduce the Bill was carried, but nobody expected it would go any further than that, and it did not. Not till Palmerston died, three years later, did a Ballot Act become practicable. And yet if one wants evidence for its necessity, one need turn no further than the graphic account written by Henry Hawkins, a lawyer, and later a famous judge, of his experiences at Barnstaple, where he stood as a candidate in 1865. Hawkins was clearly highly popular with the electors, as well he might be, since he was much the ablest of the four candidates. Yet he came bottom of the poll, through a steadfast refusal to stoop to bribery.

"Give it 'em, Orkins! Let 'em 'ave it!" they had cried at his triumphal reception into the town. Hawkins soon learnt, to quote him, "that a very different kind of influence prevailed than that of religion or political morality, and that it would be perfectly hopeless to expect to win the seat unless I was prepared to purchase the large majority of electors." "That", he added ruefully, "is what they meant by 'Give it 'em, Orkins! Let 'em 'ave it!'" After he had been defeated for Barnstaple, a friend told Hawkins that he had been making enquiries about the little borough of Totnes, but that the lowest figure required of a prospective member would be — as a first instalment — £7,000.

It was the Ballot Act, more than any other, which put an end to this kind of thing. Clearly there was no point in bribing a man if you could not be sure that, in the end, he would vote for you. "Sneaking up to a ballot-box" proved, in the end, a foundation-stone of democracy.

ODDITIES

In November, 1884, Miss Keyse, an elderly lady of Torquay, was found murdered among the ruins of her house, which there had been an attempt to burn. Her servant, John Lee, was found guilty of the sordid murder and on the morning of February 23rd, 1885, was brought out to be hanged at Exeter Gaol. Three times he stood on the drop, three times the bolt was pulled, and three times it stuck. The third time was too much for anyone's nerves, and the attempt to hang him was given up. Later the sentence was commuted. The drop worked perfectly before, between, and after the attempted executions.

Some while ago a letter was received from someone who claimed to be the son of an eye-witness, saying that in fact only two attempts were made. The letter contained much interesting and convincing detail, but it was valueless as evidence because it was anonymous. Even two failures would have been remarkable enough, though the story of three was the one that got around.

A letter from the prison chaplain to Lord Clinton says that Lee had dreamt the previous night that the attempt to hang him would fail, and that he told his warders so when he woke up. "Lee did not", adds the chaplain, "attach any weight to the dream. Up to the time of the execution he had fully believed he would be hanged. The dream did not come back to his mind while the attempts were being made, but only after he recovered from the semi-consciousness into which he had apparently fallen." And yet a signed statement from the warders confirms that he had told them of the dream when he woke up.

Lee survived his prison term, emigrated to America, and vanished from history.

Stories of the sea are not always noted for their reliability, but there is reasonably good authority for this one.

Robert Bruce was mate of a ship sailing the North Atlantic passage, round about 1830. One day, off Newfoundland, making his calculations in the cabin, he found himself sitting opposite to a complete stranger, who was writing on the captain's slate. He rushed out and found the captain, and when they came down the stranger was gone, but on the slate were written the words, "Steer to the nor-west."

Now the captain thought the mate had written it, but after conducting a handwriting test for him and for every man on board, decided that there must be a stowaway on board. They scoured the ship: no stowaway. After that, the captain stood away to the north-west, and in a few hours found a ship stuck on an iceberg. She had been there several weeks, but there were many survivors, and they were taken off. One of them was the very man Robert

Bruce had seen that morning in the cabin, and when he was asked to write "Steer to the north-west" on the other side of the captain's slate, the handwriting was identical.

What is more, the strange visitant had been asleep with exhaustion at the time of the vision, and when he awakened told his fellows that they would shortly be relieved, and accurately described the rig of the ship that was coming to relieve them.

Robert Bruce, according to a close friend, made no yarn of an old salt from this, but "always spoke of it in terms of reverence, as of something that seemed to bring him nearer to God than anything that had happened in his life."

In the second half of the sixteenth century the Fitzes were a well-known family in Tavistock. One night John Fitz and his wife, riding home across Dartmoor, were pixy-led.

Although they were only a few miles from home in familiar country, they lost the track and got into trouble in the mires. When they were near exhaustion and despair, they came to a spring and dismounted to drink. Drinking the water broke the pixy spell, and at once they realised where they were. John Fitz vowed that he would honour the spring and mark it as an aid to other travellers who might similarly be misled.

Now that sounds on the face of it very much like a sudden lifting of a Dartmoor mist. But John did in fact build a granite structure where the spring rises: it has his initials upon it, J F, and the date, 1568, and is still known as Fitz's Well. This seems a rather extravagant compliment to pay to a weather fluctuation.

John was a superstitious man. When his son, also John, was about to be born, he studied the stars, was appalled at the conjunctions he found there, and asked the midwife to delay the birth, if only for an hour. But it could not be done, and in due course the son did come to a spectacularly bad end. He did, however, produce a daughter, John Fitz's grand-daughter, and she too has passed into Dartmoor legend. For from time to time she rides at night in a coach of bones up West Street, Tavistock, and towards the moor, and if the coach stops outside your house there will be a death there. Or, if you prefer it, she rides from Okehampton to Launceston. But we have never seen the coach of bones; and you can still see Fitz's Well, near the Blackabrook, not far from Princetown.

Touchstone, in *As You Like It*, declares "I remember, when I was in love, I broke my sword upon a stone, and bid him take that for coming a-night to Jane

213

Smile... and I remember that wooing of a peascod instead of her, from whom I took two cods and giving her them again, said, with weeping tears, 'Wear these for my sake'."

Peascod wooing lasted a long time in the countryside. When the maid is shelling peas, she keeps an eye open for a cod with nine in. And when she finds it, she lays it on the lintel of the door, and knows that the next man to enter will be her husband, or at least her sweetheart. "Winter time for shoeing, peascod time for wooing", they used to say in Devon. And in Cumberland, when a girl lost her sweetheart, the lads of the village would rub her with peas-straw, which was supposed to provide consolation for a wounded heart — the straw, that is to say, though possibly the lads did as well.

There was a variation of peascod wooding in the North. It was called "a scadding of peas." they were boiled in the shell, and a single bean was put among them. Who drew the bean would be the first to draw a husband.

"Excuse me, sir", said the butler. He was reluctant to interrupt the master when the family had just suffered a bereavement, but nevertheless there was a duty to be done.

"Yes, Jenkins."

"The recent sad loss to the family, sir. Will you be informing the bees yourself, or is it your wish that I should?"

This incident, which is credibly reported in the early nineteenth century, does not stand alone. It was widely believed, especially in the West Country, that if the bees were not kept informed of a family death, they would desert their hives. The news had to be whispered separately to each hive. Sometimes, that the bees might observe the occasion with due ceremony, the hives would be draped in black.

They are susceptible creatures, bees. They are liable to leave if a man and wife quarrel. In Devon they were never paid for in cash, but always in commodities; and the only day it was safe to move them was Good Friday. When a man died, as his body left the house, the beehives were turned gently round. As the coffin of a Cullompton farmer was being carried to its hearse, the usual order was given, "Turn the bees." But the servant, who was unfamiliar with the custom, turned the hives upside-down. The bees reacted with such vigour that the mourners were despatched in a turmoil of flying hats and wigs, and the bees — with the corpse — left in possession of the field.

January 25th, 1753, was a Thursday, and therefore market day at Devizes, in the county of Wiltshire. Four women decided to go shares in buying up a sack of wheat. When one of them had counted up the money, there proved to be a deficiency, and it was suggested that a woman named Ruth Pierce had not paid her full share. She denied it with indignation, wishing she might drop dead if she had not paid in full. She repeated it. "May I drop dead if I haven't!" Whereupon she dropped dead. The missing money was found concealed in her hand.

Before you dismiss this story as old wives' moonshine, consider these points. The authorities were so impressed by the incident that they recorded it on a stone tablet, now in the Devizes Museum. Another stone inscription was set up in the Bear Hotel, and later transferred to the Museum. You may read yet another, although this was put up later, on one side of the Market Cross. More important than all this, and undoubtedly contemporary with the event, is the record of the inquest.

So it certainly happened that the unfortunate Ruth Pierce died in this way. And if you choose to rule out a supernatural explanation, you are at least left with a very striking coincidence.

Many of you will know Lulworth Cove, on the Dorset coast. The sea comes in at one narrow breach, and all the rest of the cove's circle is surrounded by high forbidding white cliffs. On September 7th, 1892, an 11-year-old girl slipped and fell from their summit. The distance of her fall was 300 feet.

It seems unbelievable when you look at the cliff, but she was not killed. By a happy coincidence, *Sir* Frederick Treves, the leading surgeon of the day, and a Dorset man, was staying at Lulworth, and was quickly on the spot to deal with her injuries. "She came down", he says, "with her back to the cliff. Her clothes were torn into strings, and it would appear that the catching of her garments on the rough face of the precipice, together with the circumstance that certain slopes and ledges were encountered in her descent, help to explain... her escape."

A further coincidence was that although *Sir* Frederick had never met the girl, or her family, he was reading a book by her father at the time he was called from his cottage to help.

She not only survived, but suffered no permanent ill-effects from her injuries.

In the seventeenth century, a leading citizen of Wimborne Minster, in Dorset, was Anthony Ettrick. He was a magistrate — indeed, it was he who committed the wretched Duke of Monmouth when he was captured after the battle of Sedgemoor. But Ettrick quarrelled with the people of Wimborne, and — the story goes on — swore that he would never be buried in their church nor out of it. It sounds an odd way of striking terror into the inhabitants, but in fact his executors solved the difficulty by setting the coffin in a niche halfway through the church wall. A fine coffin it was too, constantly and brightly repainted, because Ettrick left twenty shillings a year for the job. As a tourist attraction, the tomb has ensured that Wimborne did pretty well out of Ettrick after all.

The other interesting thing about the coffin is that it carries an extra date. Ettrick had it made to enliven his declining years, and since he was convinced that he would die in 1691, had that date inscribed upon it. But he was no prophet: he lived twelve years longer, and so you may see the second, true, date — 1703.

This is an incident recounted by the late L.A.G.Strong. Strong was always interested in the supernatural, and his evidence on such things is valuable, because he was too shrewd a man to be taken in easily and because he set out to prove no preconceived theory and, therefore, reported what he saw, and not what he wanted to see.

In his Oxford days he took part in a series of experiments in telepathy. He and a friend concentrated on a picture in Oxford, while in London a lady — she was a charwoman, as a matter of fact, who had shown some telepathic gifts — relaxed and tried to envisage the picture. Strong was satisfied that there was no possibility of cheating.

The picture was one of Charles I on horseback. The charwoman got it pretty well right, but in the details despatched to Oxford, there was one addition: what she described as a "blinkin' great cannon" in the foreground. There was nothing like this in the Charles I picture. Later, however, it was discovered that another picture in the book, quite a different one, sixteen pages away, did have a large gun in the foreground in just that position. Neither Strong nor his friend knew that such a picture was even in the book.

In the year 1822 the town crier of Plymouth announced on his rounds that Mr. James Brooks of Modbury was about to dispose of his wife by auction. Modbury was a small market town about fifteen miles away. Wife-selling was a fine old English custom, though it had never been legal, but it is surprising to find it going on so openly at so late a date.

Mrs. Brooks was advertised as young, handsome, and likely to succeed to an inheritance of £700. (What could have been the defect of this paragon? Probably she had a tongue). She would attend the sale in person, on horseback, The auction had already been "called" three times in Modbury market. This was apparently a process equivalent to taking down the banns.

The husband himself was auctioneer. The first bid was five shillings. After that the price rose slowly to £2. Then the ostler of the Lord Exmouth, who was attending Mrs Brooks, called £3, and he would have got her if two watchmen had not intervened (having no doubt taken care to see the fun first). The party marched off to the Guildhall, where both husband and wife defended their conduct vigorously. They were bound over and dismissed. It turned out that the auction had been rather a fraud. The wife had expected a "Mr. K" to come and bid for her; but Mr. K had been faithless, and in her disgust Mrs. Brooks told the ostler to buy her with her own money. This improper action on the part of Mrs. Brooks lost her the sympathy of the moral-minded public. And so far as we know, back she went to Modbury and her husband.

We do not know if all of this story is true. Some of it bears the marks of legend, but it also has a respectable ancestry, and the people in it were undoubtedly real people.

Sir Richard Hawkins was the son of *Sir* John Hawkins, the great Elizabethan sailor. Naturally Richard went to sea himself, and was captured by the Spaniards. They claimed the enormous sum of £12,000 in ransom, and although his famous father left £3,000 towards it in his will, *Sir* Richard spent nearly ten years in captivity before the amount was made up.

Now before his captivity Richard Hawkins had married a girl called Judith, and a proper miss she seems to have been. When they went from the Manor House to church (they lived at Slapton, on the South Devon coast) two pages went with her, one unrolling a red carpet before her and the other rolling it up behind. When *Sir* Richard at last came home, he found the village *en fête*, and was delighted that he should be so warmly remembered. But on enquiry, it transpired that the celebrations were not for him. They were for Lady Judith's wedding day.

He was just in time: and Judith stayed faithfully with him (at least there is no evidence to the contrary) until his death. He went to sea once too often, and was killed in an expedition against the pirates of Barbary.

In the year 1578 John Prideaux was born at Harford, a Devon village which hangs on the southern edge of Dartmoor. He was one of twelve children in a poor family, but he was a bright boy. In his 'teens, he applied for the post of parish clerk in the neighbouring village of Ugborough. There were other applicants, and rivalry was such that is was decided one candidate should tune the psalm for the morning service and the other for the afternoon. Prideaux was not chosen for either duty, and was much cast down. But soon afterwards, through the kindness of a wealthy neighbour, he went to Exeter College, Oxford, as a subsizar (a subsizar was allowed to study at the University at reduced rates, on condition that he acted as a servant to his more fortunate fellow-students).

In spite of this, Prideaux did exceptionally well. He became head of the college, vice chancellor of the university, chaplain to the king, and finally Bishop of Worcester. Although the puritans did not allow him to hold his bishopric for long, he died peacefully in a comfortable retirement. In his latter years he was fond of saying, as an illustration of how disappointments could prove in the end to be blessings, that "Could I have been clerk of Ugborough, I had never been Bishop of Worcester."

The perpetual curate of Brixham, in Devon, was down in the dumps. "Perpetual curate" was an official title, which meant much the same as Vicar — it did not mean that he was kept permanently in a kind of ecclesiastical fourth form. Anyway, Mr. Lyte — that was his name — was miserable. His health was bad, and getting worse. He had been trying for years to make his name as a writer of sacred poetry, but nobody thought his poems were very good. As a matter of fact, they weren't.

In his depression, he wrote a poem called "Declining Days". It was not much better than the rest, but it contained these lines:

O Thou! Whose touch can lend
Life to the dead, thy quickening grace supply.
And grant me, swan-like, my last breath to spend
In song that may not die.

Not long afterwards, Mr. Lyte's health became so bad that he went to Italy, where it was hoped the climate might help him. It did not, and he died there in 1847. But on his very last evening at Brixham, he wrote a poem and gave it to his family. Although he never knew it, for it was not published until after his death, he had at last written "the song that may not die." You may know it. It begins, "Abide with me."

Sometimes his friends would tease Isaac Foot a little because his brilliant brood of sons (two in the Commons, two in the Lords) had not all followed in father's footsteps — politically, at any rate. Then he would tell the story of Horrabridge Town Band.

Horrabridge is a little village in Devon, and to describe its musicians as "town" band must always have been a pardonable exaggeration. You go down a hill from the main Plymouth-Tavistock road. The village grows around you as you descend, and at the bottom is the bridge, the heart of the village. Immediately over the bridge, the road forks and climbs in two different directions, up the other side of the valley, the houses gradually petering out. That's Horrabridge.

One Carnival day, the Horrabridge Town Band set out in all its majesty and splendour, down the hill from the main road. At the back was the man with the big drum. It was a very big drum, and he was a very little man. So it came about that when they had reached the bridge at the bottom, and crossed it, all the rest of the band took the left fork, but the little man with the big drum, unable to see much, marched off to the right, still banging happily away, and quite unaware that he was parted from his colleagues.

But after he had gone some way up the hill, one of the villagers came running after him and shouted to him.

"Hey, mester", he said. "You'm gone wrong way. Band's took other fork. You'm all on y'r own this road."

The little man cheerfully carried on banging his drum while he digested this information. Then he smiled. "Dun matter", he said. "Dun matter at all. We'm all playin' same tune."

We wonder if there is anywhere in Britain now where groaning cake is baked. Sometimes it was groaning cheese. The cake or cheese was prepared when a wife was expecting a child, not just as a contribution towards the festivities, nor even as a guard against harm — we easily forget today that every birth was once a crisis — but so that various important rites could be carried out.

Pieces of the cake were carefully kept. It was reported of one old lady that she still had a piece of the groaning cake made for her first-born, "which she kept religiously with her Good Friday bun, full forty years unmouldy."

In the Cotswolds, the groaning cheese was cut in the middle when the child was born, and as the middle was hollowed out, gradually took the shape of a ring, through which the child was passed on its christening day. The first cut of the cheese was divided into small pieces, and each piece tossed by a young woman into the smocks of the midwives; to cause them to dream of their loves, it was said, though possibly it was also to ensure them safe deliveries in their turn. Or slivers of cheese, or cake, were put, more traditionally, under their pillows.

There was also, often, a groaning chair, in which mother would sit to receive visits of congratulation. This, says an eighteenth-century writer, "is a kind of female ovation due to every good woman who goes through such eminent perils for the service of her country." Since the proportion of births involving the death of either mother or child was then probably something like one in three, "eminent perils" was hardly overstating it.

In a Devon farmhouse a large family is gathered round the fire. It is All Hallowe'en. As the clock strikes eleven, the daughters each put a hazel nut on the lowest bar of the grate. Whose is the first to blaze? That one's who first will marry. Which nut cracks? Its owner will be jilted. Whose nut jumps? Jumping means a journey. And the nut that smoulders, but does not catch fire — that is the saddest, for it means sickness, and disappointment in love, and perhaps an early death.

As twelve strikes, the girls run out of the door and across the garden, all in different directions, and all crying out

Hempseed I sow,
Hemseed I throw,
He that's my true-love
Come after me and mow.

Out from the bushes rush the images of their future husbands, each chasing the beloved back to the house, each waving a threatening scythe. But the girls run back safely: though Mary, the youngest, says "Oh, wasn't I startled? Indeed I was, for I thought I saw Dick Harvey right in front of me as I turned holding a bright new sickle over his head!" But the prophecy was false, for Dick Harvey died soon after, on S.S.*Petrel* in an Atlantic storm.

In Cornwall, a girl is tying the front door key tightly with the garter of her left leg, wrapped between the leaves of a Bible opened at one particular passage in the Song of Solomon. She touches the tied key with her forefinger, and tries out names, and when the name of her future husband is mentioned, the key spins round.

Somewhere else in Cornwall, Godolphin way, just before midnight strikes, an unfortunate sneezer is seeking a remedy against that bane of physicians, the common cold. At this time on Hallowe'en you must eat a large apple beneath an apple-tree, wearing no other garment than a bedsheet. "A kill or cure remedy", says the ancient charm.

Earlier in the day, in Somerset, at Hinton St. George, the children have scooped out mangolds, cutting them to patterns, miniature houses and trees and whole landscapes, and are begging candles to light the tiny scenes. Down the village street they bear their offerings, and they sing

It's Punkie Night tonight,
It's Punkie Night tonight,
Give us a candle, give us a light,
It's Punkie Night tonight.

Punkie Night. The punkies, the patterned mangolds, portray the ghosts of the dead. Hallowe'en, which in spite of its name is a pagan and not a Christian festival, is the time when the souls of the dead return. Athens knew it in February, Rome in May, but at the end of October it is still the same festival, when protective magic is needed for fear of the vengeful dead. Even a hundred years ago, the magic had already descended into a half-serious game to choose a husband. Today, Hallowe'en is an excuse for a village dance, with masks and tenor solos and hearty councillors urging on the fun. Well, something has been gained, no doubt; but something, too, has been lost from the time when the festival carried with it a certain awe, a reflective moment dragged away from daily routine, when, it was said, the whole world of spirits intrudes upon the world of men with a threatening air.

Anne Jefferies was a Cornishwoman, who lived in the seventeenth century, who was carried off by the fairies, restored, and able to work great magic on her return. So much is a commonplace of mythology, but there are certain details about the story of Anne which have an unusually authentic air about them.

She was born in 1626, in the parish of St. Teath, and when she was nineteen became a servant in the family of Mr. Moses Pitt. It is his son, another Moses Pitt, who elaborates the legend in a letter, written in 1696, to the Bishop of Gloucester. Anne Jefferies was still alive then, and is believed to have died two years afterwards. The letter is printed in *Gilbert's Historical Survey of the County of Cornwall*, a reputable work of scholarship, at least in its latter part, and published in 1817.

First, as to what happened at her capture, for which of course Anne herself is the only authority. She was an intelligent and plucky girl. It was natural enough at that time that she should believe in fairies, but unlike most of her contemporaries, she did not fear them, but deliberately sought their company. For a long time they were shy of her, but one day while she was knitting in an arbour in the garden, she heard the rustle of someone approaching. She took it to be her sweetheart, and was a little irritated when he stopped outside. She

221

called out, "You may stay there till the cuney grows upon the gate, ere I'll come to 'ee." (Cuney is a Cornish word for moss). There was a peal of laughter, and six little men appeared. They blindfolded her and whirled her through the air to a place — well, she describes palaces of gold and silver, fruits and flowers, streams and lakes, fine ladies and gentlemen, dancing and singing. It is all a thoroughly conventional picture. More interestingly, she wandered off with the leading fairy gentleman, and they were passing the time very lovingly, she said, when the other five burst upon them, furious with jealousy. There was a fight, her lover was wounded, she was blindfolded and whirled through the air again, and there she was back in the arbour, lying on the ground and surrounded by anxious friends who thought she had been taken by a fit.

Now Mr. Pitt takes up the story. The first thing Anne cried out was "Look, they are just gone out of the window!" But for some time she would say little more about her experience. It was noticed that her behaviour became less assured than before, and she began to go to church regularly.

Then the cures began. Now supposedly miraculous cures by charmers and white witches were frequent enough in the seventeenth century. Anne Jefferies, however, was in a somewhat different category from the others, first because of the range of illnesses she dealt with — "all distempers, sicknesses and sores", says Mr. Pitt. The average white witch rarely coped with much more than warts, nose-bleedings and toothache. Second, Anne did not use verbal charms, but medicines and ointments — very unwitchhlike. She was never known to buy these: it was presumed that the fairies supplied them. People came to her for treatment from all over Cornwall, and even from London. She charged them no money, yet she never lacked it: the fairies again. More than that, says Mr. Pitt, "she forsook eating our victuals and was fed by these fairies from that harvest time" — when it had happened — "till the next Christmas day; upon which day she came to our table and said, because it was that day, she would eat some roast beef with us, the which she did — I myself being then at table."

Anne Jefferies fell foul of Jan Tregeagle or Tregagle, a justice of the peace, steward — and an unjust steward — to the Earl of Radnor. This Tregeagle is a recurring figure in Cornish folklore. For his sins he was ultimately sent to bale out a bottomless pool by means of a limpet shell with a hole in it. But there was a real Tregeagle, and, possibly suspecting witchcraft, he had Anne imprisoned in Bodmin Gaol and later in his own house. This suggests he was interested in her feeding methods: for though he deprived her of food, the fairies continued to oblige. After a time she was released, and went to live in Padstow, where she married a William Warren. The cures ceased — whether suddenly or gradually is not clear — and once more she became reluctant to talk about the affair. She told an interrogator, when she was an old woman, that "she would not have her name spread about the country in books or ballads of such things, if she were paid five hundred pounds for it."

One more incident is curious, for it is perhaps the only time a fairy has been known to quote scripture. The fairies called Anne from the family circle one day, and when she returned she was carrying a Bible. They had said to her, "What! has there been some magistrates and ministers saying we are evil spirits, and that it was all a delusion of the devil? Pray desire them to read the scripture: 'Dearly beloved, believe not every spirit, but try the spirits, whether they are of God'." "And", goes on Mr. Pitt to the bishop, "this place of scripture was turned down so in the said Bible. I told your lordship before, *Anne could not read.*"

In the first half of the seventeenth century western Europe, and particularly the Dutch, went wild about tulips. They were a comparatively recent importation from Turkey, and enormous prices were paid for the rarer varieties of bulbs.

A wealthy Dutch merchant, who dealt in tulips, and many other things, was one day pleased to receive a visit from a sailor, who advised him that a valuable consignment of goods had just arrived from the Levant. The sailor was an Englishman who came from Plymouth. The merchant was grateful for the information, and rewarded the sailor with a fine red herring for his breakfast. The sailor happened to spot an onion on the counter, and as he was fond of a bit of onion to his herrings, thought there was little harm in appropriating it.

A little while later, the merchant noticed with alarm that one of his most precious bulbs, a *Semper Augustus*, had disappeared. It was some time before it occurred to anyone to associate it with the sailor. They found him just as he was finishing his breakfast. He had enjoyed it very much; and well he might have done, for his "onion", at then current rates, was worth three thousand florins, or about £280.

RAILWAYS

Coaching Days
Brunel's Billiard Table
The Atmospheric
The Railway Age
The Cornish Railway
Summer Saturdays
David St. John Thomas
"A Race for Life"
The White Funnel Line

Coaching Days

The fine new roads of Macadam and Telford created, in the first thirty years of the nineteenth century, the brief but glorious heyday of the stage coach. But as with every advance, new problems were created, and there were not wanting those who looked askance at the craze for speed, and emphasized the increasing hazards to life and limb.

For instance, on July 27th, 1813, the Bath mail overturned between Reading and Newbury, the horses taking fright and bolting from the road into a gravel pit. A naval officer, on his way to join his ship at Plymouth, died from concussion, and only the softness of the ground prevented the other passengers from suffering more than bruising and shock.

At the Wiltshire Assizes in August, a Mr. Goddern brought an action against the proprietors of a mail coach, after suffering a compound fracture of the leg when the coach overturned immediately after leaving the yard of the Red Lion at Salisbury. The cause of the accident remained obscure. The coachman did not seem to have been guilty of any inattention, though it was suggested he might have done better to lead the horses out of the yard by the head. But a Wiltshire jury found for Mr. Goddern, and an assessor gave him the substantial sum of £600.

Two days later, at the Truro Assizes, Mr. Williams, a London merchant, brought an action against the proprietors of the Exeter-Falmouth coach, which had overturned on Polson Bridge. Mr. Williams had also suffered a fractured leg, and had several ribs broken as well. The negligence of the coachman was established, but a Cornish special jury took a less serious view than Wiltshire had, and all Mr. Williams got was £251. Most coach companies by then insured against these contingencies.

This kind of thing was happening fairly regularly, the damages varying widely, according to the degree of suspicion with which the fast new coaches were viewed. You had to be fairly well off to travel by them, even as an outside passenger. For the poor, the four-miles-an-hour covered wagon remained the standard means of transport, as it had been since the Middle Ages. But before long the famous coaches became as much a matter for national and local pride as the famous railway engines were to be in the next, and subsequent, generations. The *Quicksilver Mail*, for instance, one of the wonders of its short age, could take you from London to Plymouth in less than twenty-four hours, including stops. People would wait in the villages to see its maroon and silver glitter pass by. You can still trace the route of the Quicksilver by the old prints on inn walls on the old road to the west: indeed an inn at Yeovil, and probably there are others, is named after it.

When the railways came, there was much sentimental mourning for the coaches. Men spoke of the *Quicksilver Mail* as in these diesel days we speak of of the *Flying Scotsman*. It made no difference. Railway travel was cheaper, apart from being much faster: and the evening when the member for Exeter rose in the House of Commons and announced that he had been down to his constituency and returned, all in that one day: that evening the *Quicksilver* and all her gallant company were doomed, and insurance firms were facing a new and even more formidable series of hazards.

Brunel's Billiard Table

Not everyone approves of the bold engineering exploits of Isambard Kingdom Brunel. His ships were not very successful. His bridges brought criticism, though they are still holding up effectively, and he could never have been guilty of the monstrosity across the Tay which ended the career of *Sir* Thomas Bouch. His devotion to the broad gauge railway line may have been right in principle — it produced some fast times, and with the reduction in the overall mileage it is possible we could do with it now — but it went against the tide of opinion in his time, and finally the Great Western had to give in, and submit to the standard gauge which everyone else had adopted. Old people in Totnes, for one place, used to tell about that sad weekend, when navvies worked for 48 hours non-stop, all along the line from Paddington to Plymouth, and how the noise and the gas flares kept them awake, as the 7-foot road was brought down to 4 feet 8 and a half inches. Exciting, especially for children, but certainly sad: they felt that they were losing the best railway in the world. And the trains became slower, though more convenient if you had to travel long distances. The feeling was, and it still rumbles distantly on, that the West Country had been done down again by the bosses upalong.

Yes, Brunel made mistakes, as all pioneers do. He preferred illiterate men as his engine-drivers, because he thought illiterate men were less likely to be scared in the tunnels (well, that is a story long repeated on the Great Western, and offers an interesting psychological point). But his achievements were great, none more so than than his line from Paddington to Bristol. It was the first main line in the country, opened more than 150 years ago, and it remains, apart from the change of gauge, very much as he built it.

Quite soon it became known, among other engineers as "Brunel's Billiard Table". This was because he had chosen the route so carefully that the gradients were never more than 1 in 100, all the way from London to Chippenham. There he had to make a choice between a detour to the south, or a dive through the hills down to Bath. He chose the dive and the Box Tunnel was built, then and for many years the longest railway tunnel in the world. It was 3,212 yards long, and more than a hundred people died in the building. It took so long that money began to run short, so to encourage his directors Brunel took them on a visit to the tunnel, and invited them to descend from the hill covering it through an air-shaft, by means of a large bucket. To their credit, the directors went down, except one, who feebly excused himself on the ground that he had promised his wife not to put himself into any danger. Deeply impressed by the roar and sweat in the bowels of the earth, and possibly pleased with their own courage, the directors gave their approval to continuing the work.

The initiative for the line came from Bristol. Bristol still liked to think of itself as the second city in the country, and most certainly the second port, but its business men were disturbed by the growing prosperity of Liverpool, and correctly deduced that this had much to do with the Manchester-Liverpool railway, already open. They could conquer the competition, they felt, by a far more ambitious railway scheme. They found like minds in London, and set about it. Building began at both ends, and Brunel aged 27, was appointed chief engineer. It took longer to build than had been predicted, and cost more money — such projects usually do — and you may still notice that the outward and visible works of the line, the tunnels, cuttings and stations, are more impressive leaving Paddington and Bristol than they are in the middle, as cash ran short and argument increased.

The first section to be opened was London to Maidenhead, in 1838. It was 1841 before a public service was possible through to Bristol. The Box Tunnel was the major check. Even when it was declared safe for working, trains were stopped short of it, so that nervous passengers could dismount, catch a horse-drawn coach over the hill, and join a later train on the other side. A thousand men, a hundred horses, and forty boys worked the clock round in the last desperate days of finishing the tunnel.

Still, it was done, at heavy cost, and the question of a westward extension from Bristol had already arisen. The line towards Exeter was begun in the same year as that to Bristol was completed.

It is probable that if Brunel had had the original commission to build a line from London to Plymouth or Penzance he would not have gone directly through Bristol at all. There were easier routes to the south-west, as the London and South-Western railway later demonstrated, with its line through Salisbury and Templecombe to Exeter, and its *Atlantic Coast Express*, to travel on which was as exciting an experience as even the Great Western's *Cornish Riviera Limited*. The *Limited*, as it was always known, was hardly ever late. At school at Taunton, the sound of its passage was a sure sign that in five minutes the bell would go for the lunch break. When, years later, we lived at Totnes and the study looked out over the line, the *Limited* went through, double-headed, roaring up the Rattery bank, it was time to stroll up the hill to the *Castle* for the lunchtime pint. The *Limited* seemed to govern our lives in the west in those days. Once on the top of Cothelstone, hiking with friends, we caught its distant but unmistakable note, and paused to hear it pass. It was in the early weeks of the war, through which it kept running. No other train has had the magic of the *Limited*.

But Brunel's extension westward, though effective in keeping the L.S.W.R. out of the most attractive resorts in Devon and Cornwall, was not so successful as his bold billiard table had been. The G.W.R. cut off a loop, taking their trains through Westbury, missing Bristol altogether, but it did not bring much more traffic, and the south-western (later Southern) trains still got to Exeter — though not to Plymouth — as quickly. This led to one of the most comical situations ever to be seen on a railway line. The Southern trains from Plymouth (Friary) to Waterloo, crossed at Plymouth (North Road) with the Western trains to Paddington, going in opposite directions. The Southern line then trudged northwards off to Tavistock and Okehampton, the Western headed towards Totnes and Newton Abbot. At Exeter (St. David's) they would cross each other again. Away went the Southern down the Honiton bank, while the Western began the hard climb to Whiteball summit. No wonder that Gladstone thought, from an early date, that there was something to be said for the nationalization of railways.

The competition between these lines was intense, and probably contributed (though everyone virtuously denied it) to some accidents, notably a severe one at Salisbury, when a Southern boat train from Plymouth, driven much too fast, went over the bridge at the end of the curve through the station, with heavy loss of life.

The Great Western, it must be said, had a remarkable safety record. Only two major accidents took place on the main line to the west, both of them, oddly enough, at Norton Fitzwarren, just west of Taunton. The second of these was in 1941, and the bang woke us up in the middle of the night at school a mile away. The driver was exhausted by sufferings in the London bombing. More recently, since nationalization, there was a third nasty accident, also near Norton Fitzwarren.

From Exeter to Newton Abbot, Brunel experimented with atmospheric traction, the only serious attempt to try such a system in England. We shall return to this interesting subject. Brunel was hardly wrong about this; but a little before his time. At Plymouth where he built the Royal Albert Bridge, Brunel linked with the Cornwall Railway, and had his through line to Penzance. In these latter stages, he built, or approved, thirty-four viaducts of which the substructure was partly of wood, which sounds a perilous enterprise with all those sparks flying from the chimney. None burned down; all survived to be dismantled, and some of the stone piers can still be seen.

The engines, the Kings, Castles, Saints, Manors, which once thundered up and down the line to the west, are no longer with us, apart from museum specimens. Their successor is the Inter-City, which rattles you from side to side as you try to walk down the corridor. When the bar is reached, there is nowhere to sit down, so you stagger back to your compartment, and by the time you have reached it half your drink has been slopped on the floor. We are not against railways, do not think it. We often travel by them. But they have, to some extent, sacrificed comfort to speed. Speed is less important to a railway line than punctuality.

Much of the old G.W.R. tradition still survives on railways in the west. You feel that the staff are still pleased to be working there. You can sometimes still see an older member who wears, as it if were a badge of office, a rose in his buttonhole, as he gravely and graciously punches your ticket.

The Atmospheric

There was a time, in the middle 1840s, when many people believed that the day of the locomotive railway engine, hailed with triumph only twenty years before, was already done. Atmospheric traction, the new engineering miracle, was surely destined to supersede it.

The idea, roughly, was this. A piston was carried below the front coach of a train, and the piston fitted into a tube laid between the rails. The tube was sealed with a leather valve at the top. Stationary engines, placed at intervals of several miles by the side of the track, pumped the air out of the tube, creating a vacuum. The piston was drawn forward into the vacuum, taking the train with it. It worked on the same principle as the pneumatic tube, which we used to see shop assistants buzzing round overhead in big stores. Compared with the steam engine, there was hardly any noise, hardly any dirt, the "engine" did not have to haul its own weight, and steeper gradients could be tackled than any steam locomotive could then manage.

Four atmospheric railways were commercially operated, one in Ireland, one in France, and two in England. By far the longest was the South Devon line, engineer I.K.Brunel, from Exeter to Newton Abbot. It was intended to prolong it to Plymouth. A consequence which can still be observed is that from Exeter to Plymouth the line becomes less a billiard table than a switchback. You can still see the old engine-house at Starcross, and remnants of one or two of the others.

A good deal has been written about atmospheric railways, including a comprehensive survey by Charles Hadfield. It is a fascinating book, although occasionally he uses language which baffles non-engineers: the word "eccentrics', for instance — many of us will have no idea of its meaning, and since clearly he is not writing for engineers only, he might take the trouble to explain. But we can gather that although atmospheric railways had various problems, the chief of them was valve trouble. It has often been said that the leather valve at the top of the tube, and the grease which sealed it, had an irresistible attraction for rats, who constantly chewed their way through it and broke the vacuum. Hadfield deals with this story cursorily, while admitting it may have had a "substratum" of truth. Yet on the face of it the thing is not impossible, good historians have subscribed to it, and possibly it deserves greater attention than he gives. But however that may be, the valve certainly gave constant trouble, and though no doubt it could have been sorted out with more time, the directors were impatient for quick returns, and irritated by the breakdowns.

This was the real reason why the experiment was abandoned in 1848: it was because so many people saw in railways a quick way to fortune. The railway mania was approaching its height when the atmospheric was launched. Greedy shareholders refused to wait while the creases were ironed out, as with the improvement in materials they could have been. There was nothing impracticable about the atmospheric plan, and had the shareholders been prepared to stand the losses inevitable initially with such a revolutionary idea, we might have had an efficient and economical atmospheric railway system by 1870 or thereabouts. Robert Stephenson, who opposed Brunel on the subject, said that the atmospheric "was no better than rope haulage"; but enough had been done to demonstrate its feasibility, and the trains were quieter, smoother-running, and much less a source of pollution than the steam engines which are retrospectively so adulated.

The Railway Age

Today the problems of railways, railway men, and their passengers, seem always to be with us. If we look back, we can see that the troubles are not just a matter of declining service and poorer (relatively) pay. Partly they stem from the much lowlier position now occupied by railways in the public imagination.

In 1860 the Railway Age was going full steam ahead. The stage coaches and the canals could no longer put up any sort of opposition. The wonder of it all, the transformation of the nation's transport system in less than half a lifetime, seized public admiration. The early financial panics seemed to be over. At the beginning of the year it was announced that both the track mileage and the receipts had increased about sixfold in eighteen years. On January 31st, the railway examiners, who met daily for most of the year, investigated no less than six new lines in the west and south alone: in the Forest of Dean; an extension of the West Somerset line beyond Watchet; a line from Chard to Crewkerne; an improvement in the line from Liskeard to Caradon, and two new branch lines in mid-Sussex from Petersfield and Midhurst. This was one day's tally for one part of the country. The papers gave great publicity to it all. Every day *The Times* carried a column of Railway Intelligence. The battle between the Great Western and the London and South Western systems was closely watched. The Great Western had just introduced a Bill to extend their line from Great Bedwyn through Andover to Southampton, giving them a direct broad gauge all the way from Bristol. The L.S.W. were countering with an amalgamation with the Portsmouth Railway. Two hundred and two Railway Bills were introduced in the first session of Parliament.

In these circumstances it was not surprising that railwaymen lived in a nimbus of popular glamour, from the comparatively humble clerks, and "boys to attend first class passengers" — a recognized rank on the G.W.R. — to the exalted guards, conductors, engine-drivers, and "bobbies" (the old term for signalman). Men thought of an engine-driver as today we think of a jet pilot. And yet it was a working man's job, and we have noticed Brunel's experiments with illiteracy. The railway police, who had all sorts of duties, including inspecting the permanent way and ticket collecting, were splendid in their uniforms, and their truncheons, which in the G.W.R. were inscribed with a crown hand-painted in gold, picked out with red, green and white. The guards wore frock coats and top hats: at one time even the porters wore top hats with their green plush or brown corduroy uniforms. The station-masters, as the grade developed, were frequently as important figures in their localities as the mayors and chairmen of councils. And the staff had a sense of excitement, of pride, of limitless opportunities opening before them. The railways had their critics, notably in the pages of *Punch*, but to the great mass of the people they brought a sense of liberation. Fifty years earlier, if a man crossed England in search of work, what were his chances of seeing his family again?

The 1860s were one of the more prosperous periods of Victorian England, taking society broadly. The industrial population were certainly much better off than they had been in the "hungry forties", it was still a decade and more before foreign competition would cause the slump in agriculture. All the same, there was still much poverty and hardship about, and this was mitigated by a good deal of philanthropic work, a remedy which wealthy Victorians naturally preferred to the drastic social surgery recommended by the radicals, to say nothing of a German exile called Marx who was working away in cheap rooms in Soho on the first draft of *Das Kapital*.

Here is a characteristic extract from the *Exeter Gazette* in 1860:

> Mr William Palk, who has for some time evinced a kind and very great interest on behalf of the "navvies", gave a supper to more than 100 of them. Through the liberality of Lady Rolle, the men were supplied with some delicious venison pasties. After supper the navvies presented their friend, Mr Palk, with a silver goblet, subscribed for by men working in all parts of England.

As you will gather, William Palk was well-known for this kind of activity. Lady Rolle was married to the largest landowner in Devon. It is no disparagement of their kindness to suggest that a better way of handling industrial distress was through legislation, the way assiduously pursued by Lord Shaftesbury. He was no radical, but among his many other preoccupations at this time were the sufferings of the boy chimney-sweepers, which we have touched on in discussing Kingsley. The laws against this savage abuse were inadequate and often disregarded (as a matter of interest, Bristol had a bad reputation in the matter and Bath a good one), and it was to be many years before it was ended.

The "navvies" had long been familiar figures all over Britain, from the days of building the new roads and through the canal period, but they reached their peak under the railways. At one time they became almost a tribe of their own, a sort of industrial Romany. Many of them were Irishmen who had come over to provide cheap and plentiful labour. They lived in moving camps, with their own chapels and missionaries. The Great Western now had its through line (twelve hours Paddington to Penzance) but more and more the South-Western were stepping into the picture. An extension from Yeovil would soon link Exeter and London direct — it was on this task, one imagines, that Mr. Palk's navvies were engaged. The Great Western people were a little worried at the challenge, but felt ahead in the race, and in the assurance of their safety record. There were forty-five railway collisions, involving passengers, in the year 1860. Only one of them, and that causing no death, was on the Great Western.

Now that the branch lines close one by one, and the rockets occupy the headlines, now that six hours from Plymouth to Paddington is counted a slow train, now that the railwaymen are no longer the unchallenged aristocrats of the working class, we cannot expect to find things the same.

The Cornish Railway

Although, as must be manifest, we have always been interested in railways, we do not belong to that inner circle of expert enthusiasts for whom the sun and moon revolve around the permanent way, and whose conversation is all aglow with 4-4-0s and 2-4-2s, with domeless boilers, cylinder saddle tanks, and inverted queen post arrangements. But it does not need technical proficiency to appreciate the drama of railway development in the last century, particularly in a county such as Cornwall, whose geographical position and terrain presented special difficulties.

One is struck by the touching faith which the public, and investors large and small, continued to have in the marvellous new invention. Cornwall needed to have essentially one railway down its long, narrow spine. All the rest would be branches from that, likely to run at a loss. In fact the losses were so regular, and often so large, that very few of them survived. The complicated network in North Cornwall, made worse by the rivalry and lack of common planning between the G.W.R. and the L.S.W.R. was an added difficulty. Even the main line itself, even after the Royal Albert Bridge provided the juncture with the Great Western, was only profitable part of the time, notably at summer week-ends. And yet every time a new line was proposed, however thin and scattered the population it was to serve, it found ready supporters. *Punch* published a map of England as it might be in the twentieth century — the country almost obliterated by criss-crossing railway lines. The internal combustion engine, whatever its drawbacks, at least saved us from that. It is astonishing how *much* railway track there has been in Cornwall at one time and another.

Of course some of the branch lines had their own beauties. The line from St. Erth to St. Ives, which still survives, partly through the support of local government, is one of the most lovely in the country, with its magnificent views across St. Ives Bay. The line from Liskeard to Looe passes through some fine country, and was a considerable feat of engineering. But inland Cornwall does not have much natural beauty. The coast is its glory.

Leslie Woodfin wrote an enjoyable history of the Cornish railway to mark its centenary. At least, it is less a history than a source-book for historians. Every imaginable fact about the Cornish railways, their engines and rolling-stock, their viaducts and bridges, is crammed in. There is no perspective, no attempt to tell the story in its social and historical setting. At the same time, there is a mass of information, much of it fascinating. The battle of the broad and narrow gauges, for instance; the building of the Royal Albert Bridge — in the early days you could buy a threepenny ticket and walk across, the company accepting no responsibility for your safety; the remarkable agility of the repair gangs of Brunel's old wooden viaducts; the gradual development of lavatories, and dining cars, and sleeping berths. There were fifty-nine varieties of Great Western restaurant cars, and Mr. Woodfin knows the lot. It is impossible not to be touched by such devotion.

Summer Saturdays

Summer Saturdays in the West is one of those railway books which has considerable appeal for laymen, though for the specialists there are lovely long statistical appendices. In his introduction, David St. John Thomas, who is the managing director of the publishers, David & Charles, tells us how the book came to be. Simon Rocksborough Smith, with some colleagues, made a detailed record of the working of the main line to the west on 27th July 1957, probably the busiest day in the history of the West Country lines. Peter Gray provided many appropriate photographs to go with it. This was a famous day among the public as well as the railwaymen, for its ferocious delays and the desperate expedients with which British Rail tried to cope with them. It was a day which must have made a thousand or so more families determined that whatever happened next year, they would manage to buy a car. It was one of the days when the steam locomotive, nearing the end of its life, was manifestly incapable of doing the work put upon it. But it would be hard to tell all this from Simon Rocksborough Smith's detached notes, full and careful though they are. So David St. John Thomas himself wrote an introductory chapter, giving the setting for the day, and calling to mind — he was a railway journalist himself once — many other hot and steamy Saturdays in the holiday season; and this gives the book depth and balance. Perhaps, even so, the authors might have allowed themselves an occasional glimpse of something other than the trains: particularly the people.

For instance, the 9.05am from Birkenhead to Plymouth, arrived at Newton Abbot just under four hours late. What did they look like, what did they say, all those Liverpudlians travelling with families of five, when they arrived at Newton Abbot four hours late, with hours still to go unless they happened to be going to Torbay? Were there any buffet cars on? Improbable, in those days; perhaps an expensive restaurant car. Were the lavatories working? They were very likely clogged up with nappy liners before they reached Crewe. Every train to go on the down line through Newton Abbot that afternoon was at least two hours late. The Atlantic Coast Express, on the southern line from Waterloo, arrived at Exeter two hours before the express which had left Paddington at the same time. Of course, the southern region did not have to cope with the holiday trade from the midlands and the north. What did the people on the up trains say, those who were not quite so severely delayed but had finished their holidays, when they found their trains held up so that a clear run could be given to the Millbay-Paddington Ocean Liner Express, which of course took precedence because it contained a higher proportion of first-class passengers, and tourists helping the export drive? Probably they were never allowed to know. The authors make a comparison of that day in 1957 with a similar day in 1971. Things were much better then. That was to be expected, because the number of passengers was far fewer: all the same, it does seem from the evidence that the diesel is more reliable and manoeuvrable than the steam locomotive, and that, no doubt partly as a consequence, British Rail in the west is much more swift and sure in dealing with emergencies. Delays and awkwardness there will always be: but if some of those who were put off rail travel for life by their experiences on those summer Saturdays thirty years ago, were to return and try it again today, they might be pleasantly surprised.

David St. John Thomas
(A personal reminiscence by Alan Gibson)

Regionalism is becoming fashionable, but you would not expect a leading publisher to operate from a railway station in South Devon. At Newton Abbot, however (change for Torquay) you will find the headquarters of David & Charles. The choice was not accidental. The chairman of the firm, David St. John Thomas, had always had a passion for railways. He was a railway journalist before he was a publisher, and the first David & Charles book I remember seeing, indeed I think one of their very first titles, was *A Regional History of the Railways of Great Britain: Vol . 1, The West Country*, written by the chairman. That was just at the beginning of the boom in railway books. They still publish a lot of them, but their range now is very wide, excluding only fiction and memoirs.

I first met David St. John Thomas in about 1947, and in what now seem improbable circumstances. I, then in my early twenties, had been asked to preach at the Sunday School Anniversary service of Teignmouth Congregational Church. The lessons were read by the star boy and girl pupils of the year, and the star boy pupil was David. He read the lesson flawlessly, but, I fear inaudibly to everyone except I who was sharing the pulpit with him. He was a quiet, shy boy, inclined to hold his head to one side. Some years later, when I was a producer at the B.B.C. in Plymouth, he sent in a script on some railway subject, and came in for an audition, and I regretfully told him that we should have to get somebody else to read it. I added, cockily, that I was afraid he would never make a broadcaster, and felt a bit of a fool when his voice became acceptably familiar on the West of England Home Service. Gradually his shyness fell from him; but his friends were still startled when he embarked on publishing without much resources or experience behind him. Well, there he is, employing about 150 people last time I heard, trotting round the world once a year to brush up his overseas contacts, and beaming at the top of a full-page advertisement in the *Sunday Times*, on the occasion of the opening of his Baker Street bookshop, with Lady Antonia Fraser on his left and a clergymen on his right whom one instinctively feels must be at least an archdeacon. We should have remembered, I suppose, that his father, Gilbert, was a poet. Trains were one of father's favourite subjects, and I remember some lines of a poem on the old railway days:

Did you, in Wessex, keep slow company
With the Tanks (Royal) of the S & D,
Which waited, as it seemed, till crack of doom,
While they performed strange rites at Templecombe.

Gilbert Thomas was also a biographer of William Cowper, and liked to quote the lines beginning "God moves in a mysterious way".

One of David Thomas's inspirations was reprints. New techniques made it possible to reproduce, photographically, books long out of print. Other people had done this, but David's approach to it was audacious. When he announced that he was going to reprint, just as it stood, an early edition of *Bradshaw's Railway Guide 1922*, there was much mirth. While we were tapping our heads, he was tapping the market. Bradshaw sold enormously and is selling still. Certainly not all his efforts have been so prosperous. He once confessed to me that he was a bit down on his reprint of three Victorian telephone directories. He could not really understand why. He found them fascinating himself, especially the advertisements. David & Charles reprints have become famous: furniture catalogues, old magazines, scarce and expensive classics such as Camden's *Britannia*. He does not like to be described as a reprint publisher, any more than a railway publisher, nor would the descriptions now fit him or his firm. But they have had much to do with his success, added to the inherited curiosity and love for words of a poet's son.

I do wonder sometimes whether he publishes too *much*. If you read two books a week — which is as much as I have ever been able to manage — and have an adult reading life to 50 years, you will read 5,000 books, which is far less than the number of books published in this country every year. Who any longer can call himself a well read man? David & Charles, as I write, have just published the seventeenth volume in their history of inland waterways, with nine more in preparation. Many of these are no more than extended essays, and a generation ago we should have said that the best place for them was the transactions of a county historical association. Presumably they are commercially sufficient, but I suspect they are slightly debasing a different, uncommercial coinage. Still, this criticism could be made of many other publishers, and there is no doubt that David St. John Thomas is a remarkable man, who has greatly enlivened the publishing scene. I don't know what he will be up to next. It would not totally surprise me if he moved his office a couple of floors downstairs, and became station manager at Newton Abbot.

"A Race for Life"

Although the record of the Western Region of British Railways is remarkably good, accidents will happen from time to time, perhaps most commonly in the early days when the G.W.R. was only the senior of a group of not always harmonious partners. This is the story of a misadventure on the Cornwall Railway, happily without fatalities, on 29th. October 1872. It was an unusual kind of accident, so much so that the newspapers in their headlines called it "A Race for Life".

That day a clay train left the old Burngullow station, between St. Austell and Grampound Road, in the middle of the afternoon, going east. It was nearly all single track then in Cornwall, and the clay train had to cross with the westward-bound North Mail at St. Austell. It is not a very steep one, but the heavily-loaded clay train began to run away. It carried two guards, Cawsley and Peters, who saw the danger, and jumped from their vans before the speed became too high — omitting to put on their brakes first. The driver stayed on his footplate, but could not hold the train, which went clean through St. Austell and on down the rather steeper gradient — 1 in 60 — gathering speed all the time.

The North Mail had duly left Par, and was tackling the hill. On what Mr. Woodfin, the historian of the Cornwall Railway, describes as "about the only stretch of straight line in the section", they came in sight of one another.

The driver of the clay train was helpless. Driver Westlake, on the Mail, applied the brakes. Because of the gradient, he was able to stop quickly. He then started in reverse, back towards Par — luckily there was no train behind him. But it takes a good deal of time to reverse a long railway train, and all the while the runaway was rushing down the hill. The engines, according to the contemporary accounts, were within twenty yards of each other before Driver Westlake, on full throttle, began to draw the Mail clear. An upward gradient just before Par brought the runaway to halt.

It was luck, of course, that the trains met on the one straight stretch. All the same, it was a quick-thinking piece of work by Westlake. Whatever had been the case earlier, by 1872 the increasing complexity of the system, and the speed of the trains, required intelligent men to drive. Westlake was one to the Great Western's early heroes. He was given a gold medal and £15. His fireman and guards were rewarded too. The driver of the clay train, it was discovered, was unfamiliar with the section, and there were then no gradient boards to guide him. It was because of this accident that the Cornwall Railway decided to put indicating boards on all their principal gradients. Cawsley and Peters, the guards who had jumped from the clay train, were reprimanded. A year later Guard Cawsley was gaoled for stealing beer from a goods wagon at St. Germans. We wonder if this chapter of accidents to a possible ancestor might provoke a poem from a distinguished descendant?

As for the smash itself — the smash that didn't happen after all — well, "A Race for Life" does not, at this distance, seem an extravagant description.

The White Funnel Line

In writing about Hugh Redwood we have said something about the Campbell Steamers, the White Funnel Line. Robert Wall, in *Bristol Channel Pleasure Steamers*, makes civil gestures towards other companies which have run pleasure steamers in the Bristol Channel, but the author's heart is with the Campbells. And this is reasonable, because not only were they the dominant power in the traffic for nearly seventy years, but the public took pride in them, and felt a warm affection for them. Since their demise is relatively recent, many of you reading will be able to confirm this. At the end of the summer of 1889, the second season, Captain Alec Campbell — one of the founding brethren — was presented with a testimonial from "season ticket holders and friends", and already, says Robert Wall, Bristol "looked on the Campbell firm as its local property." Welshmen also felt justly that they had a stake in them. Somerset used to play the Glamorgan match at Weston, confident that the morning Campbell would bring over an enthusiastic crowd from Cardiff. At the beginning of the 1946 sailing season, when the service restarted after the second war with an excursion to Clevedon, an hour before departure from Bristol the queue stretched half a mile back along the road from the Hotwells pontoon.

The rivalries with other firms were sometimes intense. Campbells, like Cunard, officially denied racing, but in 1893 a Campbell ship and a Cardiff ship collided as they struggled to be first at Weston Pier. All the Campbell steamers were paddle-driven except one. In 1939 Campbells laid down a screw steamer for trips to France, but by the time she was in service, currency restrictions prohibited trips to France, and she had a miserable time of it blundering alongside small piers for which she had not been designed. This was *Empress Queen*. She did good service as an anti-aircraft ship in the war. Indeed, in both wars many of the steamers were naval auxiliaries. *Brighton Queen* was sunk in the evacuation from Dunkirk, although her Bristol crew survived.

It was not the Germans, but the motor car, that was ultimately too much for the Campbells. The company was taken over in 1959, but the direct Bristol connection had ended in 1956, when headquarters were moved to Cardiff. That same year *Britannia*, the favourite of the fleet, went to the breakers'. There were many arguments about whether *Britannia* or *Cambria* was the faster ship. Both, at about 20 knots, were listed in the early years of the century among the fastest merchant ships in the world. But not all of them were flyers. There was *Sea Breeze*, which had a single diagonal engine with an interesting habit of jamming at slow speed as the ship was approaching a pier. And there was *Bonnie Doon*: she was the first pleasure steamer proper ever to operate from Bristol, before Campbells came. Campbells bought her, and lived to regret it. She had, early in his career, acquired a nickname on the Clyde, and lived up to it: the *Bonnie Breakdoon*.

Well, so much for the ships. What of the passengers? There must be many besides Hugh Redwood for whom the Campbells bring lively recollections. It seems to us there is the makings of a good radio programme here. We could contribute one or two recollections ourselves. Anyway, we make Radio Bristol a present of the idea.

SHIPS AND THE SEA

Mayflower — The Myth and the Achievement

Some years ago, you may remember, an imitation of the *Mayflower* was built at Brixham and sailed across the Atlantic to New Plymouth. The motives of this expedition were never clear, but they were not very similar to those of the first voyage. The *British Weekly*, then in the brave old days of Shaun Heron, published a cartoon which spoke for most Free Church opinion in this country. There, on Plymouth Rock, stood two of the original Pilgrim Fathers, in their Puritan dress, watching the new Mayflower heave out of the eastern sea. And one said to the other, hands raised in dismay, "No, no, *no*, brother Carver! Definitely not one of ours!"

It is in such a mood that anyone familiar with the history of the Pilgrims contemplated the relentless series of junketings which faced us in 1970, the year of the three hundred and fiftieth anniversary. it is said that such things do no harm, but when all the apparatus of modern publicity is brought to bear on a subject of this kind, when legend is piled on half-truth, the original significance becomes lost. The wrapping is so vast and gaudy that one forgets about the contents: unless it is to wonder whether there *are* any contents at all. Intending, perhaps, to revere our forefathers, we only bring them into doubt and discredit. For instance, as C.M.MacInnes has pointed out, "It would take many modern liners to hold all the alleged genuine Mayflower articles to be found in New England today." What chance of recognition, therefore, is left for the odd one that might *not* be spurious?

So the first thing to emphasize, about the Pilgrim Fathers, is that theirs *was* an achievement of valour and of importance. This becomes more clear, not less, as the flummery is stripped away.

In 1606 a gathered congregation of Protestant Christians, fearing persecution, emigrated from Lincolnshire to Holland. After a brief and unhappy stay at Amsterdam, where there was a number of other English Protestant groups in exile, they moved on to Leyden. At Leyden they stayed for some years, preserving their souls and, rather more uncomfortably, their bodies. Then they decided to emigrate to the New World. This was a course which had been recommended as a future hope to his brethren by John Penry, one of the Protestant martyrs in the reign of Elizabeth. After many difficulties, they found some merchants who were prepared to invest in them. They sailed in 1620 from Southampton. There were more delays, but they reached New England before the end of the year. The loss of life in the first winter was terrible, but the settlement survived, and after a few years thrived.

Several footnotes must be added to this bald account. The pilgrims from Leyden were not the only ones to travel in the *Mayflower*. There was not enough of them to make a full complement, and at Southampton they were joined by others who had been enlisted by the English sponsors. These "strangers", as the pilgrims at first called them, were not actuated only, and in some cases not at all, by religious motives. G.M.Trevelyan wrote of the early American settlements that "free land, not free religion, was the promise held out by the companies promoting the emigration." This was true even of the *Mayflower* expedition, for the strangers outnumbered the pilgrims. Yet it was a religious belief that stamped its character and that of the society which sprang from it.

It was now more than a century and a quarter since the famous voyage of Columbus — longer than separates us from Stephenson's *Rocket* — and crossing the Atlantic, while still hazardous, was no longer a novelty. There had been many attempts at settlement by various European countries, but in the north few of them had been successful. One of the reasons for the failures had been the poor quality of many of the settlers. It was no use trying, as it was said, to turn "the scum of the old world into the cream of the new." The pilgrims, on the other hand, most of them devout, hard-working craftsmen, with the experience and the toughness gained already from years of exile, were just the men for the situation.

By 1620 there was a Dutch settlement at the mouth of the Hudson, and an English settlement at Jamestown, both were ruled out because it was Anglican, and because of its tobacco plantations, beginning to flourish. The Dutch were more sympathetic in religion, but one of the reasons prompting the pilgrims to leave Holland in the first place had been the fear of losing their English identity. In any case they were anxious not just to find a new home, but to build a new society on their own lines.

They obtained a grant of land to the north of Jamestown, but in fact made their landfall well to the north even of that, off Cape Cod. They happened to settle at a place which had already been given, by previous travellers, the name of Plymouth. The last town they had touched in England had been Plymouth, where they had had to put back for repairs. The association of Plymouth with the Pilgrim Fathers was thus accidental at both ends, unless indeed, as Isaac Foot would argue, it is to be regarded as special providence of God.

Now since it was a religious belief that guided the Pilgrim Fathers, it is important to remember what that belief was. It had one distinguishing characteristic, which was concerned not with sacraments or vestments or the precedence of angels, or many other such things with which Christians have needlessly stressed themselves and distressed each other. It was concerned with the nature of the church. The people who were variously called Brownists, Separatists, Independents, and later Dissenters, and nowadays Congregationalists and Baptists, or more vaguely Nonconformists or Free

Churchmen; these people held that a church was sufficient authority onto itself in all spiritual matters. In this belief they set themselves against Roman Catholics, Anglicans, and Presbyterians alike. All believers are priests. In the calling of God, no believer may naturally take precedence of another. They did not quite say "all men are equal", and they gave respect of temporal things to squires and even, for a while, to kings — the *Mayflower* pilgrims declared themselves loyal subjects of their dread Lord James. But they did say, "all members of this church are equal." And while they recognized that it was useful and probably necessary for a community to have elders, and deacons, and pastors, they insisted that such men could only be appointed by the will of God: and since, despite prayer and fasting, the will of God did not always make itself unanimously manifest, they allowed it to manifest itself through election. The word "election" had also a theological sense, but it is not in that sense that John Owen was using it when, in the seventeenth century, he wrote *The True Nature of a Gospel Church:*

> As to the nature of this election, call, or choice of a person known, tried and judged meetly qualified for the pastoral office, it is an act of the whole church; that is, of the fraternity with their elders, if they have any, *by way of common suffrage*, not of authority or office-power; for election is not an act of authority, but of liberty and power, wherein the whole church the fraternity is equal.

There is a good deal of the American constitution in that. You might even say that the bit about candidates first being "tried and judged meetly qualified" suggests the system of primaries.

What happened, both in England and America, was that these sons of the gathered churches, gradually becoming accustomed to holding elections and administering their own affairs, and finding that this system answered well, decided to offer it more widely. Thus it was that the rise of Dissent in the seventeenth century went hand in hand with the development of parliamentary institutions. You elect your minister, and (this was insisted upon by such writers as Owen) you give your minister reverence as one in authority: because you elected him, and if the worst came to the worst you could change him. But who elected the king? "A nobleman, a gentleman, and a yeoman", Cromwell considered the natural order of society. Not many of the Dissenters objected to that. Among the Pilgrim Fathers, William Brewster, who was a gentleman, socially speaking, was always accorded deference for his status and his education. But he only had one vote in the church meeting. When he held office, it was the church which elected him, and the church which could dismiss him. But who could dismiss the king? What were you to do with the king, if he was a bad king, and you could not dismiss him since you had not chosen him? The emigrants at least saved themselves the unpleasant logic of this problem.

The Pilgrim Fathers were not, then, the only, or even the first group of people to settle in what is now the United States. They were, perhaps, the best. They were certainly, for long time, the most influential. And it was of great importance to the future of that country that they went there, not as individuals, but as a kind of ready-made pocket democracy, which with a king far away was obviously likely to develop into republicanism.

There was another aspect of their beliefs which was noble, but which was less effectively fulfilled. The pastor of the pilgrims at Leyden had been John Robinson, who had gone with them from Lincolnshire. He had been educated at Cambridge University, and he was a man of graciousness and wisdom. Growing old, he intended to follow them to America once they were established, or so it is said; in any case he died before he could. Upon leaving Leyden, the pilgrims held a special day of prayer and worship, and Robinson preached a sermon. Although the version of the sermon which we have was printed many years afterwards, it conforms so much with what we know of the thought of Robinson and other Dissenting leaders of the time, that there is no reason to doubt that he uttered some such words as these:

> I charge you that you follow me no farther than you have seen me follow the Lord Jesus Christ. I am verily persuaded, the Lord has more Truth yet to break forth out of His holy Word. For my part, I cannot sufficiently bewail the condition of the Reformed Churches, who are come to a period in religion and will go at present no farther than the instruments of their reformation. The Lutheran can't be drawn to go beyond what Luther saw. And the Calvinists, you see, stick fast where they were left by that great Man of God — who yet saw not all things. I beseech you, remember, 'tis an article of your church covenant, that you be ready to receive whatever truth shall be made known to you from the written word of God. It is not possible that the Christian World should come so lately out of such thick Antichristian darkness, and that perfection of knowledge should break forth at once.

The whole sermon, spoken as it was at a time only a couple of generations removed from the Catholic atrocities at Smithfield and the Protestant atrocities at Tyburn, breathes a high and passionate hope in the love of God and the capacities of man. The pilgrims were to seek new spiritual frontiers; so it was appropriate that they should be seeking new physical frontiers as well.

They did not quite live up to this vision. Theirs was to be a strict society. To call them Puritans is not to denigrate them, for there were many different kinds of Puritans, and they were not all gloomy killjoys. Their Sabbatarianism, for instance; even in the first few weeks, a time of great urgency, they adamantly refused to work on the Sabbath. But it was the Reformation belief that the calendar had become so cluttered up with holy days, many of them of trivial importance, that it was best to sweep the lot away and set aside only the one holy day each week which God had ordained. They had no objection to working on Christmas Day, and in fact on that day in 1620 they felled the first tree.

But their society, for all its expressions of toleration, soon tended to become set in its ways. There was equality within the Calvinist church-state they founded, but little room for minority opinions. In 1630 they were joined by Roger Williams, a warm lively character with, said one of his contemporaries, "a windmill in his head". Threatened with arrest, he escaped to Rhode Island, and there founded a settlement which, in the words of Professor Bury, was "the first modern state which was really tolerant and was based on the principle of taking the control of religious matters entirely out of the hands of the government." So the contribution of the Pilgrim Fathers to this principle of the American constitution was only an indirect one.

All this is enough to show how genuinely important the voyage of the *Mayflower* was to be in American history. And not the least of their contributions was simply the example set by their courage. The Americans have built a replica of the original village at New Plymouth, a work of piety no doubt, though it can hardly look much like, still less smell much like, the original: certainly not in that first winter when sickness smote them so hard.

William Bradford, later their governor, wrote of this time:

> And in this time of most distress, there was but six or seven sound persons, who spared no pains, night or day, but with abundance of toil and hazard of their own health, fetched wood for the sick, made them fires, dressed their meat, made their beds, washed their loathsome clothes, clothed and unclothed them. And all this willingly and cheerfully, without any grudging in the least.

When the spring came, only nineteen men survived out of forty-five; and only six women out of twenty-four. But the women had not sacrificed themselves for nothing; they had saved the children. Only seven children out of thirty-four had died. It was the pilgrim mothers as much as the fathers who created New England. They had also, by that time, established friendly relations with the Indians, for though they had to be ready to protect themselves, the pilgrims came in peace.

So even though the veneration may sometimes seem a bit extravagant, one may doubt that a nation could have better heroes than Carver and Bradford, Brewster and Standish and the rest:

..those adventurous ones who went
Forth overseas, and, self-exiled,
Sought from far isle and continent
Another England in the wild,
For whom no drums beat, yet they fought
Alone, in courage of a thought
Which an unbounded future wrought.

The Rescue of Robinson Crusoe

Two frigates left Bristol on August 2nd, 1708. They were the *Duke*, 320 tons, 30 guns, a crew of 117; and the *Dutchess* (sic), slightly smaller, 260 tons, 26 guns, 108 men. They were useful but not formidable ships of war. Not ships of the Royal Navy, but privateers, members of what one might call the unofficial naval reserve, with royal commissions which, broadly, empowered them to make war on the enemies of the Queen — Anne was on the throne — and also to make what they could for themselves in the process. The two vessels were financed by Bristol merchants, and their objective was something that had only been done once before, and that well over a century earlier; to capture the Manila Galleon.

England was at war with France and Spain, the long and complicated affair which we call the War of the Spanish Succession. The Bristol privateers, however, under the command of Woodes Rogers, were not concerned with the Spanish Succession. They were concerned with loot. Spain still retained the Empire in South America which provided Drake and the Elizabethan seamen with such spoils. But raiding the east coast of South America was no longer a simple business. The Spaniards, in spite of their unwieldy imperial organisation, had learned some lessons, and the east coast ports were much more strongly defended than in Drake's time. Once a year the Spanish Plate Fleet sailed across the Atlantic, and the whole economy of Spain depended — or was believed to depend — on its safe arrival; but it was so well defended and its movements so successfully kept secret, that no Englishmen had ever taken it, though a Dutchman, Piet Hein, once did. The Dutch even still have a nursery-rhyme about him:

Piet Hein, Piet Hein,
His name is little but
His deeds are great.

On the other side of South America, however, on the west coast, it was a different matter. The ports there were very lightly defended, for the most part, because there was no-one to attack them. The Pacific was a Spanish lake. And once a year, from the Phillipines, the Manila galleon crossed the Pacific, bearing all the fruits of Spain's far eastern trade. It was not as rich a prize as the Plate Fleet, but still a very rich one — and a good deal easier to take, once you had got there.

Once you had got there: that was the rub. It still required a very considerable feat of seamanship to go round the Horn or through the Straits of Magellan. Ships and men that accomplished it were unlikely to be in very good shape for a tough fight on the other side. And the lack of harbours for refitting...and the tropical diseases which bore especially hardly on men from the cold, wet north. Cavendish, it is true, when he sailed round the world a few years after Drake, had taken the Manila galleon, but the few other attempts on the prize had failed dismally.

The men on the *Duke* and *Dutchess* did not know that this was the object of the expedition: if they had, they would probably never have gone aboard. But the leaders did. Woodes Rogers himself, who commanded the *Duke*, was a young man of wide seagoing experience and high ability. His pilot was that remarkable man William Dampier, explorer, buccaneer, naturalist, writer, who had more knowledge of the South Seas than any living Englishman. These two made a powerful combination. Unfortunately, however, the shareholders laid it down that all "enterprises of great pith and moment" on the expedition were to be decided by a council, consisting of the senior officers of both ships. As almost always happens, such a system meant divided command, and indecision at critical moments. It was especially so in this case since the council included Captain-Doctor, as he was styled, Thomas Dover. Here was another extraordinary man: full of energy and a spirit of adventure, wealthy — he was one of the chief investors in the expedition — a fashionable Bristol surgeon. Although later his reputation as a doctor suffered because of his fondness for prescribing quantities of mercury for almost every complaint, he was undoubtedly well in advance of the general medical knowledge of his time, and you can still buy Dover's powder — indeed, it was regulation issue as a bromide to the Italian army in the second world war. Dover was a man of dogmatic views and a stubborn will, which did not make him an easy colleague.

Under his council of mixed personalities the *Duke* and *Dutchess* sailed to Cork, to pick up more men. As a number of others took the opportunity to desert, the operation was only moderately successful. They also, however, were able to replenish their supply of liquor, which was already running low. The amount of liquor which was consumed on the *Duke* and *Dutchess* was, to put it mildly, substantial. As they ran south they found it necessary to put in at Madeira, and then the Canaries, to keep their stocks up. They also, on a fairly uneventful trip down the Atlantic, collected several small but useful prizes. And then they were off the Horn.

They rounded the Horn after a desperate and prolonged effort. To the normal difficulties of the passage a plague of scurvy was added, and many of the men died. Once round, they badly needed to pause to refit, but of course no port was open to them. So they headed for the remote, uninhabited island group of Juan Fernandez, a difficult landfall but likely to be safe from interruptions. When they got there, they were alarmed to see fires burning. It turned out to be, not a Spanish squadron, but a solitary British seaman, Alexander Selkirk.

Selkirk, who was to become the original of Defoe's "Robinson Crusoe", had been marooned at Juan Fernandez five years earlier. He was dressed in goatskins, just as we recall from the coloured pictures of our childhood. He was, however, in the best of health and spirits, and had organised his solitary life with remarkable efficiency. He had, for instance, been much troubled by hordes of rats, but had kept them at bay by capturing and domesticating a large number of wild cats, who slept around him at night and kept the rats at a distance. Woodes Rogers gives a vivid account of how Selkirk, during his years on the island, had slowly conquered his initial mental agony, and had come to find a deep sense of tranquil well-being in his strange life. It was, alas, a tranquillity which was never to return to him. But for the moment he was happy to throw in his lot with the expedition, to which his many skills and experience of the south seas made him a powerful reinforcement.

The *Duke* and *Dutchess* completed their refit and progressed northwards along the South American coast. They took a further number of prizes of varying value. they did not obtain much satisfaction from the capture of "near five hundred bales of Popes Bulls... we throw'd most of them overboard to make room for better goods, except what we used to burn the pitch of our ships bottoms when we careened 'em." The War of the Spanish Succession was not a religious war, but the English still retained their distrust of "popery". Woodes Rogers never loses an opportunity in his journal to comment upon its follies. At one point, he released a young prisoner, a Spanish priest, and — the journal continues:

> gave him, as he desir'd, the prettiest young female negro we had in the prize, with some linen and other things... The young padre parted with us extremely pleas'd, and leering under his hood upon his black female angel, we doubt he will crack a commandment with her, and wipe off the sin with the church's indulgence.

Arrived at Guayaquil, the expedition, its clarity of action as usual blurred by the council system with Dover being particularly difficult, decided after some hesitations to attack the port. It was a Pyrrhic victory. There was little to be got, except several tropical diseases which reduced the numbers still further. But they had not come so far to abandon the quest now. They pressed on, via the Galapagos islands, to the coast of Mexico, where they might hope to cross the path of the Manila galleon.

From August until December of 1709 they hung about, finding nothing, tormented by the fear that they had missed it, and by the endless arguments of the council. Their supplies were almost exhausted, save for the bare minimum necessary to carry them to the Dutch East Indies, when the galleon, it seemed miraculously, turned up, and after a sharp fight they captured her. It was a fabulously rich prize — worth perhaps a quarter of a million pounds, even as money went then, though the exact amount was never settled. Success, however, was not complete. For the first time the Spaniards, partly because they had heard rumours of the raid, had divided their treasure between two ships. *Duke* and *Dutchess*, though battered, attacked the second one when it came along, but after a fierce engagement it proved too strong for them. It was probably as well, for the master-gunner of the galleon had locked himself in the gunpowder-room, and sworn by all he held most sacred to blow up the ship rather than let it be taken. So the bigger prize of the two got away; but the one that had *not* got away was ample compensation even for such a voyage. As they brought her home on their way across the Pacific, a journey made even more hazardous by the inaccuracy of their charts, the conquerors were constantly sustained by the sight of their prize and thoughts of its unprecedented richness. One and all reasonably expected to retire in comfort on the proceeds.

But it did not work out like that. Their welcome in Batavia was reserved. The Dutch and the English were theoretically close allies, but this was a long way from the war in Europe, and the Dutch could not help casting envious eyes on the Manila galleon. Tact and bluff finally got them away from Batavia without having to pay too much, and then home, joining a Dutch convoy at the Cape, and rounding the north of Scotland before they anchored in the Thames in October, 1711, more than three years after they had left Bristol.

After such a genuinely heroic voyage, the long wrangles about the distribution of the prize money, and its final allocation, make depressing reading. First of all the British East India Company, who made a legal claim on the cargo, had to be bought off. By the time the directors and the officers had had their share, the ordinary sailors, "the poor South Sea sailors", as they described themselves in an unavailing petition to the House of Lords, ended up with just fifty pounds apiece for their three years of travail.

Captain-Doctor Thomas Dover did well out of it, in spite of having been more of a liability than an asset throughout the trip. There is a certain melancholy satisfaction to be derived from the fact that he subsequently lost all his money in the financial lunacy that we know as the "South Sea Bubble". William Dampier died three years after the voyage, not indeed in poverty, but not in affluence either, even though he was the only man who had been three times round the world. The cousin who was his heir received, after advances which Dampier had already spent, twenty pounds. Woodes Rogers had an up and down life until 1732, and died in the Bahamas, where he had been appointed governor, rather ironically, with a mission to stamp out piracy. Most of his gains from the voyage were spent in this service.

And Alexander Selkirk? Selkirk never recovered the peace he had found on Juan Fernandez. "Oh, my beloved island! I wish I had never left thee! I never was before the man I was on thee! ...I have not been such since I left!" He was in trouble with the law, tried to recapture his island conditions by retiring to a Scottish cave, found that didn't work, ran off with a girl, married either her or somebody else (or maybe both) went to sea again, and died at sea, serving on H.M.S. *Weymouth*.

The voyage of Woodes Rogers and company will stand comparison, both in its achievement and in the gallantry of its participants, with any epic of the sea. Londoners who saw the fabled Manila galleon riding at anchor in the Thames felt that British seamanship and courage had been fitly rewarded. And yet the expedition had no discernible effect upon the outcome of the war with France; and hardly any of those who sailed on it were ultimately much better off as a result. It could no doubt be considered a triumphant success, if heroism is held to be its own reward: but we would like the comments of some to the "poor South Sea sailors" on that. The lasting effect was that it enabled Defoe to write a classic.

A Note on William Dampier

When the world goes to East Coker, which is a picture-book village near Yeovil in Somerset, it does so because T.S.Eliot lived there for a while, and wrote a famous poem about it. Yet East Coker has associations with greatness which are less famous. A simple memorial in the church reminds us that it was the home of the Dampier family, and that the remarkable William was born there, the son of a tenant-farmer, in the middle of the seventeenth century.

"Remarkable" is a pale adjective for Dampier. He was a man with a passion for knowledge, particularly of the sea and of distant lands, an explorer but even more a hydrographer. When he was still in his 'teens and sailing before the mast, his painstaking observations had begun, and ultimately he was to make vast additions to the charts and maps of the world. Yet he was also a pirate — some of his expeditions do not even deserve the face-saving description of "privateering" — and heavily involved in some very avaricious and blood-thirsty work indeed. He declared that he "abhorred drunkenness", but his company and his conduct belied him. His record of voyages was second to none of his age — round the world, we have seen, three times — and yet as captain of a ship he was so incompetent that he was formally debarred from ever again holding a royal command. He took part in some highly successful expeditions, besides that with Woodes Rogers, and yet he did not die a wealthy man. His whole career speaks of a boldness: yet he was frequently accused of cowardice.

Usually, studying men of the past, one is able to form some conclusions about the kind of people they were. To put it at its simplest, were they nice or nasty? Were they clever or silly? Rough and ready conclusions, of course, but one instinctively makes them. Dampier is quite baffling. It is hard to understand how a man so sensitive could also have been so cruel, how a man so intelligent could also have been so stupid. Gulliver speaks of "my cousin, Dampier". *Sir* Walter Scott said that Gulliver's character "is exactly that of Dampier, or any other sturdy wanderer of the period, endowed with courage and common sense'. But there was much more to Dampier, both for better *and* worse, than there was to Gulliver.

What one can say is that Dampier's work has been a help in time of trouble for tens of thousands of seamen. In hydrographical matters he was hardly ever wrong, except when he forsook observation for conjecture. He deserves his modest monument in East Coker: which brings us to a final contradiction, for who would have expected a village deep in the Somerset countryside, where in the seventeenth century the sea was scarcely more than a rumour, to produce such a seaman?

"The Father of American Colonization"

Looking through the notes we made, when undergraduates, on the origins and growth of the British colonies — they were quite ample, for we were both interested in the subject — we find Ferdinando Gorges is hardly mentioned. Yet the notes were not, we think, slipshod, nor is the title of this chapter fraudulent. In fact it is only in comparatively recent years that Gorges has begun to receive widespread recognition for his colonial work. New research has helped, particularly a massive thesis by Professor Preston, of the Royal

Military College of Canada, and a perceptive essay by Dr. Rowes. Yet there has always been plenty of evidence of *Sir* Ferdinando's experience. The reasons why it did not make much impression on the majority of historians will become apparent in the course of this narrative. In 1859 Mr. John A. Poor, reading a paper to the Historical Society of the State of Maine, actually referred to Gorges as "the father of English colonization in America." He found few to agree with him, and many to scoff: Massachusetts' historians in particular resented it as an attempt by Maine to snatch undeserved pioneering glory. One of them, Erastus Benedict, dismissed Gorges as "a man of pretension, a favourite and a parasite of a powerful monarch, who was always unsuccessful. Whatever he touched failed." Perhaps his enthusiasm for Maine had drawn Mr. Poor on a bit, but all the same his judgement was sounder than that of Mr. Benedict. Let us consider the record, and, in the light of it, the subsequent fluctuations in the reputation of *Sir* Ferdinando Gorges.

He was born of an old and gentle Somerset family — "Ferdinando" was not an uncommon English Christian name in those days: two English sovereigns had married Spanish consorts. The traditional year of his birth is 1565, and it was on that supposition that various celebrations were held in America in 1965, and exhibitions in Bristol and Plymouth. Professor Preston has suggested that the year of his birth should be 1568, and he has the weight of the evidence on his side. But it does not matter very much, since our practice of remembering distinguished men upon their anniversaries is after all only a convenient way of ensuring we do not forget them. Gorges died in 1647, so whichever is the correct date of his birth he had, for those days, an exceptionally long life, which spanned the whole of the first, formative period of British colonization in North America. In 1658 Hawkins returned from his third slaving voyage, and at Vera Cruz had been involved in what in retrospect is seen to have been the first major act of war in the long struggle with Spain. In 1647, Parliament had won the Civil War, and though emigration had fallen away — since most of the emigrants had fled to escape religious persecution, and they no longer needed to do that — there existed a natural sympathy between the dominant powers in the colonies, and the dominant powers in England, which offered a real prospect of mutual co-operation and progress. This prospect was to be swept away at the Restoration of the monarchy, and never returned.

Gorges possessed all the zest for living which we associate with the great Elizabethans: "try anything twice" might have been their motto. He began as a soldier, fighting in the various campaigns which England conducted in France in support of the Protestant claimant to the French throne, Henry of Navarre. Gorges was always a firm Protestant, but of the Anglican, not the Calvinist, variety. In 1595 he was sent to command the new fort of Plymouth.

He lost the job, and might well have lost his head, through getting involved in the revolt of the Earl of Essex in 1601 — he had served under Essex in France, and had been knighted by him at Rouen. But when James I came to the throne Gorges was back in favour and back to Plymouth.

His active interest in colonization began in 1605, when he was one of the sponsors of the North Virginia Company. This was the first major attempt to establish a real colony in North America. To begin with, the English had been interested in America because they believed vague tales of gold and silver cities; more practically, because America was a source of naval materials — timber, cordage, canvas, pitch — which could normally be obtained only with difficulty from the Baltic and White Sea; because of the Newfoundland fisheries; and because there was still hope of a north-west passage and an easy route to the spices of the east. There was also the thought of military bases against Spain, and "Virginia", a large area, not corresponding to the present Virginia, was expected to be "a bit in the enemy's mouth." It was only slowly that anyone came to envisage a colony as more than a source of these material advantages. It was *Sir* Walter Ralegh who declared, "I shall yet live to see Virginia an English *nation*." In 1605, there was peace with Spain, and Ralegh was in the Tower. This was surely the moment when it was appropriate to press on with the peaceful development of colonies, but someone was needed to take over Ralegh's ideas and leadership. Gorges did not regard himself as Ralegh's successor, did not like him very much, often differed from him: but this central thing the two men had in common, that they were concerned not with economic outposts, but new English nations. Of course, Gorges hoped to make money out of his ventures, he would not have been averse to finding an El Dorado, but that was not his principal motive. He was not a wealthy man, though he married fairly well, and often. His fourth and last marriage, to Elizabeth Smyth of Ashton Court, near Bristol, enabled him to give up his post at Plymouth and concentrate entirely on his American projects. They swallowed up most of the money which his wives brought him.

The Virginia settlement staggered along from crisis to crisis, and Gorges gradually transferred his attention further north, to the other main settlement area, New England. In 1620 he founded the Council for New England, but the Council's attempt to establish a settlement in Massachusetts Bay was a failure. He tried again a few years later, but by that time the Pilgrim Fathers had established themselves, and a steady stream of Puritan emigrants was going out (they would probably have included Cromwell if Parliament had rejected the Grand Remonstrance). The Puritans were suspicious of Gorges, whom they regarded as a creature of the Stewart monarchy. In 1634, Archbishop Laud created the Commission for Foreign Plantations, and it was planned that Gorges should be made Governor of all New England. In 1639 he was actually granted a charter for the province of Maine, and his agents began the process of setting up a government there. But civil war came, the plans were postponed, and in 1647 Maine was absorbed into the Massachusetts Bay colony. The Virginia settlement was doing well by this time, but Gorges had given up his direct concern with that, in order to concentrate his efforts in New England. It therefore has to be admitted that both his major efforts at colonization brought him no personal success. Furthermore, and this was perhaps the crucial thing, he never crossed the Atlantic. He was obviously not a figure to catch the public imagination. The governor of Plymouth Fort, the Somerset country gentleman, did not cut much of a dash beside such a man as Ralegh, or even lesser heroes such as John Smith or Miles Standish. Gorges' claim to distinction rests not upon what he achieved, but what his teachings and example enabled others to achieve. Here, two points may legitimately be made.

First, it is quite arguable that he was right in saying that the colonization of North America was too difficult a business to be left entirely to private enterprises. When the Virginian settlement was in trouble, he urged that it should be taken over by the crown and given naval protection. The Council for New England was intended to work under the close control of the Privy Council. The early history of the English in North America is studded with tragedies which could have been avoided with proper aid from home. Gorges had in mind, probably, no more than the security and welfare of the colonies themselves. But to the stern Puritans of Massachusetts, many of whom had made their journey simply to *escape* royal control, his ideas were anathema. Laud and the Stewart kings were only too anxious to let the Puritans go to America, and had far too many more immediate problems to make any serious attempt to impose an episcopalian church and an authoritarian constitution on the settlements. It is understandable that the Laud commission alarmed and angered Massachusetts, but it was a paper tiger. The motives of Gorges in supporting Laud were very different from the motives which were supposed to animate the Archbishop; but the association was fatal to his reputation with the colonists.

The second point arises from the first, and brings us back to Gorges' philosophy of colonization. It is ridiculous to suggest, though it has been suggested by a reputable historian, that he attempted to impose serfdom in America. His anxiety to draw up formal contributions, and to maintain close links with the crown, arose *just because* he wanted to treat the colonies as more than trading-posts. If he was unduly paternalistic in his ideas, he had what he believed to be the true interest of the settlers at heart. He was intelligent enough to revise some of his notions had he ever been able to study the situation at first hand.

This is how he expresses himself in his *Brief Narration*, which he wrote near the end of his life. It was intended to publicise the province of Maine, but it also gave him an opportunity to reflect upon his life's work.

> I began when there was no hopes for the present but of loss, in that I was yet to find a place, and being found, itself was in a manner dreadful to the beholders, for it seemed but as a desert wilderness, replete only with a kind of savage people and overgrown trees. So as I found it no mean matter to procure any to go thither, much less reside there; and those I sent knew not how to subsist, but on the provisions I furnished them with.
>
> Secondly, I dealt not as merchants or tradesmen are wont, seeking only to make mine own profit, my ends being to make perfect the thorough discovery of the country (wherein I waded so far with the help of those that joined with me) as I opened the way for others to make their gain, which hath been the means to encourage their followers to prosecute it to their advantage.
>
> I dealt not as merchants or tradesmen are wont... I opened the way.

It is a proud, rather wistful apologia. But the historians would have none of it. It is not altogether a misfortune that the principal English-speaking historians were for so long Whigs. Macaulay is still properly a magic name. But it could hardly be expected that once Ferdinando Gorges had got off to such a bad start, identified by his contemporaries with the despised and defeated Stewart autocracy, the Whig tradition would do much to retrieve his reputation. Well, since 1965 something has been done, both in England and in America, and both in Bristol and in Plymouth, the two places where he spent most of his life. And not before time.

What kind of man was he, this "father of American colonization"? the best advice ever given to a student of history is "Keep on reading until you hear them talking!" But I doubt if even those who have read most widely about Ferdinando Gorges have ever "heard him talk". Although an enormous amount of material about his activities exists, he remains, in himself, elusive. We said that he had the Elizabethan zest for living. He was a soldier and a sailor, a trader, a ship-designer, indirectly a bit of a pirate, a courtier, a country gentleman, a J.P. — all this apart from his major work as a colonizer. Yet even Professor Preston confesses, at the end of his researches, that we do not really know the man. Perhaps this is above all the reason why he has been neglected. He does not throw himself at you out of the books, larger than life, as so many of his contemporaries do. Was he timid or rumbustious, mean or generous, querulous or genial, slow to anger or quick to wrath? Had he a sense of humour? We cannot answer any of these questions with conviction. But we do know of his work and his ideas, and for these we are right to salute his memory — whenever he was born.

Tobias Furneaux

Tobias Furneaux was born at Swilly, Plymouth, in 1735, and died there in 1781 on the 19th. September. When we think of Plymouth seamen it is naturally the great Elizabethans who hold the forefront of our minds, and perhaps this is why an eighteenth century sailor, such as Furneaux, has been neglected. He already had a varied and successful naval career behind him when, in 1722, he was appointed to command the *Adventure*, under Captain Cook, who was setting out for his second expedition to the Antarctic.

The *Adventure* and the *Resolution*, which Cook himself commanded, called at the Cape and sailed east. Then they lost contact in fog, and were separated for three months, a time which Furneaux spent usefully in charting the coast of Tasmania. He thought Tasmania very like Devon, and christened several of its landmarks with Devon names, including a Swilly Bay. (It is therefore untrue, though some Australians purport to believe it, that this area took its name from a more modern Australian institution, the six o'clock swill).

Furneaux met Cook again at a rendezvous, arranged in case of such an emergency, off New Zealand. They paid a successful visit to the Friendly Islands, which had been well named, since the natives, though astonished, were anxious to fraternize and to trade. But then the two ships separated again, and in the end Furneaux came back on his own, arriving almost exactly two years after he had set out. He had lost a midshipman and boat's crew to the cannibals, and brought back a South Sea islander with him. This man's fortunes were happier than most of such cases. He survived two years of the English climate and was taken back home on Cook's third voyage.

Tobias Furneaux had sailed round the world twice, in opposite directions. So far as we know, he was the first man to do this: westward, under Captain Willis of the *Dolphin*, in 1766, and now afterwards under Cook. He fought in the War of American Independence, but died, at home, before it was over. He does not seem to have been a very pleasant or popular person; his portrait by Northcote shows a wilful lip and a proud eye. Yet he was certainly one of the great seamen of the west, and he deserves remembrance.

Thomas Cochrane

Political scandals are nothing new, and the year 1813 produced a juicy one. The central figure was Thomas Cochrane, later tenth Earl of Dundonald. He was one of the most striking figures of his time, and his life has been brilliantly chronicled by J.P.W. Mallalieu in his book, *Extraordinary Seaman.*

Cochrane was born at Annsfield, Lanarkshire, in 1775, and at the age of eighteen joined the Navy. He had quite a distinguished fighting career during the first part of his life there, and when peace was declared in 1802 he enrolled as a student at the University of Edinburgh. He pursued his studies earnestly, living in secluded lodgings. There was, however, a rugged, self-sufficient streak in his character which was likely to bring him into trouble sooner or later. In 1803 when the war broke out again, he was ordered to Plymouth, and appointed to command an old collier which had been brought into the service and was being fitted as a ship of war. When ready for sea she was sent to the Downs and ordered to keep watch on the enemy in Boulogne. Cochrane soon found that the ship was useless for such a service, and represented this to the Admiral in command. His letter was forwarded to the Admiralty, and he was then ordered to cruise to the north-east of the Orkneys to protect the fisheries. This sounded more within his ship's capacities, but there appeared to be no fisheries to protect. At least he believed that this service was invented as a mark of the board's displeasure. It lasted for fifteen months, and he was not permitted to return to English waters until there was a new First Lord of the Admiralty. He was then appointed to a new 32-gun frigate and ordered to cruise for a month off the Azores.

After this, there was a vacancy for a parliamentary candidate at Honiton, in Devon, and Cochrane offered himself as a candidate. He soon found that it was a mere question of bribery, refused to sanction it on his own account, and was consequently rejected. In February 1807 there was a general election, and this time Cochrane stood for Westminster, one of the few divisions where at that time there was a popular suffrage. He was returned head of the poll. He then brought a motion in the House on naval abuses. They were real abuses, but it was an unjudicious step as regards his own career, and the Admiralty then ordered him out to the Mediterranean. His constituents agreeably gave him leave of absence.

In 1809 he returned to England again, and was immediately summoned to the Admiralty. The French had mustered the whole of their western fleet in Aix Roads, and it was contemplated to launch an attack on them there. He submitted the outline of a plan, and the Board asked him if he would put it into execution. As a junior officer, Cochrane (this is his account of the matter) naturally demurred, saying that this would cause a lot of bad feeling and jealousy, but after repeated and urgent solicitations, and after the First Lord had given his assurance that he would do all he could to allay any jealousy which might arise, Cochrane agreed. The plan worked well, but would have worked even better if he had had the co-operation of his commander, Lord Gambier. When Cochrane returned he was honoured with the Order of the

Bath.

This did not mollify him, and then he learnt that the House of Commons was to propose a vote of thanks to Gambier for his part in the affair. As member for Westminster he opposed the motion on the grounds that Gambier had done nothing to merit a vote of thanks, but had neglected to destroy the French fleet when it was clearly in his power to do so. Lord Gambier applied for a court martial, and though it seems that Cochrane's charges were probably correct, Gambier was acquitted by a friendly court, and the Admiralty found Cochrane guilty of falsely libelling his commanding officer. That proved to be effectively the end of his naval career. The Admiralty refused to consider any of the plans which he submitted to them, and he was not even allowed to rejoin his ship. He made several fiery speeches in Parliament, which proved so offensive to the Admiralty that he was again directed to the Mediterranean. He refused to go, and was promptly placed on half pay.

In 1813, he made the acquaintance of Captain de Berenger, a French refugee. Berenger was a swindler, and had been found out in a particularly unsavoury bit of business. Cochrane, it seems clear, did not know what had been going on, but he knew and liked Berenger, had visited him at his house, and was charged with complicity. He had made a good many enemies by this time, chiefly through the Gambier affair. He was found guilty, and sentenced to a year's imprisonment. He was also fined £1,000. He was expelled from the House of Commons, struck off the Navy list, and expelled from the Order of the Bath. His constituents returned him to Parliament at the By-election, and he resumed his attacks on the Admiralty's shortcomings.

In 1817, still only in his early forties, he went to Chile to command their Navy, doing so with great success in the war against Spain. He had a spell in Brazil, where he found the administration too corrupt for comfort, so he went to Greece, and commanded the Navy there against the Turks.

He returned to Britain in his last years, campaigning for reinstatement on the Navy list. He was so far successful that he obtained a free pardon from the crown, but nothing else. He had said too many hard and true things about the Navy, and the Admiralty remained unforgiving to the end.

Looking South

One of our ancestors, in the last century, was lost with Franklin in the search for the north-west passage. You can see his name on the memorial to the expedition in London. Ever since then, our family has considered itself expert in polar exploration. The terrible, moving story of the Scott expedition was one of the first stories father told me, and when we first came to Plymouth we made a prompt pilgrimage to Mount Wise, where Scott, who was of course a Plymouth man, stands looking to the south.

It was in 1912 when he reached the Pole. He had thought he was there on January 17th., but further sightings decided him that he was a few miles out, and so it was on January 18th that he reached what he calls the "actual final spot", and left the Union Jack flying there. He had known for some days that he was not the first. He had seen Amundsen's tracks, and now he found Amundsen's camp, with the Norwegian flag flying.

The arguments about the Scott expedition have been going on ever since. Of course he made mistakes. It was surely a mistake to take five men on the last stage, when all the planning had been based on four. They were even a pair of skis short: the tent was not big enough. The composition of the party was open to question, particularly Scott's own preference of Petty Officer Evans, who was past his best, to such other candidates as Lashly. For some things Scott has been criticized unjustly. Amundsen preferred dogs (they could be eaten, perhaps by other dogs, perhaps by men) but Scott's chosen route, which he had already prospected, took him up the Beardmore glacier, where dogs could scarcely go. His plan, combining motor-sledges, ponies, and man haulage over the last stages, seemed reasonable enough at the time, though certainly the motor-sledges had not been adequately tested. He did not miss by very much: a few weeks, and unexpectedly bad weather on the way back, were all that stood between him and his goal, all the difference there was between triumph and tragedy.

Amundsen started later, and got there first. His dogs took him there with what seems, by contrast, ridiculous ease. He never lost a man. But Amundsen's objective was the Pole, and very little else. Scott was engaged on a scientific expedition, and his interest in the Pole sprang at least partly from the knowledge that, without some such dramatic objectives, he could never raise the funds for the trip. Amundsen achieved his aim. Scott's aims were manifold, and they did not all fail. If he was not first at the Pole, his men brought home three eggs of the Emperor penguin, won at a cost of hardship and stress little less than suffered by the Pole party itself.

And then, there is the sheer gallantry of it, that still, as one reads the story, leaves one humbled.

A Note on Drake

We doubt if it is an exaggeration to say that ten books have been written about Drake for every time he went to sea. The question to ask of any *new* book about him, therefore, is — was it necessary? There is a strong case for *Francis Drake, Privateer: Contemporary Narratives & Documents*, edited by John Hampden. It attempts something which has not, so far as we know, been done before. Dr. Hampden prints, in one volume, the principal early accounts, the best we have, of Drake's privateering voyages. He links them with a commentary that is both learned and succinct. Where there is matter for controversy — and there was plenty of that in Drake's life — he indicates the latest state of scholarly opinion, but leaves the documents to speak for themselves. He has not changed them, except to modernize the spelling. Where he has abbreviated them, he tells us. The result is a book which, even though it confines the voyages after 1580 to an epilogue, makes a gripping and vivid whole.

The most tantalizing question about Drake is not at precisely what points of the American continent he landed; or what he said just before the Armada arrived; or even whether he deliberately deserted his command in the middle of the channel fight, for booty. The tantalizing question is — and we have seen it to be much the same in the case of Dampier and Furneaux — would you like him if you met him? At times he seems a repellent as well as an avaricious rogue. At times he seems kind and gracious. At times — when he was Mayor of Plymouth, for instance, and brought water to the city — he is a planner, thoughtfully measuring possibilities. At times he was unbelievably casual and inefficient in administration. In his last voyage with Hawkins, he hopelessly over-manned and under-supplied his half of the fleet. Nearly always he was a hero: but once, on his first voyage with Hawkins, he was either a coward or a traitor: a traitor to his commander, anyway — and Drake held high views about the rights of commanders at sea, as his treatment of Doughty showed, Dr. Hampden's book leaves no doubt, we think, that in both these episodes — of the *Judith* and of Doughty — Drake behaved badly. But nor does it leave any doubt that he was a man of extraordinary courage and imagination, and that there was in him a touch of the true glory. But would we *like* him? Five minutes in a pub on the Barbican should be sufficient to find out. At least this book gives us the evidence on which we can argue.

Mother Weston

In the last war, the Navy produced a poet: one of the outstanding British poets of the last decades — Charles Causley. These are some lines from his "Song of the Dying Gunner":

Farewell, Aggie Weston; the Barracks at Guzz;
  Hang my tiddley suit on the door;
For I'm sewn up neat in a canvas sheet,
  And I won't be home no more.

He used the words *Farewell, Aggie Weston* for the title of his first book of poems. It is a tribute to the place which Dame Agnes Weston's Royal Sailors' Rests have come to fill in the lives of seamen.

A new one at Devonport, opened in 1960, is so luxurious that it has been suggested it should be called "The Royal Sailors' Ritz". The bed-sitting rooms have hot and cold water, electric shaving-sockets, foam mattresses, and everything else you would expect in a good hotel. They can be booked for long periods, so a man can spend his whole leave there. The cabins, for shorter stays, are smaller but equally comfortable. At 1960 prices, a bed-sitting room cost two shillings, with bacon and egg. Inflation has caused rises, but the Rest still gives splendid value for money. There is a main hall seating 400, a smaller hall, a games room with two full-sized billiard tables, a television room, a quiet room, electric lifts, film projectors, radio in the public rooms. The decor is striking: modern but not garish, functional but not bleak. The Royal Sailors' Rests have always recognized the importance of decor: it was written of the first Devonport Rest — which was the first of all — opened in 1876: "As the building was to compete for trade with the many public houses round about, the furnishings and decorations were made as attractive as possible. Gold leaf played a distinguished part in the brightening-up process, while many mirrors looked on the animated scene most reflectively." Gold leaf and mirrors are not the distinguishing motifs of the new building, but the principle remains the same.

For the aims of the society are clearly defined. They are "the spiritual, moral and physical well-being of men of the Royal Navy, their wives and families, and of other service men." But though the word "spiritual" comes first and always has done, and the Rests were partly begun as a challenge to the furious drunkenness of naval ports in the last century. Agnes Weston herself laid it down that the physical comforts were in no way to be conditional on spiritual or moral amendment. She insisted that the Rests were to be open to anyone, the pagan as well as the saint, the drunk as well as the sober. She was heavily attacked for this in her own lifetime by many worthy people who considered she was condoning sin. She took no notice.

The new Rest at Devonport was in fact in use for some time before its official opening in 1960, and there was a precedent for this. The day before the opening in 1876, three sailors went to Miss Weston. They had watched the building grow, and now, they said, they wanted to be "the first birds to roost there." They had special shore leave from the captain. When she said it was not possible, they asked, "Couldn't you throw the red tape overboard for once, Miss Weston, and let us in?" Miss Weston knew all about red tape, and the appeal went to her heart. They came in, and she always treasured a photograph of them: the first of uncounted thousands.

"Mother Weston" — so the sailors called her in her own day, and the name tells you the important things about her went on throwing bucketsful of red tape overboard for the rest of her life. She never flinched, whether the problem was a drunken Petty Officer, an awkward Admiralty official, or an over-zealous evangelist. She stuck — the old phrase seems appropriate — to her guns. She would joke with the sailors, pray with them, break up their street fights, put them to bed when they were drunk, write them innumerable letters. She lived and died for them: an astonishing woman, a formidable woman, and yet clearly a lovable woman. When she died, her work was recognised by a funeral with full naval honours.

Who Discovered America?

Pause before you answer. You cannot just say "Columbus, 1492" and have done with it. Certainly Columbus landed in the West Indies in that year, and that was the first direct connection western Europe had with what soon came to be called the New World. Columbus has been variously depicted as a hero and a stumbler, but there is no doubt at all that he made that famous voyage and made his landfall.

Whether that entitles him to be the man who "discovered America" is a more complicated question. There have been all sorts of claimants. Bristol has two of them. There is St. Brendan in the sixth century, and John Cabot in the fifteenth. Neither of them was strictly a Bristolian. We presume St. Brendan visited Bristol at some point of his travels, because of Brandon hill, which used to have an oratory dedicated to him, at the top, where the Cabot Tower now stands. Cabot was a citizen of Venice, probably born in Genoa, certainly an Italian; but he sailed from Bristol, and returned to Bristol, and was backed by Henry VII. He sailed several years after Columbus, but it is possible, so many people have thought, that his landfall was on the mainland of North America, and as Columbus had only touched the fringes, the offshore islands, it was John Cabot who had really discovered the proper America. Indeed, at about that time, Bristol had a sheriff called Richard Amerike, who may have been one of the people who put up money to help Cabot. And that, of course, is how America got its name...well, it is not all that more unlikely a story than the usual one, that the continent was named after Vespucci, one of Columbus's successors in the southern hemisphere, whose Christian name was Amerigo.

We shall return to these points. First let us consult Samuel Eliot Morison, an American historian, who has written a life of Columbus, a history of the American Navy in the second world war, and various other works which have found general approval among both historians and sailors. Admiral Morison's more recent work, *The European Discovery of America: the Northern Voyages* is a large and admirable survey written with a scholarly and open mind. He has the sailor's eye for wide horizons. Consider his brief summary of Bristol, with which he introduces his chapter on the voyages of John Cabot:

> Bristol, where Cabot, his wife, and three sons settled shortly after they came to England in 1495, was the right place to gain local support. "Bristowe", as it was then pronounced and often spelled, is a truly extraordinary city. By making the most of its few natural advantages and surmounting every disadvantage, it had by 1400 become, and for four centuries remained, the second seaport in the kingdom. Bristol has never decayed. It welcomed the age of steam, built the first iron screw steamship *Great Britain*, and hundreds of other steamships, created great industries out of its Spanish trade in sherry and its American trade in cocoa and tobacco, survived some very severe bombing in World War II, and in 1969 enjoyed a trade not far short of £300 million per annum.

Well, that is a fair and spacious tribute. Admiral Morison spent some time in Bristol pursuing his researches, and one of the people who helped him was P.V.McGrath, Reader in History in the University of Bristol. McGrath has these recollections of Morison, the seadog and scholar:

> Seadog and scholar? Yes, but in reverse order. Scholar first, seadog second, and primarily in order to be a better scholar — though he knows and loves the sea. He was a Harvard Professor of History with a long list of scholarly publications, including a majestic book on Columbus, when in 1942 he suggested to President Roosevelt that he should write a history of American naval operations in the war

— not an "official" history, but "Morison's history". He was given access to all the top-secret documents, but he was no armchair historian. He took part in many naval operations. Of Guadalcanal, for example, he says "We cannot pretend to write of that stinking island with the detachment and objectivity expected of trained historians, for both Commander Shaw [his collaborator] and I had a part in the torment and passion"; again, he says, "I know from personal experience how great a part luck plays in naval warfare. I am probably more charitable towards mistakes than many writers who never get their feet wet."

When I was asked to help show him Bristol, I didn't know quite what to expect. A top-ranking scholar with degrees from a dozen or so Universities, an admiral, an American — the result might be formidable, even frightening. He turned out to be completely charming, courteous, thoughtful, modest, and anxious to get to know Bristol. One felt he really wanted to know, not just to get something he could stick in for a bit of "local colour". It was in line with his practice of trying to get to the heart of the matter — going in a small boat over much of Columbus's route, flying over the coastline along which Cabot must have sailed.

In his book, Morison deals with all the European exploration of north America, up to the year 1600. Obviously we cannot deal with all the interesting points he raises, but there are two things we should touch on. The first concerns the early voyages of the Norsemen; the second of course concerns John Cabot, and his son Sebastian, and the claims which they made, and which have been made on their behalf. And these aspects of the subject illustrate very well one of Morison's favourite themes, that matters of national and even local pride tend to obscure, indeed have repeatedly obscured, the natural light of scholarship. In other words, the questions of who got where first have become a battleground where even good scholars find patriotism dominating reason.

Here is an example. October the twelfth, in the United States of America, is Christopher Columbus day. Then they specially celebrate the man who first introduced the New World to the Old.

But in 1965, on the eve of Columbus Day — and we doubt if the date was chosen by accident — the University of Yale published a book called *The Vinland Map and the Tartar Relation*. This book contained a map, now widely known as "The Vinland Map", which suggested that Columbus had been forestalled, several hundred years earlier, by the Norsemen.

This was by no means a new suggestion. The old Norse sagas contain accounts of voyages which have usually been thought to be descriptions of landings at various points in North America. Archaeological research has confirmed this supposition. That there were such landings is accepted by Admiral Morison, though he was inclined to think the map is a forgery. He is probably right, and later carbon fourteen dating tests have gone some way to confirm it. The arguments are technical, and any way that is not our present point. The thought that there should be a *map*, dating apparently from before the time of Columbus, showing that people in Europe knew a great deal about America already, infuriated many Americans, who had no doubt where their loyalties lay. This was the comment of Mr. John La Corte, head of the United States Italian Historical Society:

> The University's report has the flavour of absolute prejudice. We very much regret the release, even if it is true, and it isn't. Columbus colonized the New World. We've got the facts. You and I are here. We're going to put Yale University against the wall.

In the *New York Herald Tribune*, it was reported that:

> Italian-American societies, scholars, and politicians, rallied to Columbus's defence as parades throughout the nation, including one with one-hundred-thousand marchers on New York's Fifth Avenue, stepped off in his honour.

The President of the New York City Council, Mr. Paul Screvane, had a practical point to make about Leif Ericsson, the Norseman whose alleged discovery of America the Vinland Map (and also the less questionable Tartar Relation) could be held to substantiate:

> If Leif Ericsson in fact really discovered this hemisphere, I must say he and his Vikings did not exploit it. In my travels round this town, I find very few Vikings, and very many Italo-Americans.

And the matter was summed up, from an Italo-Spanish-American point of view — remember Columbus was an Italian, like Cabot and sailed under the Spanish flag — in a chalk-scrawl on the wall, in east Boston, which declared:

LEIF ERICSSON IS A FINK.

Now that is all very comical, we may think; imagine anyone thinking it made any difference who had got there first. Just like those Italo-Spanish-Americans. But we find Admiral Morison, in a footnote to his chapter on the Cabot voyages, saying this:

> The reader should keep in mind that English and Anglo-Canadian historians are desperately eager to prove that Cabot touched the American mainland, so that they

can claim a "first" for him as a discoverer of the continent, Columbus not having set foot on the *mainland* before 1498.

And he goes on to explain why the English historians, including J.A.Williamson, whom he agrees is "the greatest authority on the Cabots", are wrong in thinking that John Cabot touched the mainland. It is conceivable that this argument might work both ways, even against the valiant admiral. For instance, after fully recognizing the existence of the Norse settlements and giving proper credit to Leif Ericsson and the others, he says:

> What relation do these early Norse colonies bear to the great discovery of Columbus? In my opinion, nothing.

Yet if there was, through the northern discoveries, to say nothing of rumours of the ancient world — if there was this knowledge, these rumours that a new land lay to the west, how can one say it had *nothing* to do with Columbus, or for that matter Cabot?

We know what they were both trying to do. They were trying to find a quick sea route to the Spice Islands. Spices in those days — "when there were no refrigerators", as Admiral Morison puts it — were precious, the only way to keep food and make it eatable, the only way (so it was thought) to fight off disease. Columbus looked for the spice lands in the south, Cabot in the north, but both of them found America in the way.

We do not really know much about John Cabot. He left Bristol in the ship *Mathew* in 1497, made a landfall on the northern tip of Newfoundland — this is Morison's account — and returned to Bristol after a trip of eleven weeks, including nearly a month exploring by sea the Newfoundland coastline. He had a fine reception when he got back, and dashed off to London to report his success to Henry VII, who rewarded him, not over-lavishly. He was conscious of his glory, and inclined to make sweeping Latin gestures of goodwill, such as promising an island to his barber. He set off with five ships on another voyage in 1498. One of the ships soon had to put back to Ireland. The others were lost, John Cabot with them. His history was subsequently confused by extravagant statements by his son Sebastian, who may have accompanied him on his first voyage, and was certainly a sailor himself, but inclined to attribute to himself the deeds of his father. He seems to have been a good companion, a fine man at a party, but he has not made it easier for subsequent historians.

Let us call in Paddy Mcgrath again for his comments:

> History is full of examples of historians being influenced by national bias. Professional historians like to think themselves above such things, but it breaks

through all the same. Local pride comes in, too, like the story, first put out in 1910, that the name America comes from Richard Amerike, the sheriff of Bristol, who paid Cabot his pension. The French-Canadians, the Portuguese, the Scandinavians, the English have all been involved in claiming what Professor Morison calls "firsts" for their nationals. Morison, as an American, can afford to look on these things with a twinkle in his eye, with detached amusement. But I think he pushes this nationalism too far. What seems to be more to the point is that scholars are much too inclined once they have taken up a novel position, to cling to it too tenaciously, to be reluctant to say "I was wrong." I think this bedevils the Discovery Industry — a fairly close preserve. The evidence is scanty, and different interpretations are possible. Thus we have scholars on the basis of a document that turned up in 1956, arguing that America was discovered by Bristolians before Cabot, but that they then couldn't find it again. Alwyn Ruddock writes: "All the evidence points to a discovery of the coast of North America by Bristol men at some uncertain date prior to 1480, but their landfall was lost again in the Atlantic mists until John Cabot rediscovered it in 1497." The Atlantic mists seem to add a touch of authenticity.

Another scholar, with the same evidence, argues that it wasn't in fact lost in the Atlantic mists. Bristolians just kept quiet about it and kept it as their own secret — maybe to discourage others from getting in on the Newfoundland fisheries.

Professor Morison has great fun with such views — I think he is a shade too rough with some of those who put them forward, although in the present state of knowledge I think he is right. But the point is not nationalism, but the attachment of scholars to a point of view they have put forward. In the Discovery Industry, every scholar hopes yet another document will turn up which will prove him right, and equally fears lest a rival will get hold of something which will prove him wrong.

As to the Cabots,

...The question is whether John Cabot in 1497 landed on the mainland or whether he merely landed on the island of Newfoundland. If he landed on the mainland, he beat Columbus to it, and England can claim a "first" since Columbus didn't land on the mainland till his third voyage in 1498. It's a highly technical argument involving considerations of latitude, the distance you could sail in the conditions that happened to prevail at the time and the proper interpretation of the document that turned up in 1956. Williamson, who has done an immense amount of work on Cabot, argues for a mainland landing. Morison argues forcibly against this. He writes, "Williamson to my astonishment gives Cabot a Maine landfall" and produces plausible, and as far as I can judge, convincing arguments against him. Morison admits that his readers will think his rconstruction of Cabot's voyage assumes a lot — and adds, "I cheerfully plead guilt", but all the same his assumptions do seem to make sense of most of the evidence and I think he is as right as one can be, given the existing evidence. Perhaps I am prejudiced by the undoubted fact that he knows a lot about sailing and about the seas in question. I don't really think it does matter all that much — but that would be heresy to those in the Discovery business. It may well be that the first European to put foot on the American continent at this time was not Columbus or Cabot but some Unknown Seaman who leapt ashore first, but who just didn't matter to people at the time because he wasn't in command.

It is not easy to sort out the relative achievements of father and son, because the son, Sebastian, was a slippery customer in some ways; Morison is inclined to agree with the comment that Sebastian Cabot was the greatest liar in the history of discovery. Sebastian may have gone with his father on the great voyage of 1497; he *may* have been in one of the ships in the second ill-fated expedition of 1498 in which his father disappeared. Sebastian was long credited with having sailed right down the American coast on this expedition, but no one accepts that now. It seems agreed that he did go on an expedition of his own in 1508 and he was apparently looking for a way through North America to Asia — the North West passage, which wasn't there, or a passage south. He is said to have gone as far south as Cuba. Later he became a big shot in the service of Spain, but he also kept up English connections and right at the end of his life in the 1550s he was Governor of a company looking for a North-East passage to Asia. It sent out the Chancellor and Willoughby expedition in 1553 which didn't find the passage but did open up the English trade with Russia. He was inclined to give himself a lot of credit for exploration. Maybe he felt his father hadn't got the credit he deserved, and he would try to cash in on the business.

Well, John Cabot remains a remote figure; Sebastian less so, but in his way equally puzzling. Morison, to return to his book for a moment, says, "One cannot help liking Sebastian. He was a genial and cheerful liar, devoted (in so far as it helped him) to the cause of oceanic discovery." And he repeats this picture of him, drawn when he was 74 years old, having a drink with Stephen Borough, master of the *Searchthrift*, about to depart on a voyage to the north-east:

The 27th being Monday, the right Worshipful Sebastian Cabot came aboard our pinnace at Gravesend, accompanied with divers gentlemen, and gentlewomen, who after they had viewed our pinnace, and tasted of such cheer as we could make them aboard, they went on shore, giving to our mariners right liberal rewards; and the good old gentleman Master Cabot gave to the poor most liberal alms, wishing them to pray for the good fortune, and prosperous success of the *Searchthrift,* our pinnace. And then at the sign of the Christopher, he and his friends banqueted, and made me, and them that were in the company great cheer, and for very joy...he entered into the dance himself, amongst the rest of the young and lusty company: which being ended, he and his friends departed most gently, commending us to the governance of Almighty God.

The question remains, who discovered America? Leif Ericsson? Columbus? Cabot? St. Brendan? There is an American Etruscan Society, dedicated to the belief that the Etruscans got there first. The Japanese have put up a case. The Russians have more or less suggested that they would have done, and possibly did, but dismissed the matter as of no importance. Where did the American Indians come from? Twenty, thirty thousand years ago, they came — it is said — across the Baring Sea to settle, descendants of the Mongols. But let us leave the last word to Lawrence Witten, the American antiquarian who introduced the Vinland Map to the public, and who disarmed cross-examination by saying:

Well, it seems to me exceedingly likely that everybody has been here, at one time and another. Yes. You could say that everybody discovered America.

TIMES AND PLACES

Restoration Plymouth
Smeaton Tower
A Cornish View
A Fire at Wareham
White Cockades at Hambledon Hill
Cotehele House
Restormel Castle
A Poldhu Memorial
The Delectable Duchy
The Knockers of Lelant
The Enchanted Isles

Restoration Plymouth

Judging public opinion at a distance of three hundred years is a hazardous business. It seems likely that a majority of Englishmen were in favour of the restoration of the monarchy at any time between the execution of Charles I in 1649 and his son's return in 1660, and the number was certainly increased during the chaotic year which followed the abdication of Richard Cromwell. But the picture of a people unanimously enthusiastic in their reception of Charles II is false. Especially in areas which had fought with zeal and success on the parliamentary side, it could hardly be expected that joy would be unconfined.

Nearly every Devon town of any size had declared for parliament at the outbreak of civil war, and Plymouth had withstood a three years' siege. Its part in the war had been critically important, for so long as it remained undefeated it pinned down in the west royalist forces badly needed elsewhere; and it provided the navy, which was also on parliament's side, with one of its principal bases.

Plymouth did, of course, join in the congratulations to Charles II and the celebrations. He was "proclaimed... with greate triumph, the cunditts running two days with wyne, and shortly after a curious gift of rare plate was presented to his Majesty by this Corporation." A memorial to the king declared the town's abomination of "the rebellious and factious proceedings of the former Corporation", and the readiness of the people "to discharge our duty to your most sacred Majesty as you in your great vision shall see fitt." There were more celebrations when peace was made with Spain, and the ambassador who brought the ratification of the treaty was given civic honours; though since the prosperity of the town had risen upon the Spanish wars, it is doubtful if its feelings matched its hospitality. And there were more celebrations still eleven years later, when Charles II came to visit Plymouth himself.

There was, however, a jarring note towards the end of the visit. The mayor, after consulting with his colleagues how they "might further treat the king", suggested that he might care to make a tour of the civil war fortifications, which still existed in Freedom Fields. It was not exactly tactful to offer to show the king the lines which his father had failed to pierce, and Charles turned away without speaking, and left immediately by boat for Mount Edgcumbe. Thither the flustered corporation followed him, and managed to make their peace. This is the episode as it is described to us, but one cannot help wondering if the mayor was really as maladroit as all that. Possibly somebody thought the king would be none the worse for the reminder.

This supposition is strengthened when we recall that it was a fortification of a very different kind which had brought Charles to Plymouth. He had come to open the Citadel, the huge Vauban-style fortress on the Hoe which is Plymouth's most abiding memorial of the restoration. This could conceivably have had some value in repelling foreign attacks, though the points on both sides of the Sound would have been better places to mount defences; but it would certainly, from its position, also be very useful in quelling any future rebellious tendencies among the local citizenry. This was the view of Cosmo, Duke of Tuscany, when he paid a visit, and also the common contemporary view in Plymouth. (The parliamentary general Lambert, imprisoned on Drake's Island in the Sound, had a good view of it). One sad thing about the building of the Citadel was that it destroyed for ever the carved figures of the two wrestlers, out on the grass of the Hoe, which commemorated the fight between Corinaeus, the supposed first Duke of Cornwall, and the giant Goemagot. The story, which is found in Geoffrey of Monmouth, is of course nothing but legend; but the figures were real enough, and were maintained at corporation expense for many years.

Charles II paid a number of further visits to Plymouth. A mercer, John Allen, recorded that the king had been gracious enough to kiss his young wife; and on another occasion he touched for the king's evil in St. Andrew's Church. Towards the end of his reign, he further showed his affection for the town by mutilating its charter.

We have contradictory opinions on the social life of Plymouth in the years after 1660. Bernard Gomme, the engineer who planned the Citadel, called it "this wilderness town, almost out of the world, where the Presbyterian is in his most Puritanical seat, and there is neither company nor women fit for a gentleman to pass his time with." But according to John Quicke, one of the leading puritan divines, the place was going the way of Sodom, with "multitudes of devils that walk in temples and congregations, in streets, and houses, in chambers and closets, in ships and shops, upon keys and exchange." Of the two, one prefers Gomme's judgement, which suggests a reasonably large area of respectability, with the savage fringe which was only too characteristic of any large town in the seventeenth century, and particularly a port. But there was probably some general lowering of morality. Not all the restrictions of the Interregnum had been bad ones: if the travelling players came back, so did cock-fighting and bear-baiting; so did witch-hunting — one of the most famous cases in Devon, the trial and execution of the three witches of Bideford, took place in 1682. Cromwell had had some sensible ideas about legal reform: "to hang a man for six-and-eightpence", he had said, "is a thing God will reckon for"; and Barebones' Parliament had declared that first offenders for theft must not be hanged. But Cromwell died before he had made much headway against the lawyers, and now all this collapsed. Savage penalties of course produced a high crime rate, the Plymouth gaols were full — and the conditions appalling, even by contemporary standards — and every week brought its new quota of felons, publicly hanged in chains.

Gentlemen could once again settle their honourable differences in a duel. There was an example at Plymouth in 1665. Francis, a son of Mount Edgcumbe, and John Skelton, son of the governor of the fort, fell to odds over an archery match. Afterwards there was a brawl at the Three Cranes Inn, where the bystanders prevented too much violence being done; but early the next morning the contestants crept away to a higher part of the town, and had their quarrel out. Francis Edgcumbe was killed, and Skelton disappeared, not for fear of the law, but of the Edgcumbe interest, still very powerful in Plymouth.

What must have distressed the Plymouth people most in these first years after the restoration was the collapse of England's naval greatness. The Dutch sailed into the Medway and actually towed away the *Royal Charles*, the English flagship (it is difficult to imagine it happening when she had been called the *Naseby*). Their ships pranced unimpeded up and down the Devon coast. The Dutch contempt for their adversaries is illustrated by an engraving of John Skinner, a strange little man who was known as the Plymouth dwarf. Underneath a picture of him they attributed to him these words: "I challenge all those who by a thousand boasts defy my sword, as yet firmly sheathed. By and by I may draw it." The trouble was there was no sword to be drawn. The naval preparations were in complete confusion, partly because of lack of money. The Plymouth bakers refused to supply the fleet with bread unless they were paid.

But Plymouth was not an unpatriotic city; it was the city of Drake and Hawkins; only a few years earlier, in Cromwell's time, Blake had died within sight of the Hoe after his last glorious voyage. If Pepys, in London commented on the popular discontent in the change of affairs since Cromwell's time, local remarks would certainly be even more vitriolic. There were many former parliamentary soldiers in the town, and on at least one occasion they engaged in conspiracy against the crown, under the leadership of a Major Cawborne. The password was "Tumbledown Dick", the name by which the unfortunate Richard Cromwell had come to be known. One man was arrested for crying out that King Charles was doomed to an early death; Francis Buller of Saltash got into trouble, because his servant was reported to have said that if his master were tried, he doubted not that he would find friends enough to take his part, and that it might cost the king as much as the five members did his father.

But those who suffered most severely under the restoration in Plymouth were the Protestant Dissenters, those whom Bernard Gomme called "the Presbyterians". Not very many of them were in fact Presbyterians, but royalists often used the word as a general term of abuse for puritans, irrespective of their doctrines.

Plymouth, and indeed all Devon, was a stronghold of the Independents, with a good sprinkling of Quakers and Baptists. During the Interregnum a wall had been built across Exeter Cathedral, dividing the chancel from the nave, so that both Presbyterians and Independents had been able to worship in the building at the same time. The destruction of the wall was doubtless an architectural improvement, but it did mean that only one sort of Christian could use the building instead of two. The Protectorate had been a period of comparative religious liberty, remarkably wide in its scope for that age. The restoration returned to the theory of one state church, and penalties for those who refused to join it. Dissenting ministers in Plymouth, as elsewhere, were sometimes sent to prison, or forced by the Five Mile Act to retire to the country and hold their services there. A favourite place for Dissenting meetings was the Saltstone Rock, where as we have seen John Hicks preached off the coast of the South Hams; since its jurisdiction was disputed no authority would take the responsibility of arresting the worshippers. But the tide was awkward, and it was a long way to walk.

It would be wrong to make too much of the sufferings of the Dissenters, however, since the Episcopalian clergy had suffered in the same way in the days of the civil war. The numbers in Devon were about the same on each occasion, though by no means always in the same places. One ironic twist of the Anglican return was that it brought the post Herrick — a devoted royalist — reluctantly back to his living at Dean Prior. He detested Devon, and had bidden it farewell with the words,

> Dean Bourn, farewell! I never look to see
> Dean, or thy watry incivility.

And on another occasion,

> First let us dwell in widest seas,
> Next with severest savages,
> Last let us make our best abode
> Where human foot as yet ne'er trod,
> Search worlds of ice and rather there
> Live than in loathed Devonshire.

And the best that Charles II could do for him was to send him back again!

Restoration Plymouth was a turbulent, colourful place: not an unattractive town as towns went. Crowded and illegal chapels; crowded gaols; crowded inns with signs in wood-carving (the sign of the Lion and Lamb illustrated the prophecy that they should lie down together, and is described as "quaint"); the head of Colonel Alured, one of the parliamentary leaders, slowly rotting away on a spike on the Guildhall; the old fortifications crumbling in Freedom Fields; the new ones rising on the Hoe. Most of the people were doubtless glad enough of the free drink when the king came back — most people are always grateful for such mercies, and dissent was not yet associated with teetotalism; but on the whole, remembering its history and its character, it is not surprising that when the Stewarts were finally expelled, and William of Orange landed at Brixham, Plymouth was the first town formally to declare for him.

Smeaton Tower

The story of the Eddystone Light is one of the most gripping episodes in the long struggle of men against the sea. It has been told, unforgettably, by Mr. Fred Majdalany, and there is little the rest of us can add to it. It has all the elements of tragic grandeur; the brilliant, erratic, opera-bouffe character of Winstanley, the pioneer: his deliberate challenge to destiny when he declared his longing to spend a night in his lighthouse amidst the greatest storm ever known, and destiny's granting of his wish; the resumption of the toll of wrecks immediately Winstanley's light had been swept away. Then the extraordinary but successful design of John Rudyerd, who built a kind of wooden man-of-war set on its end, which succumbed only to the most dreaded enemy of the man-of-war, fire. John Smeaton's lighthouse, completed in 1759, was the third, and the first to bear any resemblance to modern ideas of what a lighthouse should be.

Smeaton was a Yorkshireman, one of the remarkable group of north-country engineers who led the way in transforming England's pattern of life in the hundred years or so after 1750. He had none of the brilliance of his predecessors, and none of their weaknesses. He was enormously capable, with all a Yorkshireman's care in checking and cross-checking. He was a religious man, and caused to be inscribed around the lighthouse walls the text: *Except the Lord build the house, they labour in vain that build it.* The combination of faith in a divine purpose and meticulous attention to detail proved as efficacious as Cromwell had found it; as, in fact, it usually is. Smeaton's lighthouse lasted more than a hundred years, and only the treachery of the rock beneath it caused it to be replaced. It is this which raises the one query concerning Smeaton's reputation. The flaw in the rock had been observed at the time of the building, and continued to cause some anxiety throughout the lighthouse's existence. It is a little difficult to see why he did not build on one

276

of the adjoining rocks, as was done with the fourth, and present lighthouse.

The decision to move the lighthouse, stone by stone, to Plymouth Hoe, was an astonishing tribute to the admiration in which Smeaton was held. This kind of operation was a great deal less commonplace in the middle of the nineteenth century than it is today. Out by the Eddystone on only a slightly rough day, one is appalled at the difficulties of building there, even with modern equipment. Why go to all the extra trouble of this careful dismantling and reassembly? But we are glad it was done. Many Plymothians, as we mention elsewhere, are rather distressed at the proliferations of statuary which tend to give the Hoe the air of a mausoleum. But nobody challenges the right of Smeaton Tower to stand there, exchanging a dignified salute with its successor on the horizon.

A Cornish View

Knill's Monument is a big triangular granite obelisk on the hills behind St. Ives. It was built by John Knill, collector of the port and mayor of St. Ives in the eighteenth century. He intended to be buried at its foot, but changed his mind and left his body to anatomists. One side of the monument are the words "Johannes Knill, 1782"; on the second, "I know that my Redeemer liveth"; and on the third, "Resurgam: Nil Desperandum", which suggests he had a sense of humour. Every five years, a ceremony is carried out in accordance with his will. Ten maidens dressed in white, accompanied by two widows and a fiddler, walk in procession to the monument, and then dance round it, singing the hundredth psalm. The ceremony nowadays has taken on a character of a holiday amusement rather then a solemn remembrance.

However, Knill was a benefactor in his way, for his monument is a convenient destination for a walk that yields one of the noblest and most characteristic views in Cornwall. Once one of us was asked to make a short broadcast that would give listeners a sound-picture of a typical stretch of Cornish country. The steps of the monument seemed the obvious place from which to do it. It is not specially high up — about six hundred feet, well below Trencrom to the south — but so placed that it commands a prospect of nearly all the west Cornish peninsula. There are the small farms in the gently rolling countryside: looking pretty and prosperous when the sun shines, though in fact farming is often hard going, particularly on the upper slopes, where the soil is thin and the granite boulders keep poking their noses through. There are the square, roofless, towered buildings, scattered all over the land like small and ugly churches — the derelict engine-houses of the old tin mines.

Wheal Speed is just below the monument itself — many of the mines had lovely names, and many of them beginning with the old Cornish word "Wheal". But the mines have followed the language into disuse. Now there are only two or three working in all the county, and even at the beginning of the century there were scores. Some of them had been in existence for centuries: one of them, Ding Dong, is always said to have been producing tin in pre-Christian times, when the Phoenicians came to trade.

Though the collapse of tin mining was a terrible blow to Cornwall, two things have helped to take its place. One is china clay, which William Cookworthy, the first maker of English porcelain, discovered in Cornwall, at Tregonnin Hill, in the eighteenth century. Today, china clay is used for a great many things besides china — in face powder and toothpaste, for instance. On a clear day, from Knill's monument, it is possible to glimpse in the distance some of the big white pyramids that are the mark of the claypits (though like the slag-heaps of the coal mines, they are only the waste). The other thing, of course, has been the tourist trade. Cornishmen at one time hated their coastline; it was too rocky and dangerous altogether, especially on the north side —

From Padstow Port to Lundy Light
Is a watery grave by day and by night

— but its noble outlines have proved to have great tourist appeal, and there are plenty of beaches tucked between the headlands. Fishing is another industry which has declined. It still goes on — looking across St. Ives Bay from the monument you can usually see some crabbers at anchor, and across in Mount's Bay (which you can also glimpse) are the inshore trawlers from Newlyn. But places such as St. Ives, and Mevagissey, and Looe, and Penzance now rely a great deal on the summer visitors to keep them going. Nearly every fisherman's wife seems to take in guests. All round west Cornwall on a fine summer's day, the beaches are crowded. It is a mild climate, almost sub-tropical; often wet, to be sure, but rarely cold. At Falmouth, we used to look at the bananas growing, rather tardily, in the open at Kimberley Park. During the war, they must have been very nearly the only bananas in Britain: not very many, not very big, but still, indisputably, bananas. They were auctioned off for good causes.

You cannot see all this from Knill's monument, but you can see enough to give you, in one vista, something of a people's history and life. And you can see the pinnacles of St. Michael's Mount, looking so absurdly like a fairy-tale castle. it is a walk worth taking, and had it not been for old John Knill I wonder bow many of us would have taken it?

A Fire at Wareham

Wareham, in Dorset, is a town of gracious churches; a town of Thomas Hardy and T.E.Lawrence, whose noble and little-known effigy, by Eric Kennington, lies in St. Martin's. It is also a town which suffered, in the eighteenth century, a fire which was startling even in those days when large fires were a much more commonplace enemy of life than they are now. With concrete and iron replacing wood, with mains water and a fire service to use it, it is not so easy today to realise how dreaded an enemy a big fire was to our forbears.

It was on a Sunday, when everybody was at church (from the figures of confirmations in the eighteenth century, Wareham seems to have been a very devout town, even in those doldrum days for the Church of England). Before it could be stopped, 133 houses had been burnt down, and most of the town's principal buildings. A good deal of the loss, incidentally, was covered by the Sun Fire Insurance Company, that pioneering organisation. One suspects that their heavy commitments were more than compensated when the word got round that they had paid up — in so many villages to this day you see those brave sun plaques by the cottage doors. In fact, one is inclined to guess that the biggest long-term effect of the fire of Wareham was the impulse it gave to the insurance business. The town itself, though sadly scarred, was rebuilt, with all the patient resource one expects from Dorset men. It was the thatched houses, of course, which caused the fire to spread so quickly, and today you are not allowed to thatch a house in Wareham. Those that still stand almost all date from before the fire; their positions are a good rough guide to the fire's extent.

The Guildhall was destroyed, and with it the original version of the town's arms. This has provided a comfortable field of argument among the local experts in heraldry ever since.

The house of John Hutchins was destroyed. It had been suggested to John Hutchins, twenty years earlier, that he should write a history of Dorset, and he set about it in the painstaking, timeless way that those eighteenth-century antiquarians did. He had, however, some ideas which oddly anticipate the mechanized historians of the twentieth century. He sent out a questionnaire to every parish in Dorset. He had an enormous response, and all these papers, together with his digest of the material, would have been lost had not his wife — so the story goes — dashed into the burning house at the risk of her life, and brought them out. The book was published in the end, an invaluable source-book for the history of Dorset, though it appeared in print only after John Hutchins was dead.

Another interesting thing about this fire was that there was an effort to provide relief for those who had not safeguarded themselves with the Sun Fire Company — and there were, too, the usual arguments, which are reproduced today, about the morality and wisdom of such a proceeding. £500 came from the king; over £300 from those ever-generous people, the Quakers.

Sir Frederick Treves, the great surgeon, who wrote a lovely book about the county, calls Wareham "the Mrs. Gummidge of Dorset town", presumably in reference to her complaint, "I am a lone lorn creetur, and everthing goes contrairy with me." "It may be", he goes on, "that its troubles in latter years have made it 'contrary'." We have never, on visits to the town, found any evidence of this ourselves. But certainly a slight contrariness is suggested by a town which, after being remorselessly pillaged through the centuries by Norsemen and Mercians, by York and Lancaster, by Roundhead and Cavalier, proceeded, when at last left to itself, to burn itself down.

White Cockades at Hambledon Hill

The episode of the Clubmen is one of the sadder passages in the English Civil War. They were countryfolk of Dorset, Wiltshire, and Somerset, who had suffered from the ravages of both sides in turn, and who banded together for self-defence. There is some evidence that Royalist agents tried to use them for their own purposes, but there is no doubt that mostly they were what they claimed to be, and that their battlecry, "England, and our homes!" represented their real interests.

There were perhaps five thousand of them at their strongest, and one theory is that they drew their name from the clubs with which they were armed. Certainly their weapons were primitive, but they must have made a brave showing as they gathered from the villages, white cockades in their hats.

They sent a petition to the king, but the king, even had he been minded, could have done nothing for them for this was July of 1645, and Fairfax and Cromwell were sweeping the west in the last major campaign of the war. After the Clubmen had attacked a parliamentary post at Sturminster Newton, Fairfax decided he must deal with this possible threat to his flank, and Cromwell with a detachment of dragoons scattered the villagers in a brief fight on Castle Hill, Shaftesbury. But the Clubmen were not done with yet. About two thousand of them took up position within the ancient fortress of Hambledon — not the cricketing Hambledon in Hampshire, but Hambledon Hill in Dorset. They were determined to fight to the death. Their leader, Mr. Bravel, the Rector of Cerne Abbas, threatened "to pistol whoever surrendered" (there was once a theory, not supported, that the ancient giant of Cerne

280

Abbas, carved on a hill, was produced by the Clubmen).

But in spite of the enormous natural strength of the position, it turned out to be neither death, save for a few, nor glory. Villagers with clubs could not fight the New Model Army. Fifty dragoons charged the hill, and it was all over in a few minutes. "I believe", says Cromwell "we killed not twelve of them, but cut very many." Some of them escaped by sliding down the hill's steep sides on their bottoms, but about three hundred were taken prisoner, including four vicars and curates, a circumstance which doubtless caused a good deal of knowledgeable head-wagging among the Army puritans.

And now, what to do with them? The day after the fight, on August 4th , Cromwell reported to his general. The prisoners were, he said, "poor silly creatures, whom if you please to let me send home they promise to be very dutiful for time to come, and will be hanged before they come out again."

Generosity, as usual, paid; and in spite of an occasional subsequent attempt to revive the movement in the king's interests, there was no more serious trouble. It had been, according to one's point of view, a last gallant flickering of the yeoman spirit, or a stupid waste of time and life. But it is ironical to think that the sons of many of those villagers whom Cromwell scattered and spared must have lost their lives when, a generation later, once again they took up their clubs and pitchforks to war: but this time for the Protestant Duke, Monmouth.

Cotehele House

Cotehele House is a Tudor manor, at Calstock in Cornwall, just across the river Tamar from Devon. Calstock, famous for its strawberries, is a pretty village in one of the loveliest parts of the Tamar valley (though in recent years the waterfront has been marred by a hideous cafe with a juke box) and Cotehele is more than worthy of the beauty of its surroundings. It is recognized as the outstanding example of its style and period of architecture in Cornwall, and probably in all the south-west. Its history is appropriately embellished with legends, from the days of the lord of the manor under Richard III, Richard Edgcumbe, who avoided the king's troops by wrapping his cap round a stone and throwing it into the river, thus convincing them that he was drowned. The current guide to Cotehele speaks of this Richard Edgcumbe in glowing terms as a Cornish hero, though in fact he seems to have been much the same kind of unscrupulous barbarian as were most English landowners at the time of the Wars of the Roses. There is also the story of the lady buried in the family vault, and wakened from a trance by a sexton who was after her jewellery. That one, as R.A.J. Walling observed, "hath a familiar sound."

Whatever his shortcomings, Richard Edgcumbe helped to found the family fortunes, and soon after his time the present Cotehele House was built. It remained the property of the Edgcumbe family until the year 1944, when it was accepted by the Treasury in part payment of death duties on the estate of the Fifth Earl of Mount Edgcumbe. In 1947 it was handed over to the National Trust, who found themselves confronted with some awkward problems of restoration. They did what they could, tackling it bit by bit, but every attempt at improvement seemed to reveal something more that needed doing. They started, for instance, treating the roof beams of the hall for woodworm, and in the process discovered that the death-watch beetle and dry rot were also in possession. Every step forward seemed to involve two steps back. "We'd have managed somehow", said Mr.Cook, the clerk to the works, who regards Cotehele with a deep affection unsuccessfully disguised by an air of detachment; "We'd have managed somehow: We couldn't have let it go. We'd have *had* to have managed" But just how, it seemed difficult to tell: until in 1958 a grant from the Historic Buildings Council of £14,000 made a proper renovation possible. The work began in the summer of that year and was finished early in 1960. Enough of it was completed in December, 1959, for the annual carol services in the great hall to become a festival of thanksgiving. These services have become a Cotehele tradition. There are two of them, one Anglican and one Methodist, because this is Cornwall — but there are no real denominational barriers, and plenty of people go to both, or are content to go to either according to their convenience, rather than their dogma.

Cotehele has been happy in its modern guardians. We have mentioned Mr. Cook, clerk to the works. Then there is Mr.Stephens, the builder, who looks on the task as the crown of a life's work. Mr.Stephens likes old buildings. You can gather his opinion of some modern architectural tendencies by the way he pronounces words such as "concrete" and "chromium". It was a real restoration, not a patching up. It required the same sort of craftsmanship as the original builders knew. The slate for the roofs came from Delabole, which has roofed almost every big house in Cornwall for centuries; the timber came mostly from Tamerton Foliot, just across the river, and in one case from a huge and ancient oak tree in the gardens.

Then there is Mrs.Down, the curator. Mrs.Down had been housekeeper for the Earls of Mount Edgcumbe, and viewed her new duties with some suspicion. But Cotehele won again, and now the visitors who come — many thousands a year — can entrust themselves to the friendliest, most un-mechanical and knowledgeable of guides.

Let us hope that in years to come many more thousands will take the opportunity of seeing the restored Cotehele. A noble ruin has its beauties: but manor houses were homes for people, not architectural or theological statements, and a dilapidated Cotehele would not have been beautiful — it would only have been miserable. Mr.Cook, Mr.Stephens, Mr.Edwards — the architect — and all the craftsmen did their work well; and how well it was worth doing.

Restormel Castle

Restormel Castle is the noble ruin which you see if you travel through Cornwall, by train or road, a mile or so to the east of Lostwithiel. There is a legend that it was once the home of the Kings of Cornwall, and it is sometimes supposed that from this legend a tradition arose at Lostwithiel which was observed on Easter Sunday well into the last century, though no vestige of it exists today.

The freeholders of the town and manor gathered together: freeholders were then a special class. For one thing, if their freeholds were worth forty shillings a year, they had the right to vote in parliamentary elections, in the county divisions. There were not very many of them; and they took it in turns, at Easter, to assume the title and dignity of the "Duke of Restormel". The temporary Duke, brightly clad and on horseback, crowned and carrying a sceptre, a sword borne before him, headed the company as they proceeded in state to the church. It was a solemn, not primarily a convivial, occasion, which distinguishes it from "boy bishops", "lords of misrule", and similar medieval junketings.

At the church, he was greeted by the parson, and heard the Easter service. Afterwards there was an enormous dinner, where the chosen freeholder continued to assume the position and privileges of a duke. Afterwards the duke disrobed; but the ceremony was not accompanied by any jocularity, any suggestion that he had had his fun and now must expect to be debagged or ducked. People who, while they did not see the ceremony themselves, but were told about it by parents or grandparents, have said that what impressed all the participants was that it was always regarded as a solemn occasion.

It is very doubtful whether it had anything to do with the Kings of Cornwall or the Dukes of Restormel. Memories of these alleged persons may have inspired the ceremony, but it sounds much more like the forty-shilling freeholders taking over an old tradition and using it for their own purposes. In the unreformed parliament before 1832, they were the one body of electors, all over the country, who could reasonably claim to be representative of public opinion. Their wishes were constantly thwarted, especially in Cornwall, by the owners of the pocket boroughs and the rotten boroughs, of which there were a great many in that part of the world. The Duke of Restormel became the protest of the freeholders against all those borough-mongering dukes who were constantly, by money and influence, overriding them.

This is only a guess: but the more we learn about folklore, the more we are convinced that many supposedly ancient customs either began, or were revived, as a result of comparatively modern situations. One is always supposed to begin any account of a Cornish custom by a reference to King Arthur; but we don't think he had much to do with this one.

A Poldhu Memorial

In 1961 the National Trust made rather an unusual acquisition in Cornwall. They were given forty acres of Poldhu, down near the Lizard. This is not, scenically, an area of outstanding natural beauty, though the coastline is magnificent and Poldhu Cove deservedly famous. The reason for the preservation of the forty acres is an historical one. They contain the site of Marconi's first transatlantic radio transmitter, and the title deeds were handed over to the Trust by the English Electric Group, which included the Marconi Company.

It was in the autumn of 1901 that Marconi and his helpers bought some land outside Poldhu village and started building there, to the perplexity of the inhabitants. Marconi had then been six years in England, and had already demonstrated that his wireless telegraphy was effective over short distances. His critics, however, pointed out — and it seemed, on the face of it, a sound argument — that since the earth was round, it would be impossible to use radio waves for anything but local communications, as they presumably travelled in straight lines and would therefore shoot off uselessly into space. Marconi did not believe that the waves behaved in this way, and a transmission from England to America would prove his point. This was what brought him to Poldhu.

The transmitter was duly built — an assortment of huge glass jars inside a wooden hut, tall masts and trailing nets without. Marconi told his staff to send out single letters in Morse regularly at every hour, and set off for Newfoundland with one assistant. They carried some box kites and balloons to make a receiving aerial. The assistant worked the aerial while Marconi listened on headphones in a tent — on the Newfoundland coast in winter. On December 12th, unmistakably, he heard Poldhu signalling the three dots that represent in Morse the letter S. It was at that moment that wireless telegraphy took the decisive step in its journey from the crank's dream of the 'nineties to the commonplace miracle of today.

The station at Poldhu stayed there until 1937, when it was dismantled. Part of the site was given to the National Trust then, but the Marconi Company retained forty acres. All that stands to recall the past is a granite column. But the Lizard peninsula is studded with radio masts of one purpose and another, so is might still be said of Marconi at Poldhu that *si monumentum requiris, circumspice.*

Places can have a value because of their associations, apart from their own merits. We cherish the houses in which the great have lived, even if their architecture is undistinguished. In the city of Plymouth, Freedom Fields is still kept an open space — the spot where the citizens threw back the king's army on a desperate Sabbath day in the civil war — and though now it is only a not-very-attractive public park, that is better than covering it with blocks of flats. In the same way, the fields of Poldhu are rightly honoured as the setting of an historic occasion.

The Delectable Duchy

Seventy-four per cent of Cornishmen think that the county gets too many visitors. Eighty-two per cent think that the tourist board should stop trying to attract them. These figures are provided by a recent survey, published in Truro. Furthermore, seventy-three per cent would like to limit the number of visitors, even if it meant setting up check-points on the boundary. And given the proposition that increasing tourism "would not harm the beauty of Cornwall too much", ninety-one per cent disagreed with it.

I used to live in Cornwall, and for many years took my holiday there. I am not exactly surprised by these figures, though I view them with some caution. Truro is not a tourist resort, and you would no doubt get a different result if you ran your survey from, say, Falmouth or St.Ives. But one can understand what prompted the replies. A summer's day in the narrow streets of what was once a pretty little fishing village, now crammed to bursting with tourists and their cars, can be a harrowing experience. For three months of the year natives effectively lose their own towns, submerged fathoms deep by the touring tide, as the lost land of Lyonaesse was drowned by the sea. We know of several people who retired to places on the Cornish coast, and left again because they could not stand the summers.

But there is more to it than discomfort, and more than any marring of the landscape. Inland, Cornwall is not very beautiful anyway. It is at root a matter of pride. Cornishmen are warm-hearted, but fiercely independent, sometimes xenophobic. Looking after tourists is not the way of life they would naturally relish. It used to be said that anywhere in the world, if you saw a hole in the ground, you would find a Cornishman at the bottom of it: but the tin and copper mines of Cornwall are almost all gone. Only the derelict stacks remain, with their resounding names — Penandrea, Wheal Grambler, Ding Dong, Wheal Bloody Nose, Honey, Trelawney — telling of a vanished prosperity. There is a good deal of sentimental thinking about the mines — it was a rough life, and when attempts have been made at reopening a few, Cornishmen have not rushed to go down — but it was more of a man's life than selling ice cream for half the year. The huer's house still stands on the cliff at St.Ives, but no longer does the cry "Hevva! Hevva!" go up from there when the schools of pilchard are sighted in the bay. The pilchard, they will say sadly, is a wayward fish. It is better in some other places, but if Cornish fishing villages actually had to depend on fishing, they would mostly have a thin time of it.

There is china clay in the east, as we have seen, there is engineering at Camborne, there are docks at Falmouth, there is an assortment of light industry, but Cornwall has become heavily dependent upon tourism, and is unhappy about it. It is not the tourists that are disliked, but the dependence. More should be done, it is felt, to attract to the county light industry which would not be subject to a seasonal trade; but tourism brings in getting on for a million pounds a year, and it would take a lot of light industry to replace that.

It is an old question, and used greatly to labour the thoughts of Q, who was Cornish of the Cornish. One of the happiest and saddest of books is *Sir* Arthur Quiller-Couch's *Memories and Opinions*; a happy book because it is the product of a wise, generous and tranquil mind, a sad book because it breaks off in the middle of the fifth chapter, with that rich and varied life no more than fairly launched on its course. This was, alas! his own fault. Many years before his death, he wrote to S.C.Roberts, "There ain't going to be no reminiscences, never — never. You're the second kind friend this fortnight to hint at such a book in view of my approaching demise." When at last he allowed himself to be persuaded, there was not enough time left to finish the book.

Nevertheless, his output in his eighty-one years (he died in 1944) was such that his admirers are left with plenty to choose from: whether they prefer his novels or his short stories, or his essays, or his collected lectures, or his criticisms. Ourselves, we are particularly fond of his short stories, especially in *The Delectable Duchy*, with its touching picture of an old Cornish couple bravely setting out for the workhouse; though there are many who say he never wrote anything better than *Troy Town*, with its picture of Fowey, which of course is pronounced "Foy". As a critic, he must have come into the rather stuffy pre-1914 academic world like a breath of fresh air. His first course of lectures as the King Edward VII Professor of English Literature at Cambridge was recast, published, and has become a classic under the title *On the Art of Writing*. In the preface he declares his faith:

> Literature is not a mere Science, to be studied; but an Art, to be practised. Great as is our own literature, we must consider it as a legacy to be improved. Any nation that potters with any glory of its past, as a thing dead and done for, is to that extent renegade... Not all our pride in a Shakespeare can excuse the relaxation of an effort — however vain and hopeless — to better him, or some part of him.

That is relevant to some current literary controversies.

Perhaps the most remarkable thing about Q as a writer was that while the quality of his work varied, as the quality of any author's must, he scarcely ever wrote a shoddy sentence. This was true even of his journalism. We have been glancing through the first volume of *The Cornish Magazine*, published in 1898. His contributions were lengthy and numerous, and he can hardly have been able to give much time to their writing, yet one searches in vain for the clumsy construction, the hasty phrase, the jarring adjective.

The Cornish Magazine, in its early issues, was full of the question of the future of Cornwall. Generally, tourists are welcomed, but there was no recognition of what would be involved. *Sir* Joseph Fayrer, Bart., pointed out that "the scenery is charming; the objects of antiquarian and historical interest are numerous; there are the usual opportunities of shooting and hunting", and clearly thought that enough for anybody. *Sir* Edward Durning-Lawrence, M.P., declared that Cornwall must be "discovered", and suggested promenades, military bands, open air cafes. This provoked wrathful replies. Mr. J.L.W. Page begged "for goodness' sake let us have some place that knows not the tripper." There was a curious letter from the Penzance medical officer of health. "Above all", he said, "I would plead for their possible infirmities of digestion. I have known visitors...driven from the field, vanquished in a brave and painful struggle with food comforts readily assimilated by our robuster selves." Four knife and fork meals a day, we suppose, and all pasties.

Q himself summed up. Because of the county's economic depression, he saw no alternative to tourist development. "Since we must cater for the stranger", he wrote,

> let us do it well and honestly. Let us respect him *and* our native land...I have dreamed...of a broad and noble coast road: but always I awoke, and lo, it was a dream.

He was dubious about promenades and bands. As for the road, the fastest form of road transport known to Q was the pushbike.

Soon they will be coming down a broad motorway to Cornwall, more and more of them, for better or worse: and a picket line across Bodmin Moor cannot stop them.

Cornwall, of course, held Q's heart, and he always seemed to add a cubit to his stature when he was writing about his native county. True love sees the flaws in the beloved, and yet loves all the more: and so, though there was no Cornishman more loyal, Q could relish Cornish foibles, and even at times be severely critical of Cornish follies. For this he sometimes got into trouble with Cornishmen whose minds had a shorter view and a narrower range.

Sir Arthur Quiller-Couch said of Johnson, "He never saw literature but as a part of life." As S.C.Roberts added, Q might well have been speaking of himself. Perhaps this is why those who knew him — of whom, and how I regret it, I am not one — those who knew him feel that the best thing of all about the writings is that they reflect the man.

The Knockers of Lelant

New Year's Eve and New Year's Day were always holidays for the Cornish tin miners. They were not paid holidays, of course, for in the last century tin miners were paid, not wages, but what was called a tribute according to the amount of tin they produced. But not even the richest lode would tempt a miner to try to earn his tribute over the New Year, for that was the time when the knockers assembled. They were found, or heard, most often in West Penwith, particularly around Lelant.

The knockers, or knackers (they were often colloquially called — possibly the term "knackered" derived from them) were always about the mines, though they were not seen. They could be heard working away in the distant parts of a lode, repeating every blow of the miner's pick; but lest you dismiss them simply as an echo, they could also be heard when work had ceased for the day, even at the head of a shaft on a still night. The miner Tregarra, in one of Kingsley's novels declares, "We used to break into old shafts and adits which they had made, and find old stag's-horn pickaxes, that crumbled to pieces when we brought them to grass."

The knockers were believed to be the ghosts of the Jews who crucified our Lord, and were sent to the mines as slaves by the Roman Emperors. They were not the same as the wicked gnomes or pixies, who were also liable to turn up in mines, and seem to occur in mining mythology throughout the world. No, the knockers were quite cheerful and friendly spirits, who would often, by their knocking, draw the attention of the miners to the places where they could make the best tributes. Perhaps, reflecting what some Roman Emperors did to Christians, they felt they had got off lightly.

At the same time, the miners always treated them with the greatest respect. The mark of a cross was prohibited underground, as it was thought to bring ill luck, lest it make the knockers cross. And when at the New Year the knockers met for their annual jamboree, the miners were careful not to interfere with them.

Legend apart, Mr.Robert Hunt, a Fellow of the Royal Society, and a notably unsuperstitious writer on Cornwall, heard the knockers in the lode of tin running underneath his house in Lelant in the last century. At least, if it was not the knockers, he did not know what it could have been.

The Enchanted Isles

The Isles of Scilly — you must always call them the Isles of Scilly, and not the Scilly Isles, though the colloquial plural "The Scillies" is permissible — lie about twenty-five miles west of Land's End. I went there (writes Alan Gibson) first when I was a youngster, and I was vilely sick all the way over. I went by sea, and it is a notoriously bad crossing. Since then I have usually gone by air, which is much easier. The ship the *Scillonian*, the principal link between the islands and the mainland, used to take three and a half hours, often more in bad weather. They proudly say "The *Scillonian* puts to sea when the *Queen Mary* stays in port." Even the new *Scillonian*, which went into service about twenty-five years ago, takes about two and a half hours. By air, from St.Just, you hop over in twenty minutes. Nowadays it is even quicker by helicopter from Penzance. The air trip used to be not without its anxious moments. As the little Rapide bore down upon the aerodrome on St.Mary's — the largest island — you thought it could never manage to land. You are going far too fast ever to stop within the confines of that tiny green pocket-handkerchief. Somehow you always did it, and when you were safely down there was obviously plenty to spare, and you wondered what on earth you had been worried about; but next time you began to worry all over again. This is as it should be, for the enchanted lands are traditionally difficult to approach.

Now many lands look enchanting from a distance, and especially from the air. Naples, for instance, is decidedly less salubrious at close quarters than from a comfortable 10,000 feet. But with the Scillies the enchantment persists. As you see them spread out beneath you, flung into the middle of the ocean in a happy confusion, more than a hundred of them, as though God had been using an irregularly-shaped pepperpot, none large, many tiny, most brightly coloured on all but the dreariest of days— then you feel that the realisation cannot equal the prospect. You always feel this, and you are always agreeably confounded.

I remember a quarter of a century ago climbing to the top of Garrison Hill on St. Mary's. It is not a taxing climb — I doubt if there is anything much above a couple of hundred feet in all the islands — but it gives a commanding view. It was a perfect summer evening. Even the Atlantic rollers were mellowed into composure. The sun was plunging down behind Samson, Mincarlo, Bryher and the western isles. I had had an excellent dinner, and England had just won the final Test match. Then into St.Mary's Pool there slowly drew a rowing boat.

It was a long, eight-oared gig, the kind of boat in which long ago the islanders would race out to meet the clippers, competing for the pilotage which was one of their main sources of income. I recalled Tennyson's lines upon the journey of Odysseus:

The lights begin to twinkle from the rocks:
The long day wanes: the slow moon climbs: the deep
Moans round with many voices. Come, my friends,
'Tis not too late to seek a newer world.
Push off, and sitting well in order smite
The sounding furrows; for my purpose holds
To sail beyond the sunset, and the baths
Of all the western stars, until I die.
It may be that the gulfs will wash us down;
It may be we shall touch the Happy Isles.

Here, I thought, is Odysseus, his journey ended at last: here are the Happy Isles, where rest the souls of the brave.

The next morning I was a little surprised to discover that not a single eight-oared gig, nor anything like one, was left in the islands. There had still been some until shortly before, but they had all been sold to Newquay (where later, as it happened, I coxed one) for sea racing. I accepted the correction with proper humility. I did not risk contumely by suggesting any explanation.

The Scillonians, I suspect, do see visions sometimes, but they do not tell you about them. Their conversation turns upon more practical matters: at that time it would probably be about income tax, which they had to pay for the first time in 1954. They felt that they were already heavily taxed through freightage costs, and there were those who did not hesitate to say that the new tax would lead to depopulation. It has not in fact been too severe.

The islands have had a chequered economic history. For centuries they depended upon a tenuous harvest from the land and a sporadic one from the sea. Neither depth of soil nor acreage was sufficient for a thriving agriculture. Fishing and pilotage were a hazardous business in those deep waters, and though there are fishermen still on the Scillies the islands have never had a predominantly seafaring population.

It was when times were hard that Parson Troutbeck would offer up his famous prayer: "We pray thee, O Lord, not that wrecks should happen, but that if any wrecks *do* happen thou shouldst cast them upon the Isles of Scilly for the benefit of the poor inhabitants thereof." And I do not know whether it was Troutbeck or another who is alleged to have made the announcement of a wreck from his pulpit one Sunday morning. This promptly robbed him of his congregation. The next time such news came, he did not disclose it, but finished his sermon, proceeded to the west door, disrobed, and turned to his flock: "Now brethren, there's a ship on the rocks below, and this time *we'll all start fair*." (This familiar story is told of many Cornish parishes, but I heard it first of St. Mary's).

There are grim stories, as elsewhere in the west, of ships deliberately lured to destruction by false lights. Smuggling was certainly a popular source of income, long connived at by parson, squire, and even preventive man. If the Queen herself came to Scilly, they were wont to say in Victorian times, she would have to smuggle like all the rest. But smuggling declined, and wrecks became more infrequent. Today you may see seven warning lights, or the looms of them, from the islands, among them the famous Bishop Rock, which welcomes transatlantic voyagers. In the old days the islanders depended chiefly upon the potato crop, and if it failed, as it sometimes did, starvation was very near.

Then, about a century and a quarter ago, Mr. Augustus Smith, the Lord Proprietor, packed up a bunch of flowers in a hatbox and sent them to London for sale. They were Scilly Whites, the delicate narcissi which grow nowhere else. It was the beginning of the industry which ever since has been the people's main support. The speed of railways, and the valiant *Scillonian* made this possible. More than half-a-million bunches a year are sent to England. This, and the growing tourist trade, as the holiday habit developed, has kept the islands going. Though great caution is expressed about the future, Scillonians have a native toughness and determination which will surely see them through crises as it has done in the past — as it did, indeed, during the war, when their living almost vanished and when any morning they might have woken up to find the enemy in possession.

The islands have their attractions for the botanists — especially the lovely gardens of Tresco — the ornithologists, and particularly the archaeologists. But for me, their prehistory has been written by Malory and Tennyson. Did not the lost land of Lyonnesse stretch from Land's End to St. Mary's, and may you not hear the bells of the churches still ringing far below the surface as the waves move them? Upon the day when Arthur received his death-wound, his followers fled, Mordred upon their heels, through Lyonnesse to the place we know now as St. Martin's Mead. And the Lord called forth the waters, and Lyonnesse was submerged, and Mordred swept away with them. Perhaps the explanation of the heart-catching magic of the Scillies is that they are the last, lone sentinels of a lost people, the last remnant of "all that glory and her goodliness."

> Low in the waves she lies,
> Sea-sepulchred, and monodied by winds
> That ever sigh o'er Lyonnesse the fair.

INDEX

INDEX

INDEX

INDEX

INDEX

INDEX

INDEX

INDEX

300

INDEX

INDEX

More books from **Ex Libris Press** *are described below:*

Bath/Land's End
WEST COUNTRY TOUR: *Being the Diary of a Tour through the*
  Counties of Somerset, Devon and Cornwall in 1797
  John Skinner   96 pages   £2.95

London/Land's End
GREEN ROAD TO LAND'S END:
  Diary of a Journey on Foot from London to Land's End
  Roger Jones   144 Pages   £2.95

South Devon
TALL SHIPS IN TORBAY:
  A Brief Maritime History of Torquay, Paignton and Brixham
  John Pike   144 pages   £3.95
IRON HORSE TO THE SEA: *Railways in South Devon*
  John Pike   160 pages   £3.95
BETWIXT MOOR AND SEA: *Rambles in South Devon*
  Roger Jones   96 pages   £2.95

Somerset
MENDIP RAMBLES: *12 Walks around the Mendip Hills*
  Peter Wright   96 pages   £2.95
COLLIERS WAY: *History and Walks in the Somerset Coalfield*
  Peter Collier   160 pages   £4.95

Wiltshire
CURIOUS WILTSHIRE
  Mary Delorme   160 pages   £4.95
TOURING GUIDE TO WILTSHIRE VILLAGES
  Margaret Wilson   160 pages   £3.95

Farming Autobiography
SEEDTIME TO HARVEST: *A Farmer's Life*
  Arthur Court   128 pages   £3.95

Ghost Stories
OUR NEIGHBOURLY GHOSTS:
  Tall and Short Stories from the West Country
  Doreen Evelyn   96 pages   £2.95

Ex Libris Press books may be obtained through your local bookshop or direct from the publisher, post-free on receipt of net price, at 1 The Shambles, Bradford on Avon, Wiltshire, BA15 1JS. Please ask for a free catalogue.